JUSTICE LEAGUE OF AMERICA
ROAD TO REBIRTH

STEVE ORLANDO
JODY HOUSER
writers

ANDY MacDONALD * **JAMAL CAMPBELL** * **STEPHEN BYRNE**
MIRKA ANDOLFO * **IVAN REIS** * **JOE PRADO** * **OCLAIR ALBERT**
artists

JOHN RAUCH * **JAMAL CAMPBELL** * **STEPHEN BYRNE**
ARIF PRIANTO * **MARCELO MAIOLO**
colorists

CLAYTON COWLES
letterer

IVAN REIS * **JOE PRADO** * **MARCELO MAIOLO**
series and collection cover artists

THE RAY created by JACK HARRIS and JOE QUESADA
KILLER FROST created by GERRY CONWAY and ALLEN MILGROM
VIXEN created by GERRY CONWAY and BOB OKSNER

BRIAN CUNNINGHAM ANDY KHOURI JESSICA CHEN Editors - Original Series ● **AMEDEO TURTURRO DIEGO LOPEZ** Assistant Editors - Original Series
JEB WOODARD Group Editor - Collected Editions ● **ERIKA ROTHBERG** Editor - Collected Edition
STEVE COOK Design Director – Books ● **CURTIS KING JR.** Publication Design

BOB HARRAS Senior VP - Editor-in-Chief, DC Comics

DIANE NELSON President ● **DAN DiDIO** Publisher ● **JIM LEE** Publisher ● **GEOFF JOHNS** President & Chief Creative Officer
AMIT DESAI Executive VP - Business & Marketing Strategy, Direct to Consumer & Global Franchise Management ● **SAM ADES** Senior VP - Direct to Consumer
BOBBIE CHASE VP - Talent Development ● **MARK CHIARELLO** Senior VP - Art, Design & Collected Editions
JOHN CUNNINGHAM Senior VP - Sales & Trade Marketing ● **ANNE DePIES** Senior VP - Business Strategy, Finance & Administration
DON FALLETTI VP - Manufacturing Operations ● **LAWRENCE GANEM** VP - Editorial Administration & Talent Relations
ALISON GILL Senior VP - Manufacturing & Operations ● **HANK KANALZ** Senior VP - Editorial Strategy & Administration
JAY KOGAN VP - Legal Affairs ● **THOMAS LOFTUS** VP - Business Affairs
JACK MAHAN VP - Business Affairs ● **NICK J. NAPOLITANO** VP - Manufacturing Administration
EDDIE SCANNELL VP - Consumer Marketing ● **COURTNEY SIMMONS** Senior VP - Publicity & Communications
JIM (SKI) SOKOLOWSKI VP - Comic Book Specialty Sales & Trade Marketing ● **NANCY SPEARS** VP - Mass, Book, Digital Sales & Trade Marketing

JUSTICE LEAGUE OF AMERICA: ROAD TO REBIRTH

DC Comics, 2900 West Alameda Ave., Burbank, CA 91505. Printed by LSC Communications, Salem, VA, USA. 5/5/17.
First Printing. ISBN: 978-1-4012-7352-1

Library of Congress Cataloging-in-Publication Data is available.

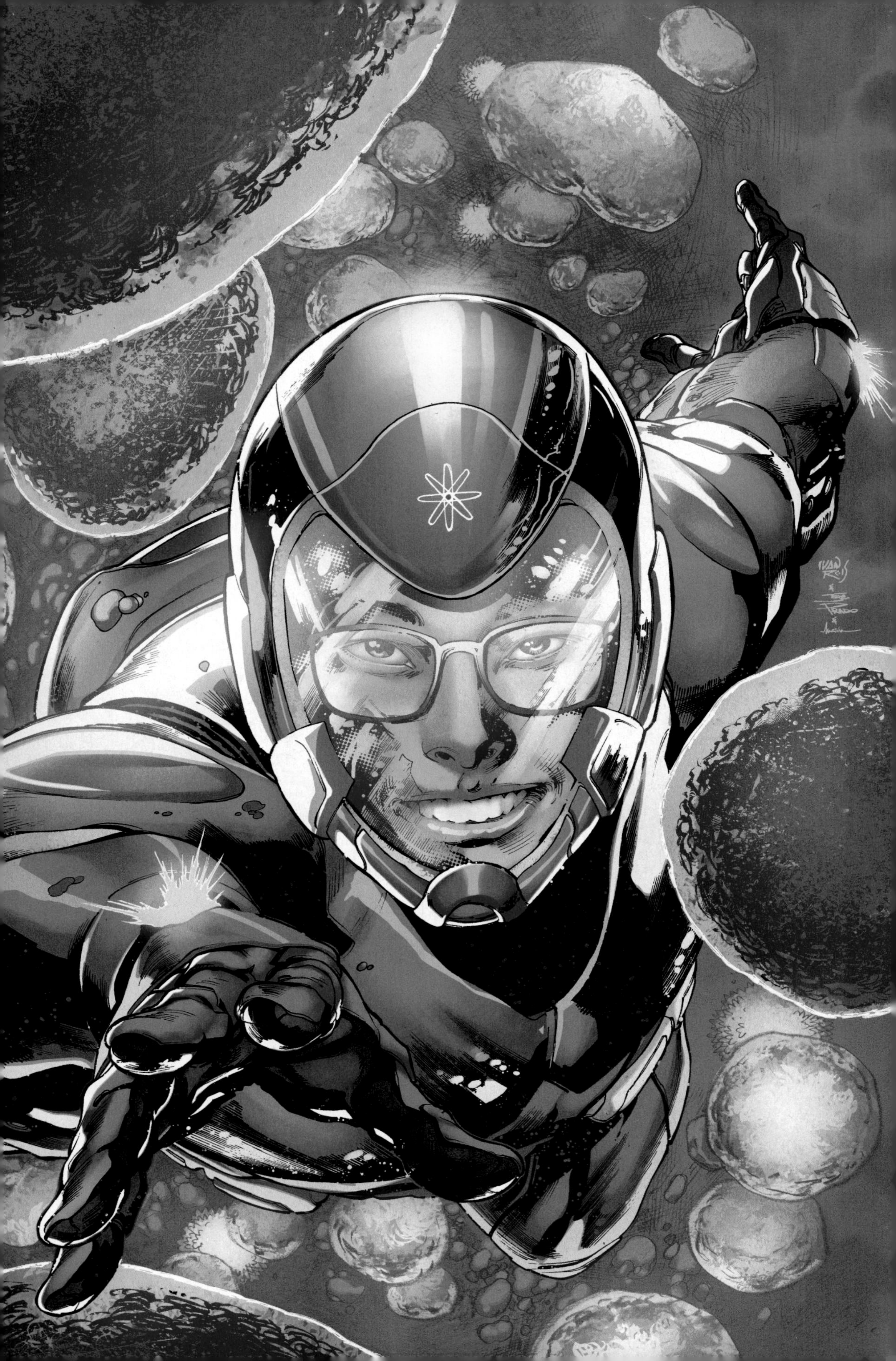

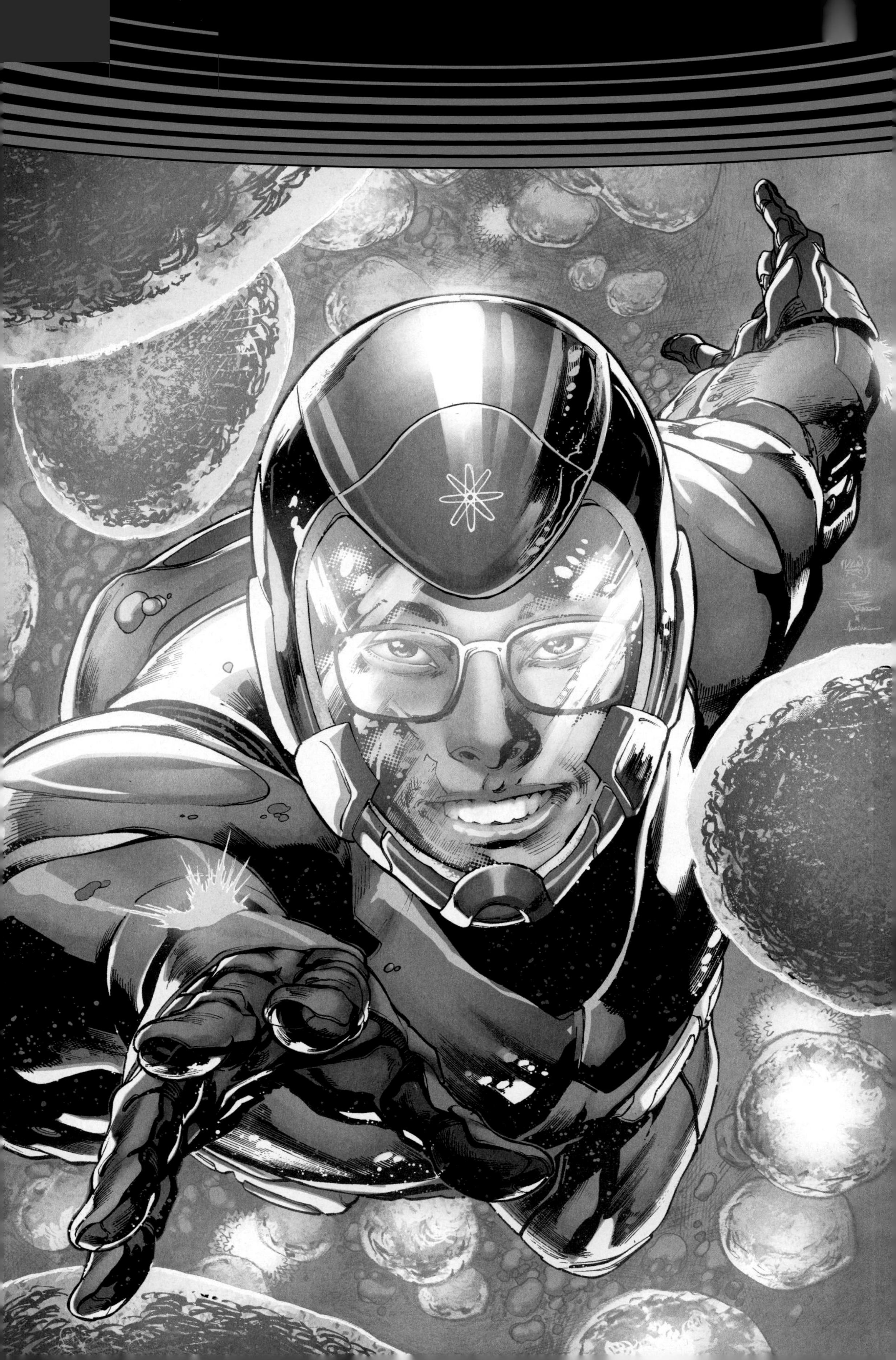

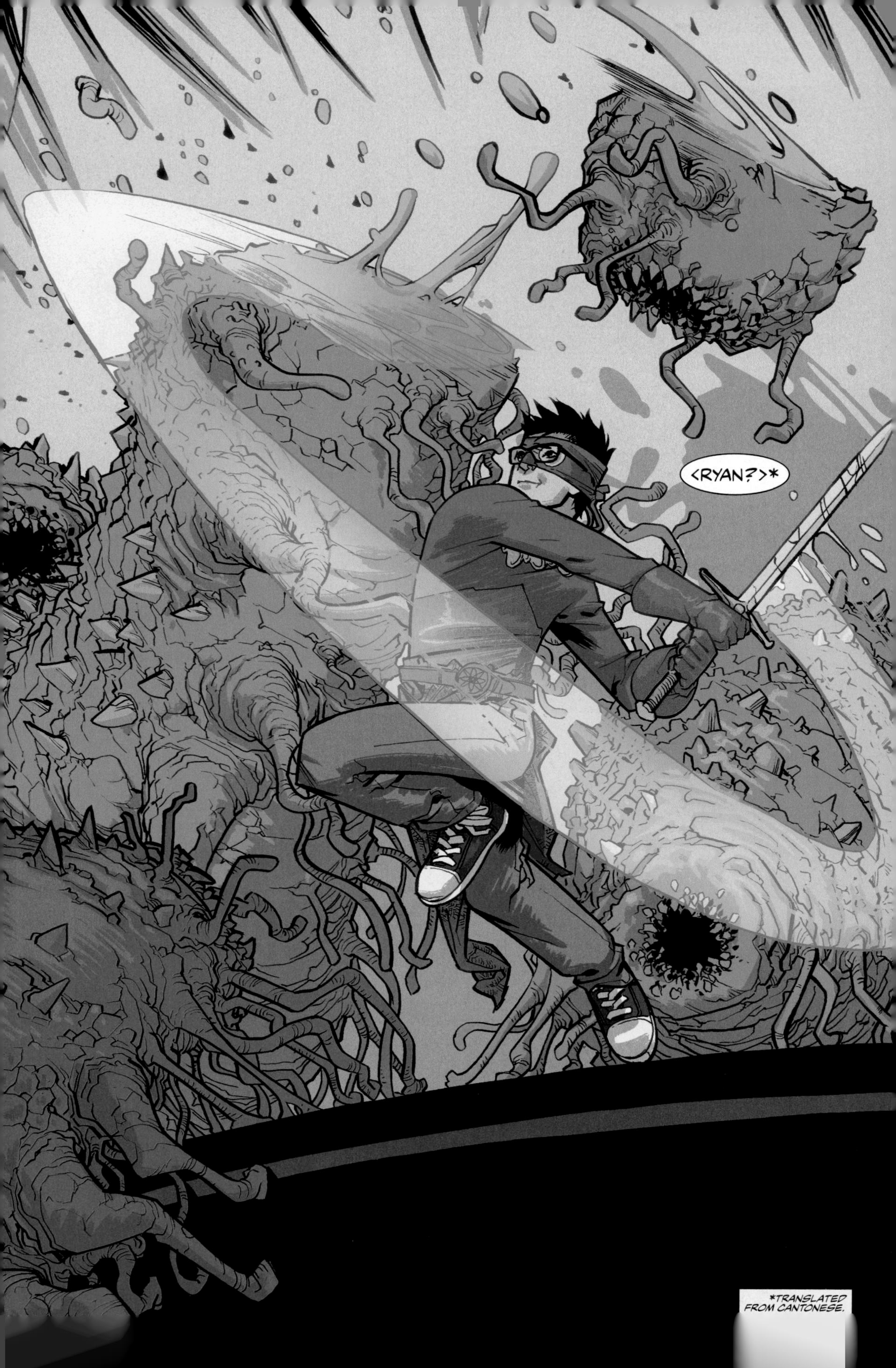
<RYAN?>*
*TRANSLATED FROM CANTONESE.

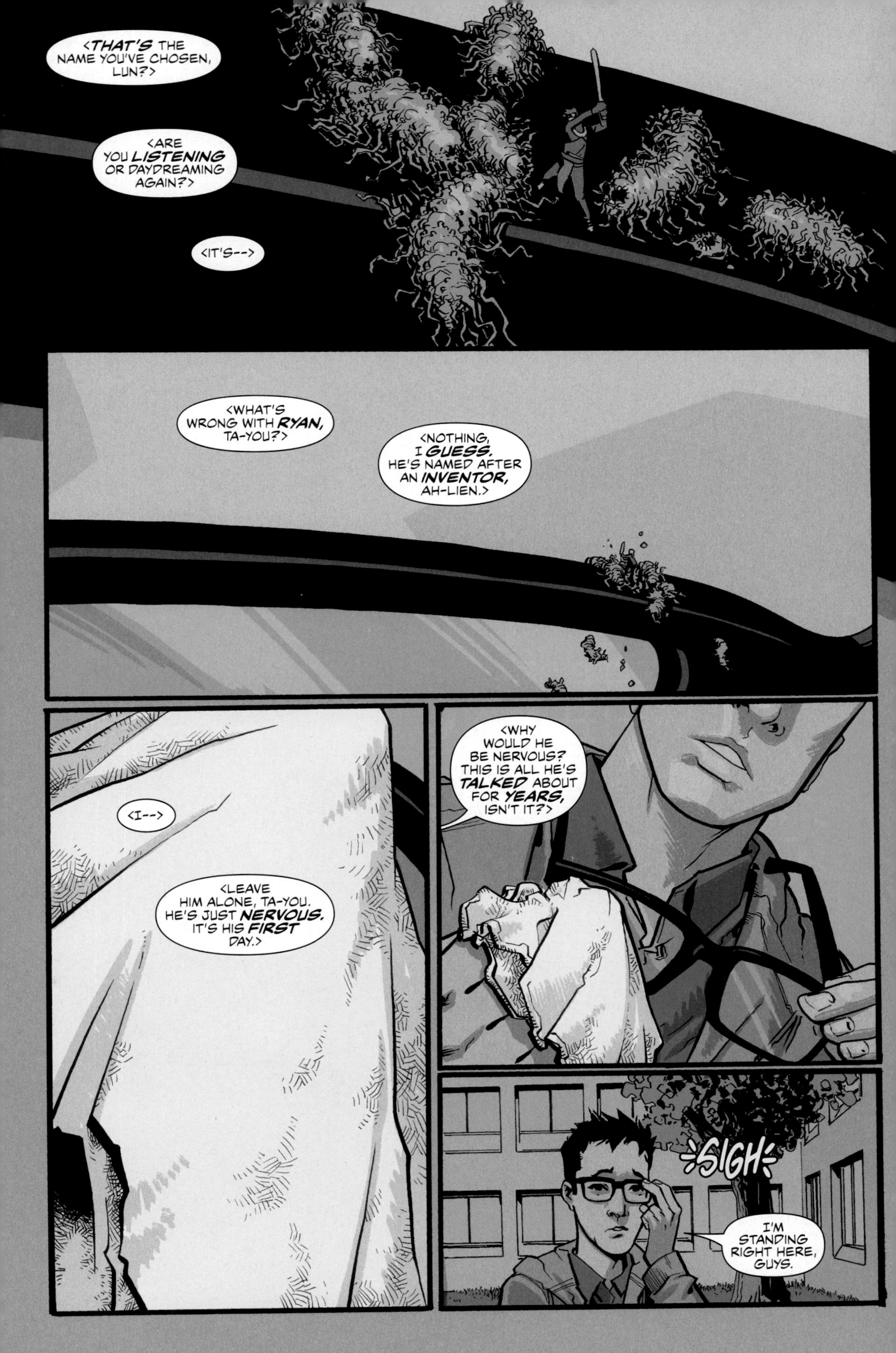
<THAT'S THE NAME YOU'VE CHOSEN, LUN?>
<ARE YOU LISTENING OR DAYDREAMING AGAIN?>
<IT'S-->
<WHAT'S WRONG WITH RYAN, TA-YOU?>
<NOTHING, I GUESS. HE'S NAMED AFTER AN INVENTOR, AH-LIEN.>
<I-->
<LEAVE HIM ALONE, TA-YOU. HE'S JUST NERVOUS. IT'S HIS FIRST DAY.>
<WHY WOULD HE BE NERVOUS? THIS IS ALL HE'S TALKED ABOUT FOR YEARS, ISN'T IT?>
SIGH
I'M STANDING RIGHT HERE, GUYS.

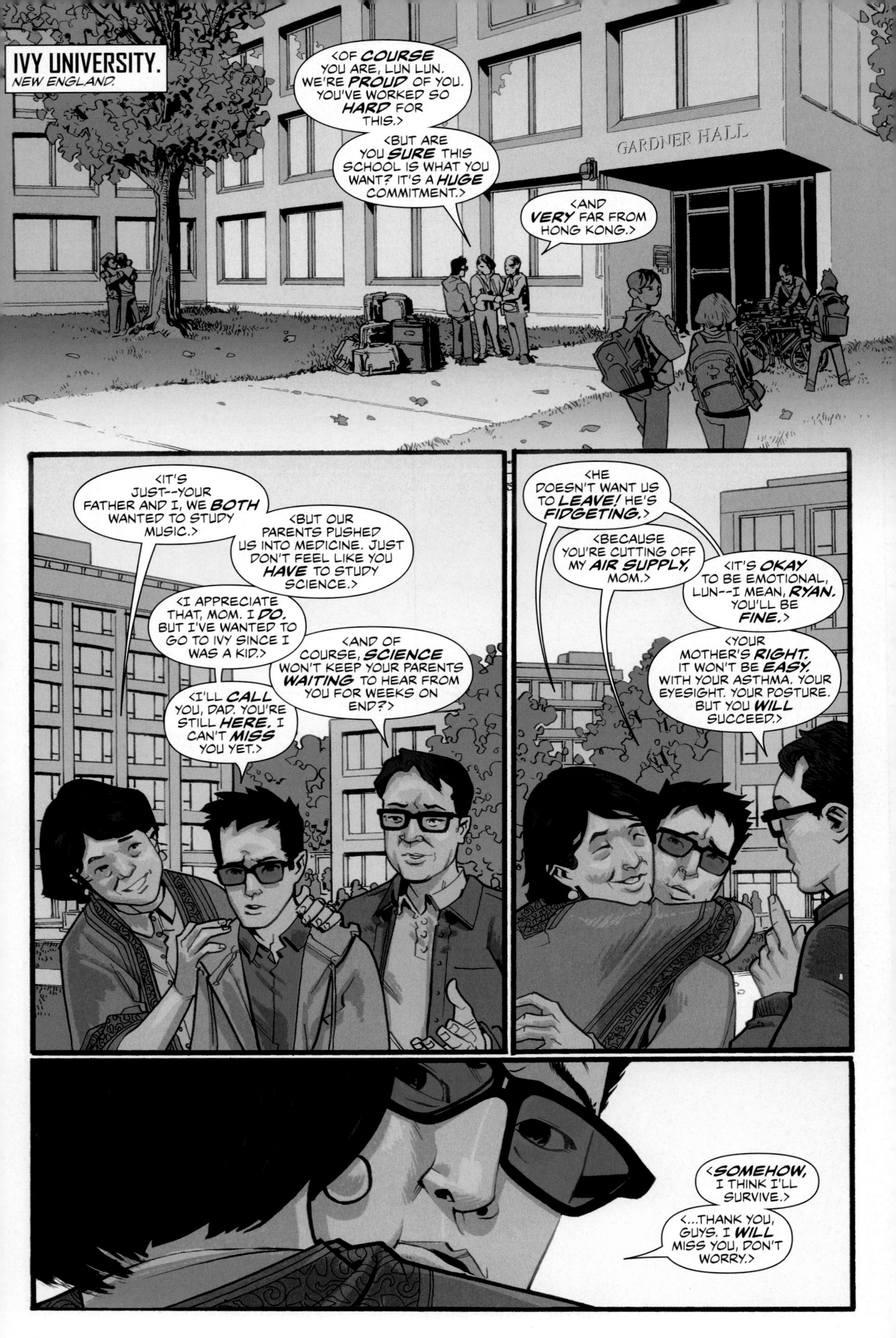
IVY UNIVERSITY. NEW ENGLAND.
<OF COURSE YOU ARE, LUN LUN. WE'RE PROUD OF YOU. YOU'VE WORKED SO HARD FOR THIS.>
<BUT ARE YOU SURE THIS SCHOOL IS WHAT YOU WANT? IT'S A HUGE COMMITMENT.>
GARDNER HALL
<AND VERY FAR FROM HONG KONG.>
<IT'S JUST--YOUR FATHER AND I, WE BOTH WANTED TO STUDY MUSIC.>
<BUT OUR PARENTS PUSHED US INTO MEDICINE. JUST DON'T FEEL LIKE YOU HAVE TO STUDY SCIENCE.>
<I APPRECIATE THAT, MOM. I DO. BUT I'VE WANTED TO GO TO IVY SINCE I WAS A KID.>
<AND OF COURSE, SCIENCE WON'T KEEP YOUR PARENTS WAITING TO HEAR FROM YOU FOR WEEKS ON END?>
<I'LL CALL YOU, DAD. YOU'RE STILL HERE. I CAN'T MISS YOU YET.>
<HE DOESN'T WANT US TO LEAVE! HE'S FIDGETING.>
<BECAUSE YOU'RE CUTTING OFF MY AIR SUPPLY, MOM.>
<IT'S OKAY TO BE EMOTIONAL, LUN--I MEAN, RYAN. YOU'LL BE FINE.>
<YOUR MOTHER'S RIGHT. IT WON'T BE EASY. WITH YOUR ASTHMA. YOUR EYESIGHT. YOUR POSTURE. BUT YOU WILL SUCCEED.>
<SOMEHOW, I THINK I'LL SURVIVE.>
<...THANK YOU, GUYS. I WILL MISS YOU, DON'T WORRY.>

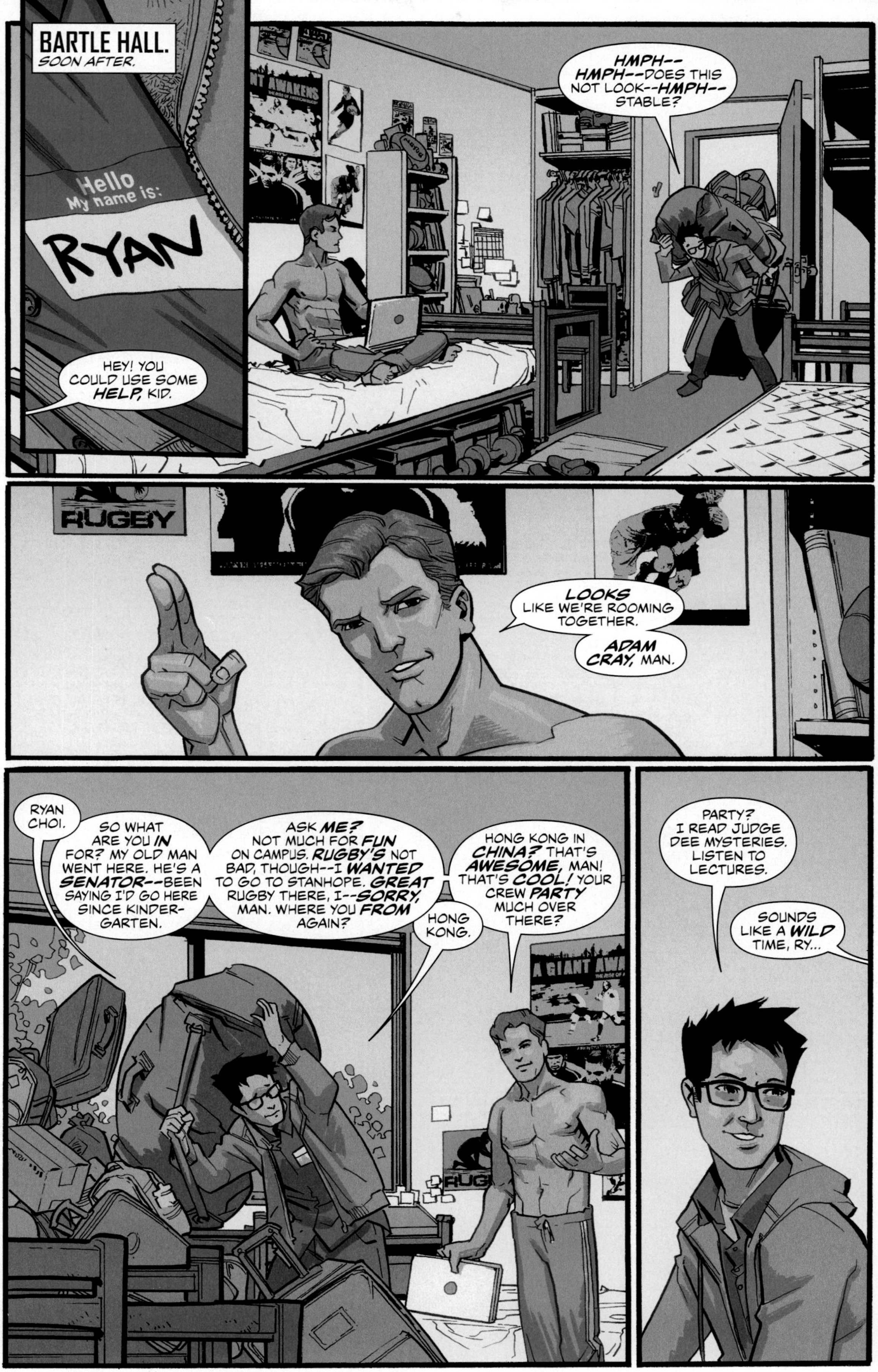
BARTLE HALL.
SOON AFTER.
Hello
My name is:
RYAN
HMPH-- HMPH--DOES THIS NOT LOOK--HMPH-- STABLE?
HEY! YOU COULD USE SOME HELP, KID.
RUGBY
LOOKS LIKE WE'RE ROOMING TOGETHER.
ADAM CRAY, MAN.
RYAN CHOI.
SO WHAT ARE YOU IN FOR? MY OLD MAN WENT HERE. HE'S A SENATOR--BEEN SAYING I'D GO HERE SINCE KINDER-GARTEN.
ASK ME? NOT MUCH FOR FUN ON CAMPUS. RUGBY'S NOT BAD, THOUGH--I WANTED TO GO TO STANHOPE. GREAT RUGBY THERE, I--SORRY, MAN. WHERE YOU FROM AGAIN?
HONG KONG.
HONG KONG IN CHINA? THAT'S AWESOME, MAN! THAT'S COOL! YOUR CREW PARTY MUCH OVER THERE?
PARTY? I READ JUDGE DEE MYSTERIES. LISTEN TO LECTURES.
SOUNDS LIKE A WILD TIME, RY...

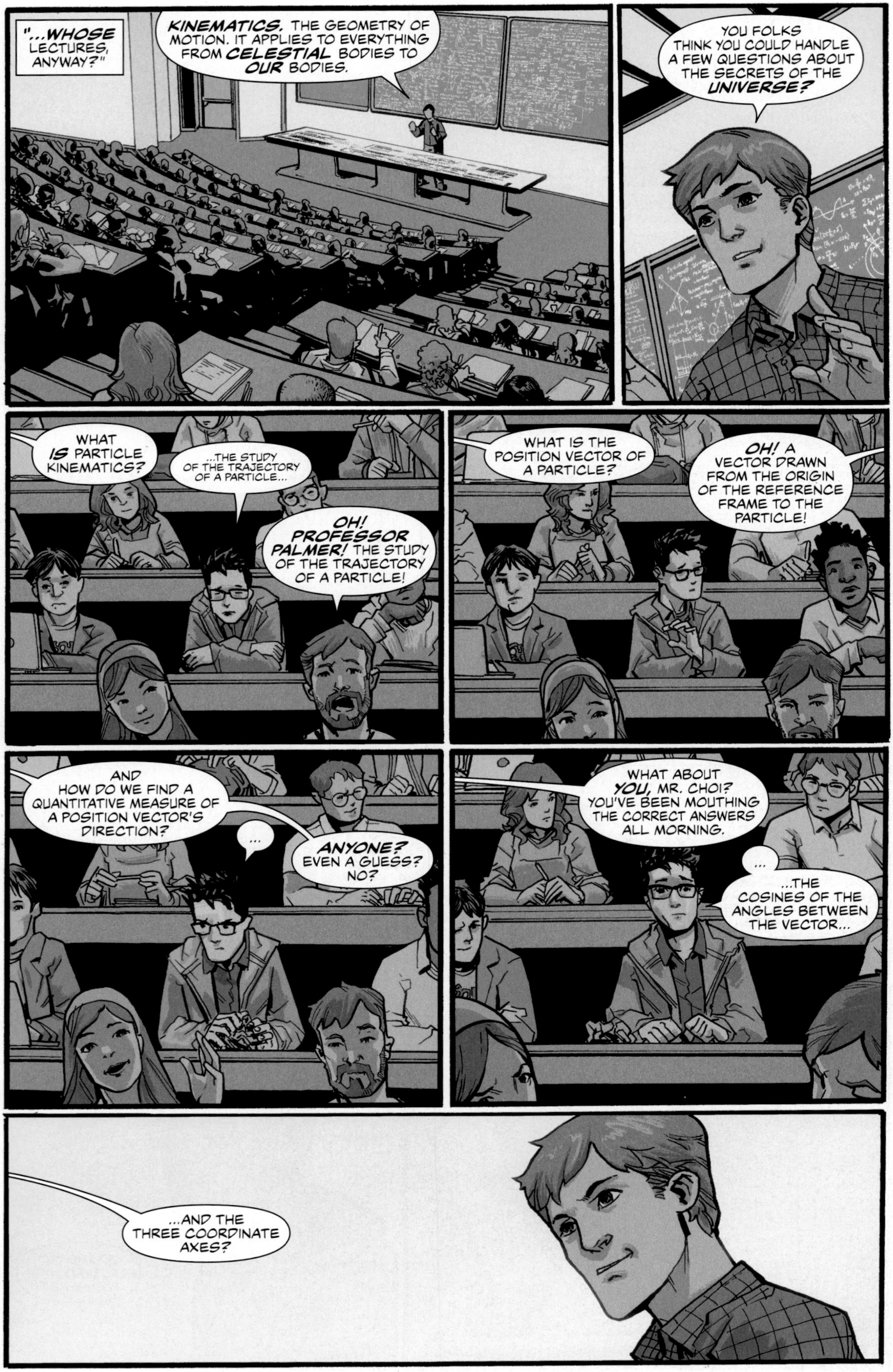
"...WHOSE LECTURES, ANYWAY?"
KINEMATICS. THE GEOMETRY OF MOTION. IT APPLIES TO EVERYTHING FROM CELESTIAL BODIES TO OUR BODIES.
YOU FOLKS THINK YOU COULD HANDLE A FEW QUESTIONS ABOUT THE SECRETS OF THE UNIVERSE?
WHAT IS PARTICLE KINEMATICS?
...THE STUDY OF THE TRAJECTORY OF A PARTICLE...
OH! PROFESSOR PALMER! THE STUDY OF THE TRAJECTORY OF A PARTICLE!
WHAT IS THE POSITION VECTOR OF A PARTICLE?
OH! A VECTOR DRAWN FROM THE ORIGIN OF THE REFERENCE FRAME TO THE PARTICLE!
AND HOW DO WE FIND A QUANTITATIVE MEASURE OF A POSITION VECTOR'S DIRECTION?
...
ANYONE? EVEN A GUESS? NO?
WHAT ABOUT YOU, MR. CHOI? YOU'VE BEEN MOUTHING THE CORRECT ANSWERS ALL MORNING.
...
...THE COSINES OF THE ANGLES BETWEEN THE VECTOR...
...AND THE THREE COORDINATE AXES?

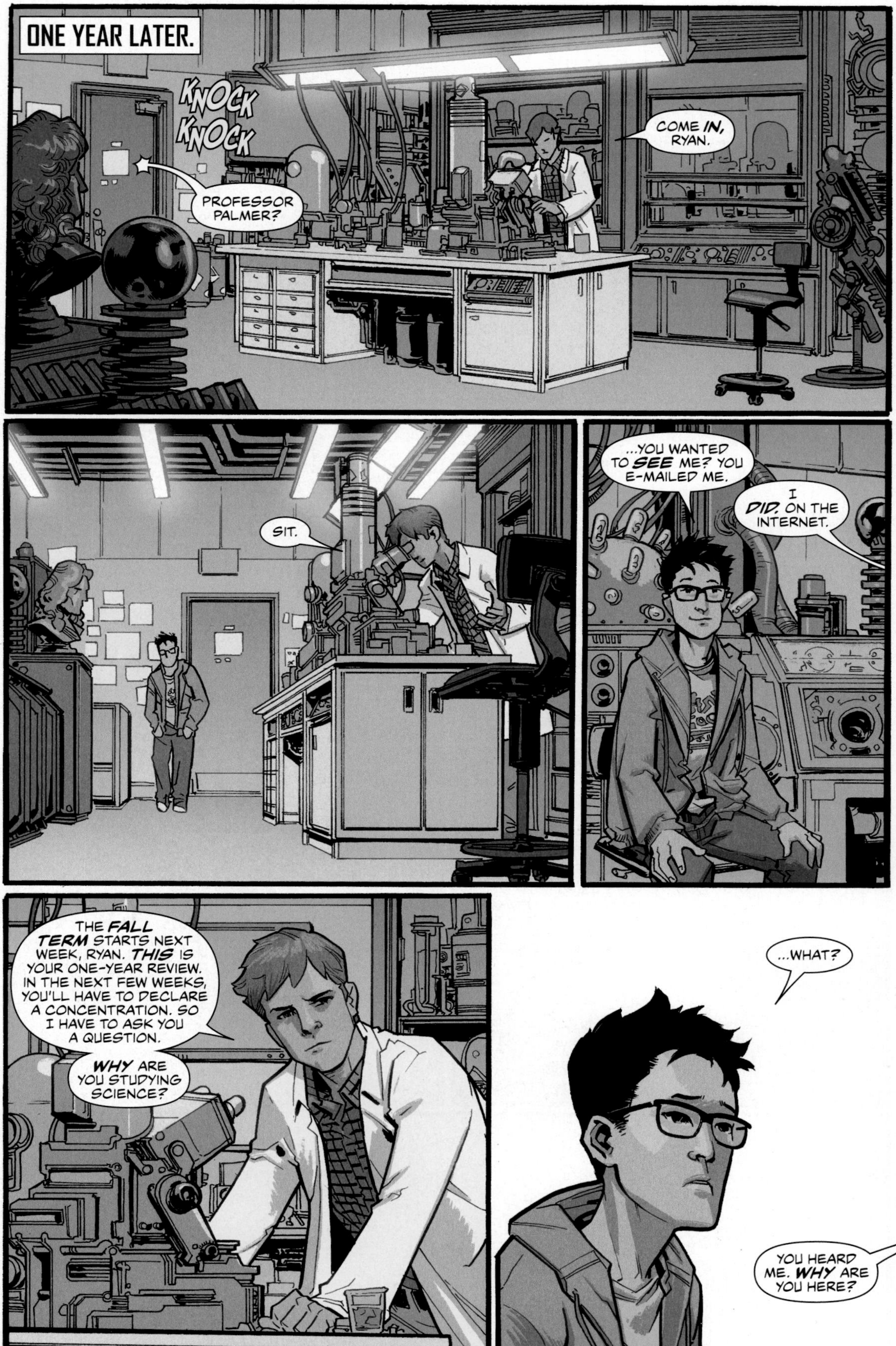
ONE YEAR LATER.
KNOCK KNOCK
PROFESSOR PALMER?
COME IN, RYAN.
SIT.
...YOU WANTED TO SEE ME? YOU E-MAILED ME.
I DID. ON THE INTERNET.
THE FALL TERM STARTS NEXT WEEK, RYAN. THIS IS YOUR ONE-YEAR REVIEW. IN THE NEXT FEW WEEKS, YOU'LL HAVE TO DECLARE A CONCENTRATION. SO I HAVE TO ASK YOU A QUESTION.
WHY ARE YOU STUDYING SCIENCE?
...WHAT?
YOU HEARD ME. WHY ARE YOU HERE?

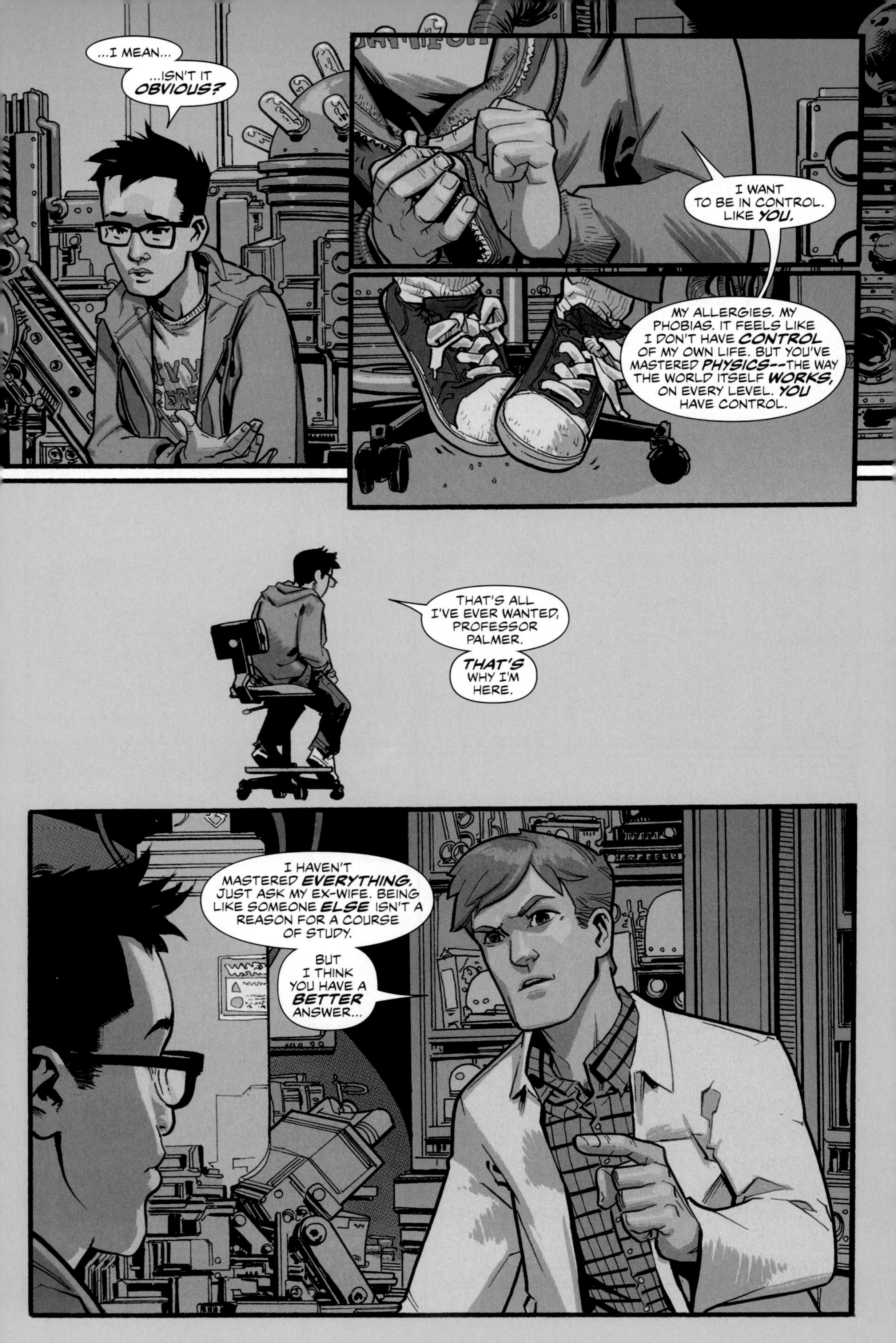
...I MEAN...
...ISN'T IT OBVIOUS?
I WANT TO BE IN CONTROL. LIKE YOU.
MY ALLERGIES. MY PHOBIAS. IT FEELS LIKE I DON'T HAVE CONTROL OF MY OWN LIFE. BUT YOU'VE MASTERED PHYSICS--THE WAY THE WORLD ITSELF WORKS, ON EVERY LEVEL. YOU HAVE CONTROL.
THAT'S ALL I'VE EVER WANTED, PROFESSOR PALMER.
THAT'S WHY I'M HERE.
I HAVEN'T MASTERED EVERYTHING. JUST ASK MY EX-WIFE. BEING LIKE SOMEONE ELSE ISN'T A REASON FOR A COURSE OF STUDY.
BUT I THINK YOU HAVE A BETTER ANSWER...

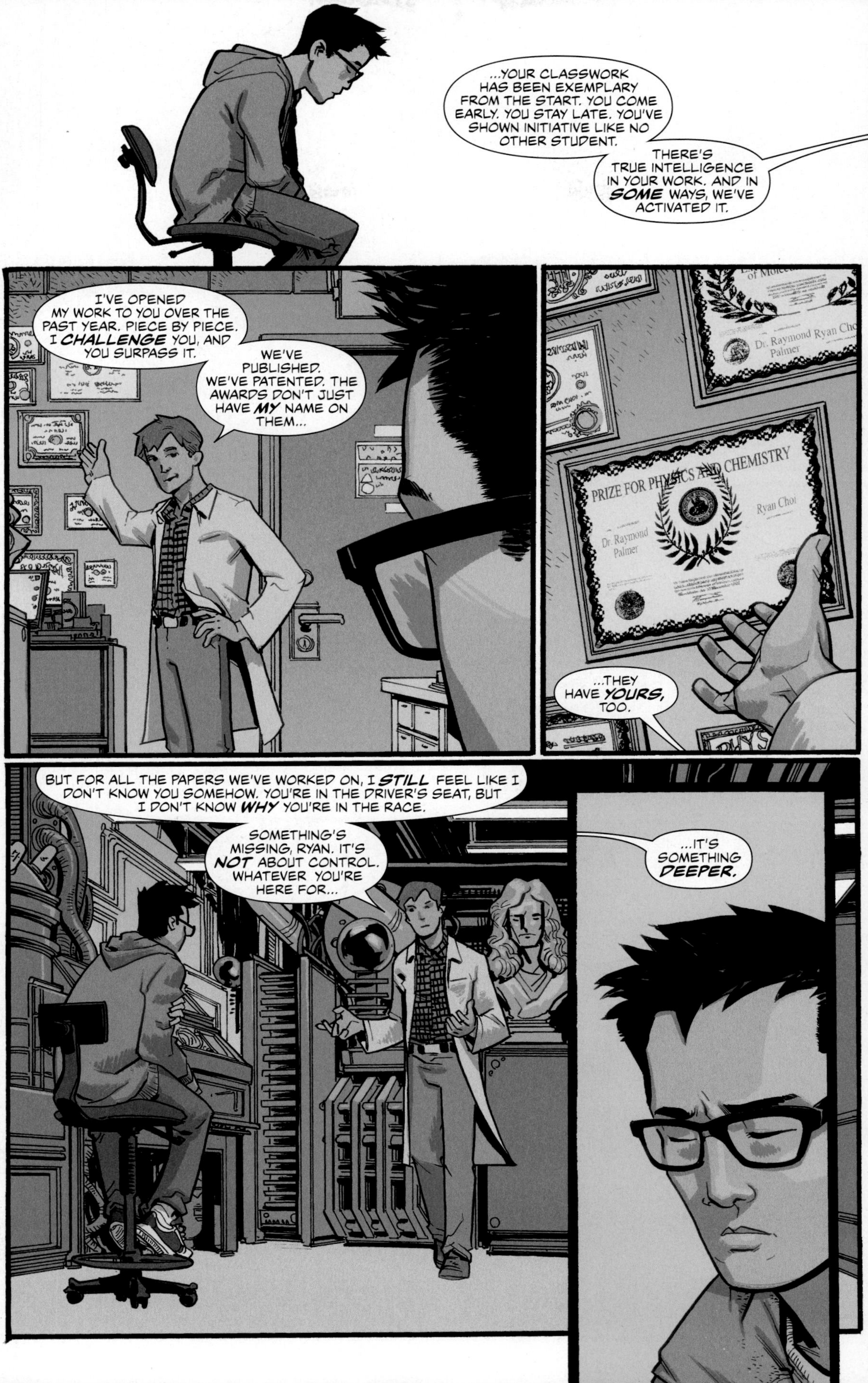
...YOUR CLASSWORK HAS BEEN EXEMPLARY FROM THE START. YOU COME EARLY. YOU STAY LATE. YOU'VE SHOWN INITIATIVE LIKE NO OTHER STUDENT.
THERE'S TRUE INTELLIGENCE IN YOUR WORK. AND IN **SOME** WAYS, WE'VE ACTIVATED IT.
I'VE OPENED MY WORK TO YOU OVER THE PAST YEAR. PIECE BY PIECE. I **CHALLENGE** YOU, AND YOU SURPASS IT.
WE'VE PUBLISHED. WE'VE PATENTED. THE AWARDS DON'T JUST HAVE **MY** NAME ON THEM...
PRIZE FOR PHYSICS AND CHEMISTRY
Dr. Raymond Palmer
Ryan Choi
...THEY HAVE **YOURS,** TOO.
BUT FOR ALL THE PAPERS WE'VE WORKED ON, I **STILL** FEEL LIKE I DON'T KNOW YOU SOMEHOW. YOU'RE IN THE DRIVER'S SEAT, BUT I DON'T KNOW **WHY** YOU'RE IN THE RACE.
SOMETHING'S MISSING, RYAN. IT'S **NOT** ABOUT CONTROL. WHATEVER YOU'RE HERE FOR...
...IT'S SOMETHING **DEEPER.**

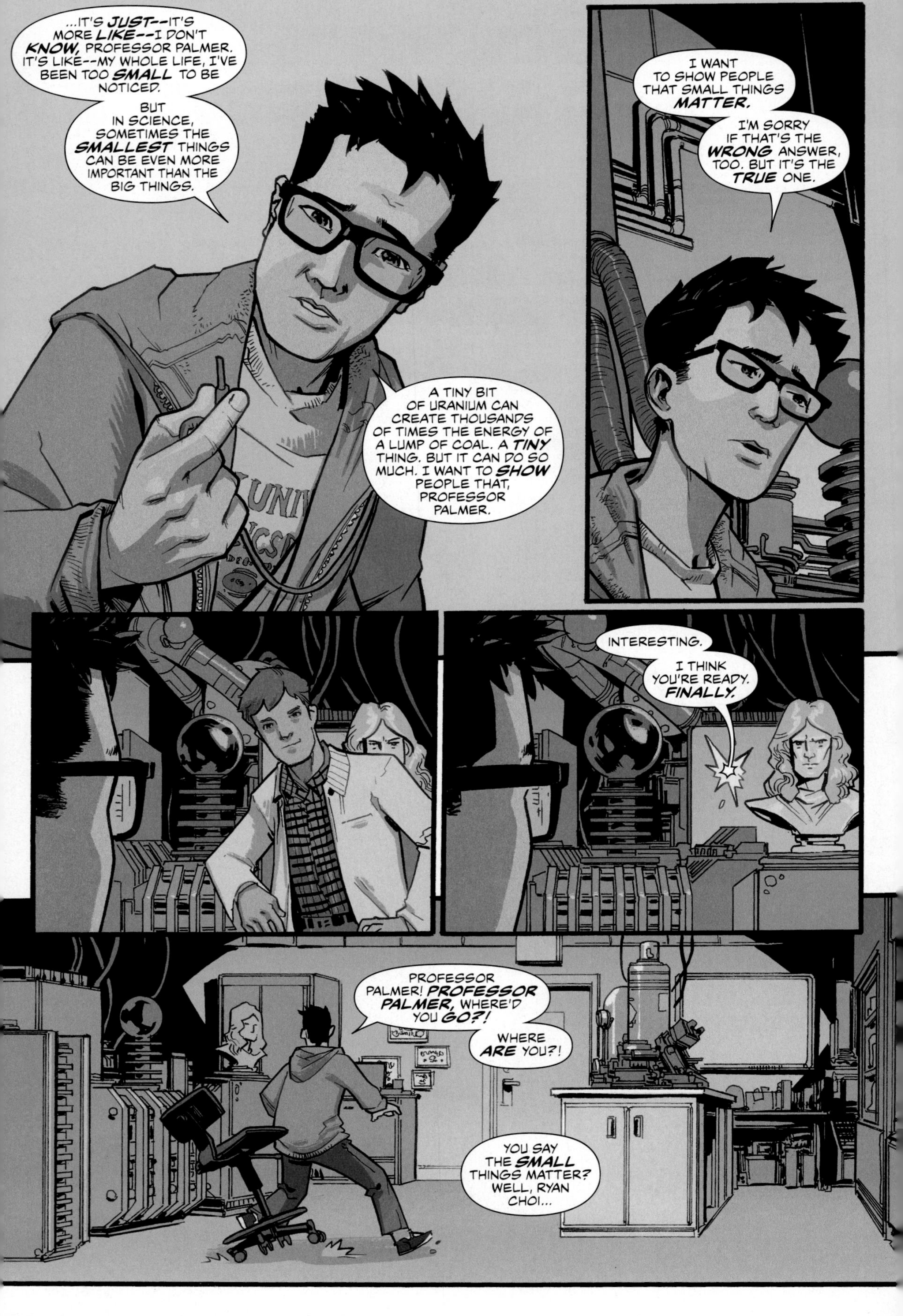
...IT'S JUST--IT'S MORE LIKE--I DON'T KNOW, PROFESSOR PALMER. IT'S LIKE--MY WHOLE LIFE, I'VE BEEN TOO SMALL TO BE NOTICED.
BUT IN SCIENCE, SOMETIMES THE SMALLEST THINGS CAN BE EVEN MORE IMPORTANT THAN THE BIG THINGS.
A TINY BIT OF URANIUM CAN CREATE THOUSANDS OF TIMES THE ENERGY OF A LUMP OF COAL. A TINY THING. BUT IT CAN DO SO MUCH. I WANT TO SHOW PEOPLE THAT, PROFESSOR PALMER.
I WANT TO SHOW PEOPLE THAT SMALL THINGS MATTER.
I'M SORRY IF THAT'S THE WRONG ANSWER, TOO. BUT IT'S THE TRUE ONE.
INTERESTING.
I THINK YOU'RE READY. FINALLY.
PROFESSOR PALMER! PROFESSOR PALMER, WHERE'D YOU GO?!
WHERE ARE YOU?!
YOU SAY THE SMALL THINGS MATTER? WELL, RYAN CHOI...

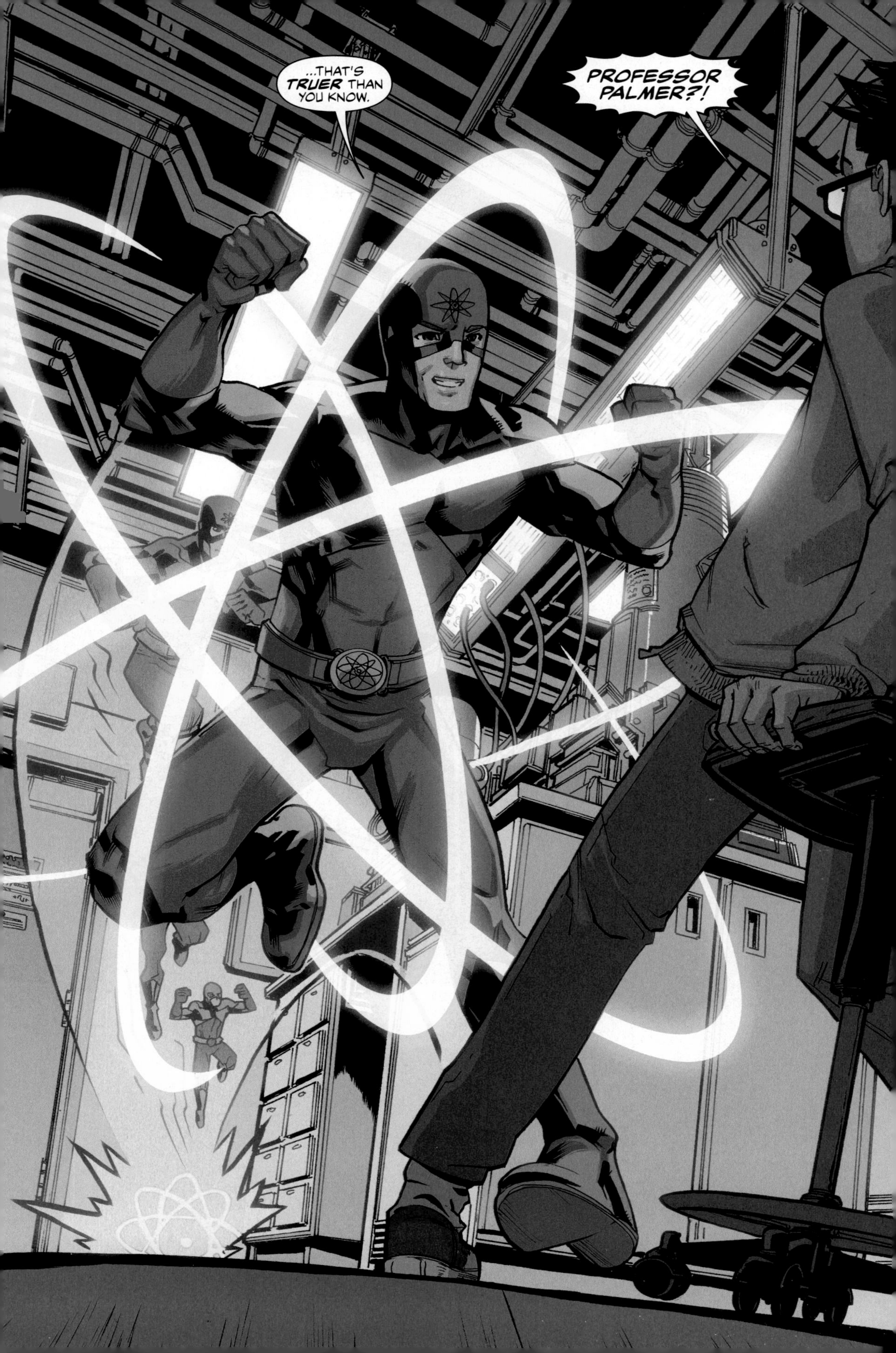
...THAT'S TRUER THAN YOU KNOW.
PROFESSOR PALMER?!

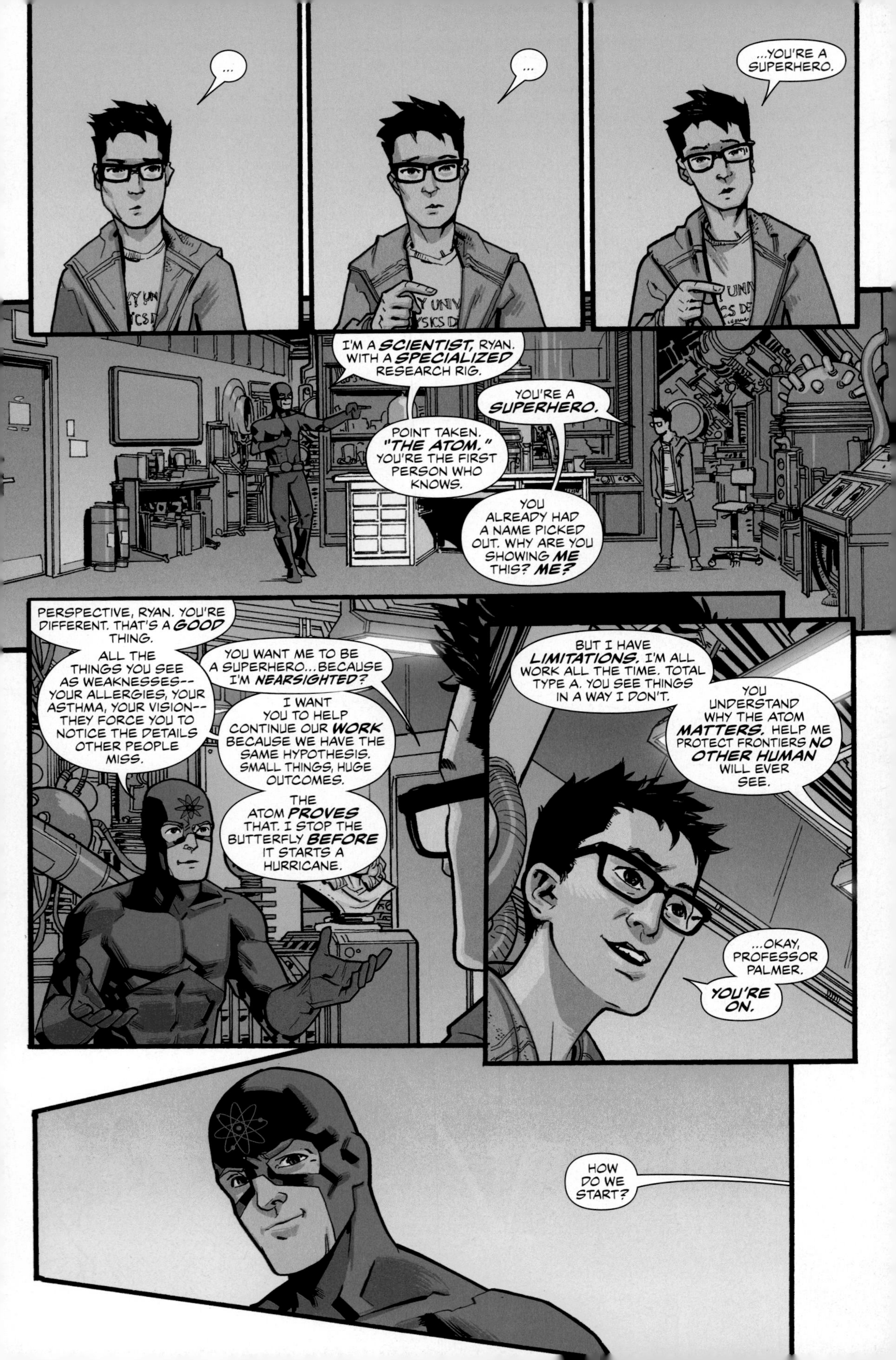
...
...
...YOU'RE A SUPERHERO.
I'M A SCIENTIST, RYAN. WITH A SPECIALIZED RESEARCH RIG.
YOU'RE A SUPERHERO.
POINT TAKEN. "THE ATOM." YOU'RE THE FIRST PERSON WHO KNOWS.
YOU ALREADY HAD A NAME PICKED OUT. WHY ARE YOU SHOWING ME THIS? ME?
PERSPECTIVE, RYAN. YOU'RE DIFFERENT. THAT'S A GOOD THING.
ALL THE THINGS YOU SEE AS WEAKNESSES-- YOUR ALLERGIES, YOUR ASTHMA, YOUR VISION-- THEY FORCE YOU TO NOTICE THE DETAILS OTHER PEOPLE MISS.
YOU WANT ME TO BE A SUPERHERO...BECAUSE I'M NEARSIGHTED?
I WANT YOU TO HELP CONTINUE OUR WORK BECAUSE WE HAVE THE SAME HYPOTHESIS. SMALL THINGS, HUGE OUTCOMES.
THE ATOM PROVES THAT. I STOP THE BUTTERFLY BEFORE IT STARTS A HURRICANE.
BUT I HAVE LIMITATIONS. I'M ALL WORK ALL THE TIME. TOTAL TYPE A. YOU SEE THINGS IN A WAY I DON'T.
YOU UNDERSTAND WHY THE ATOM MATTERS. HELP ME PROTECT FRONTIERS NO OTHER HUMAN WILL EVER SEE.
...OKAY, PROFESSOR PALMER.
YOU'RE ON.
HOW DO WE START?

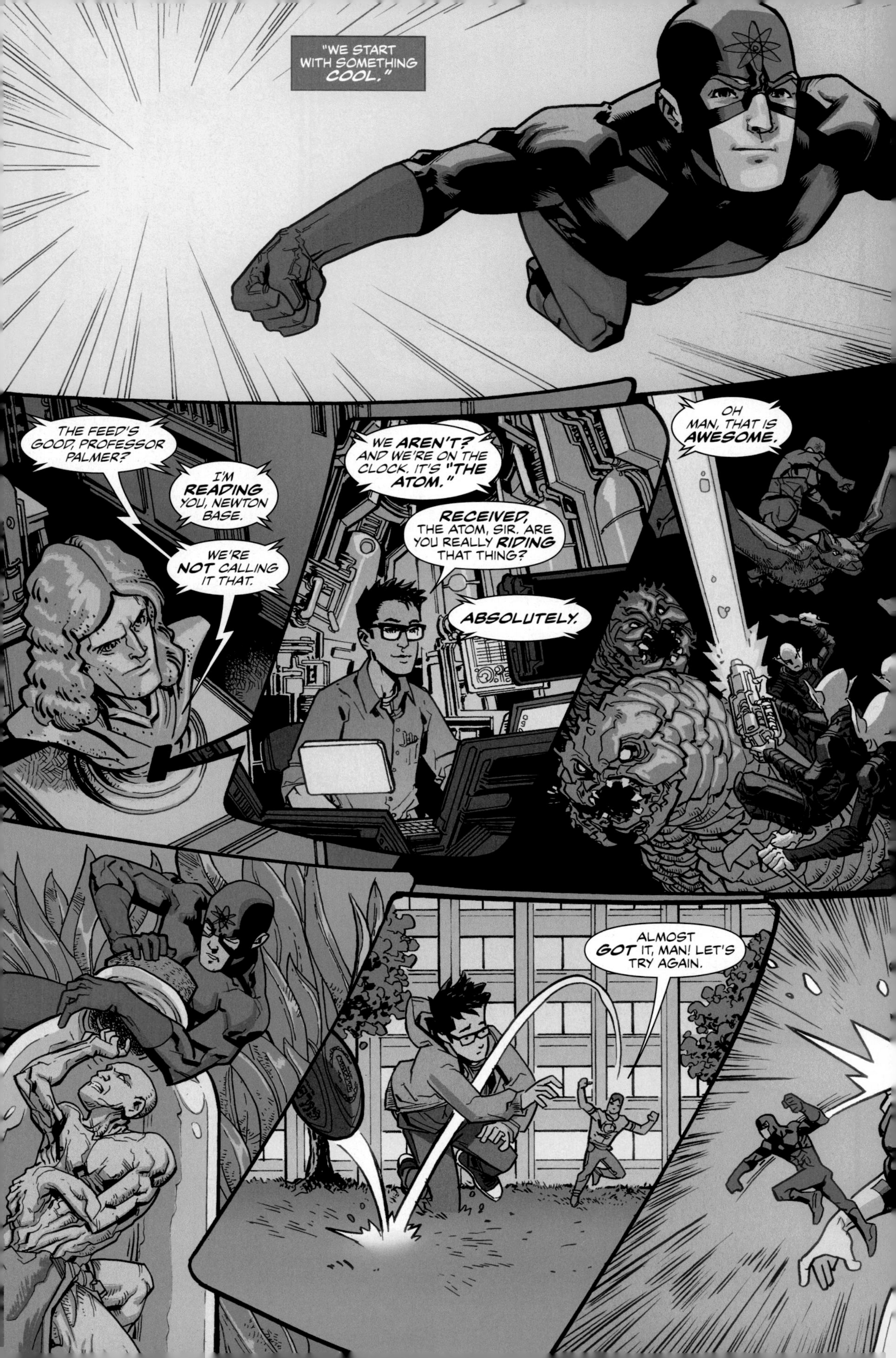
"WE START WITH SOMETHING COOL."
THE FEED'S GOOD, PROFESSOR PALMER?
I'M READING YOU, NEWTON BASE.
WE'RE NOT CALLING IT THAT.
WE AREN'T? AND WE'RE ON THE CLOCK. IT'S "THE ATOM."
RECEIVED, THE ATOM, SIR. ARE YOU REALLY RIDING THAT THING?
ABSOLUTELY.
OH MAN, THAT IS AWESOME.
ALMOST GOT IT, MAN! LET'S TRY AGAIN.

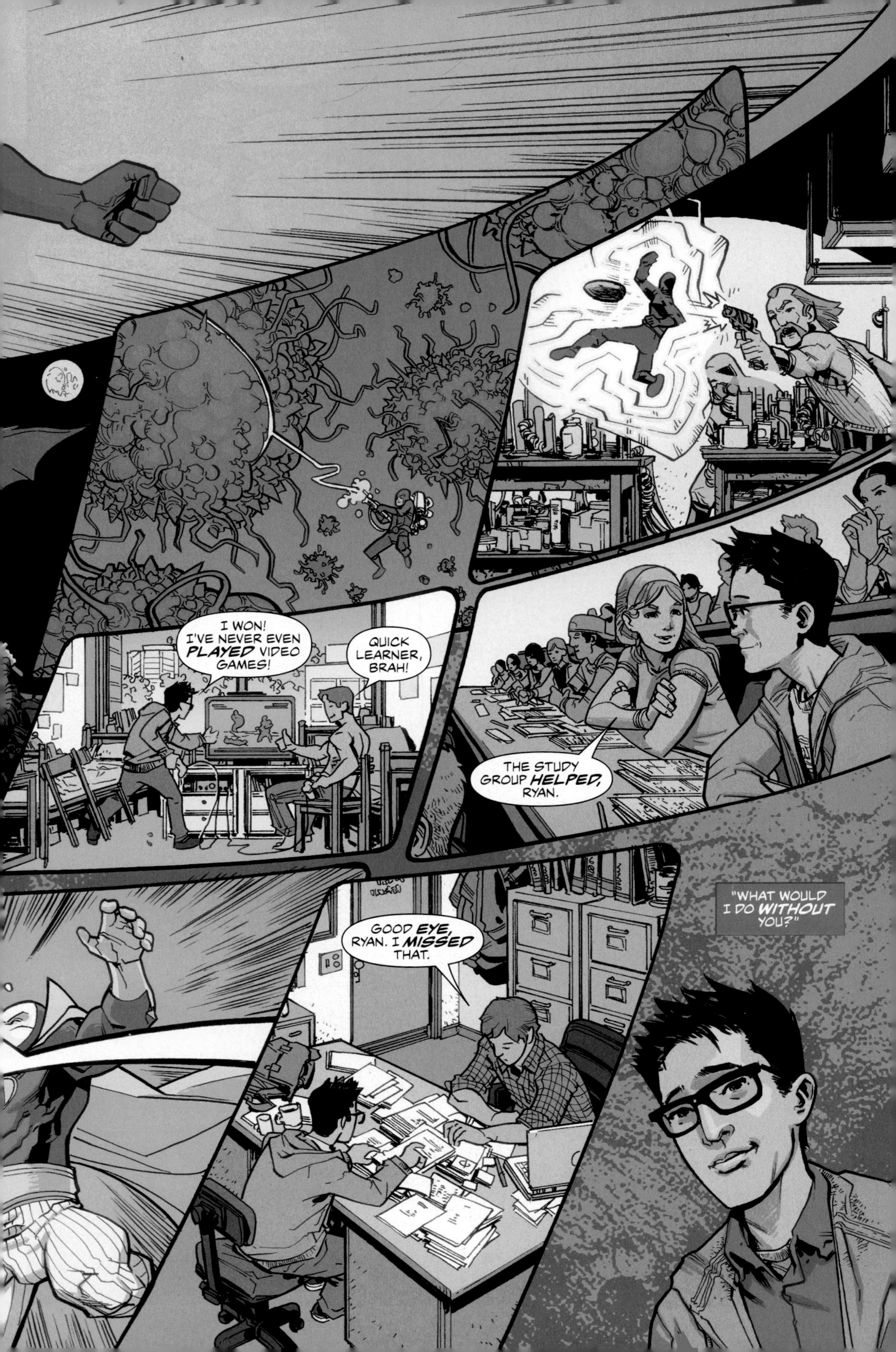
I WON! I'VE NEVER EVEN PLAYED VIDEO GAMES!
QUICK LEARNER, BRAH!
THE STUDY GROUP HELPED, RYAN.
GOOD EYE, RYAN. I MISSED THAT.
"WHAT WOULD I DO WITHOUT YOU?"

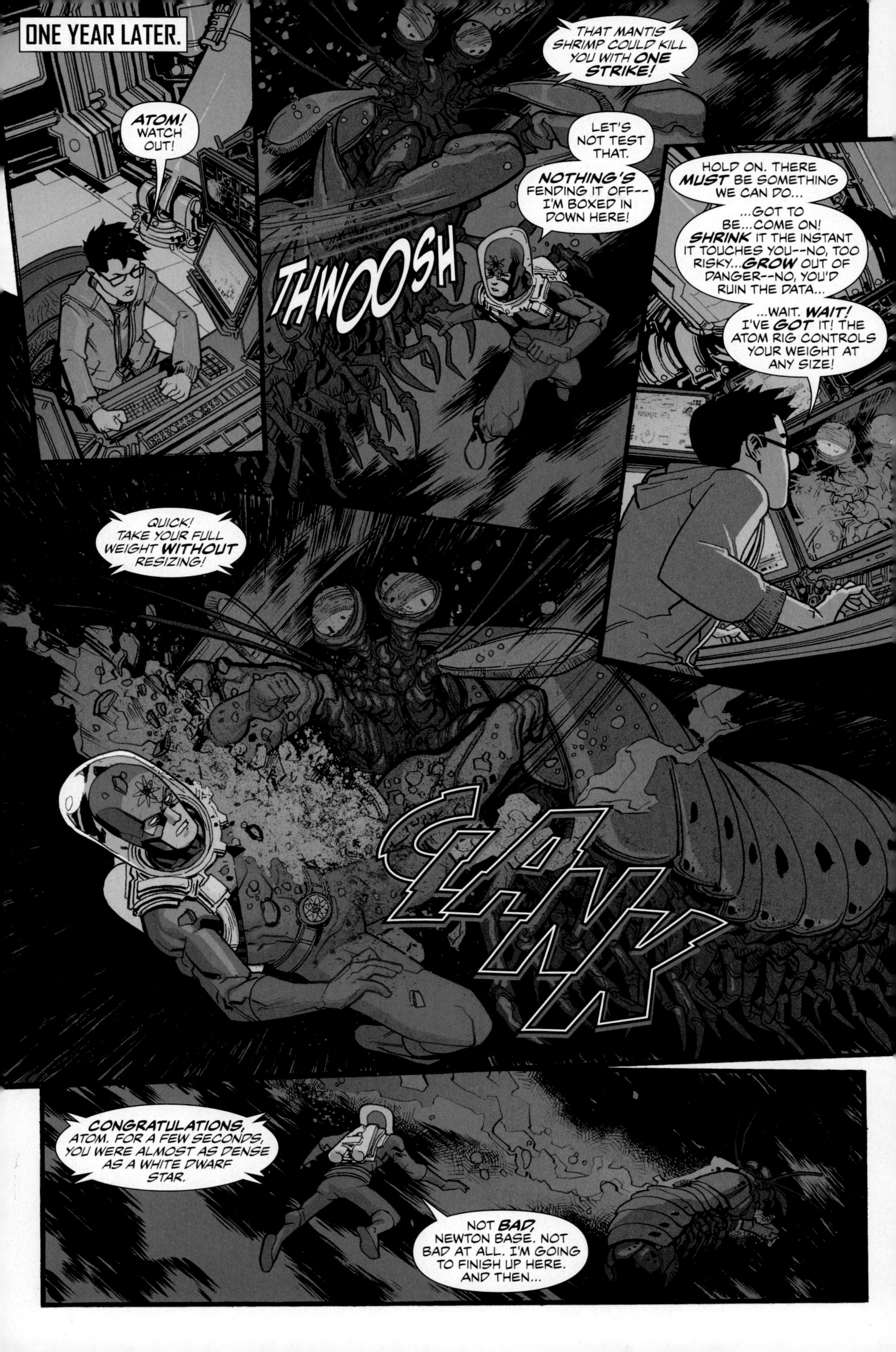
ONE YEAR LATER.
ATOM! WATCH OUT!
THAT MANTIS SHRIMP COULD KILL YOU WITH ONE STRIKE!
LET'S NOT TEST THAT.
NOTHING'S FENDING IT OFF-- I'M BOXED IN DOWN HERE!
THWOOSH
HOLD ON. THERE MUST BE SOMETHING WE CAN DO...
...GOT TO BE...COME ON! SHRINK IT THE INSTANT IT TOUCHES YOU--NO, TOO RISKY...GROW OUT OF DANGER--NO, YOU'D RUIN THE DATA...
...WAIT. WAIT! I'VE GOT IT! THE ATOM RIG CONTROLS YOUR WEIGHT AT ANY SIZE!
QUICK! TAKE YOUR FULL WEIGHT WITHOUT RESIZING!
CLANK
CONGRATULATIONS, ATOM. FOR A FEW SECONDS, YOU WERE ALMOST AS DENSE AS A WHITE DWARF STAR.
NOT BAD, NEWTON BASE. NOT BAD AT ALL. I'M GOING TO FINISH UP HERE. AND THEN...

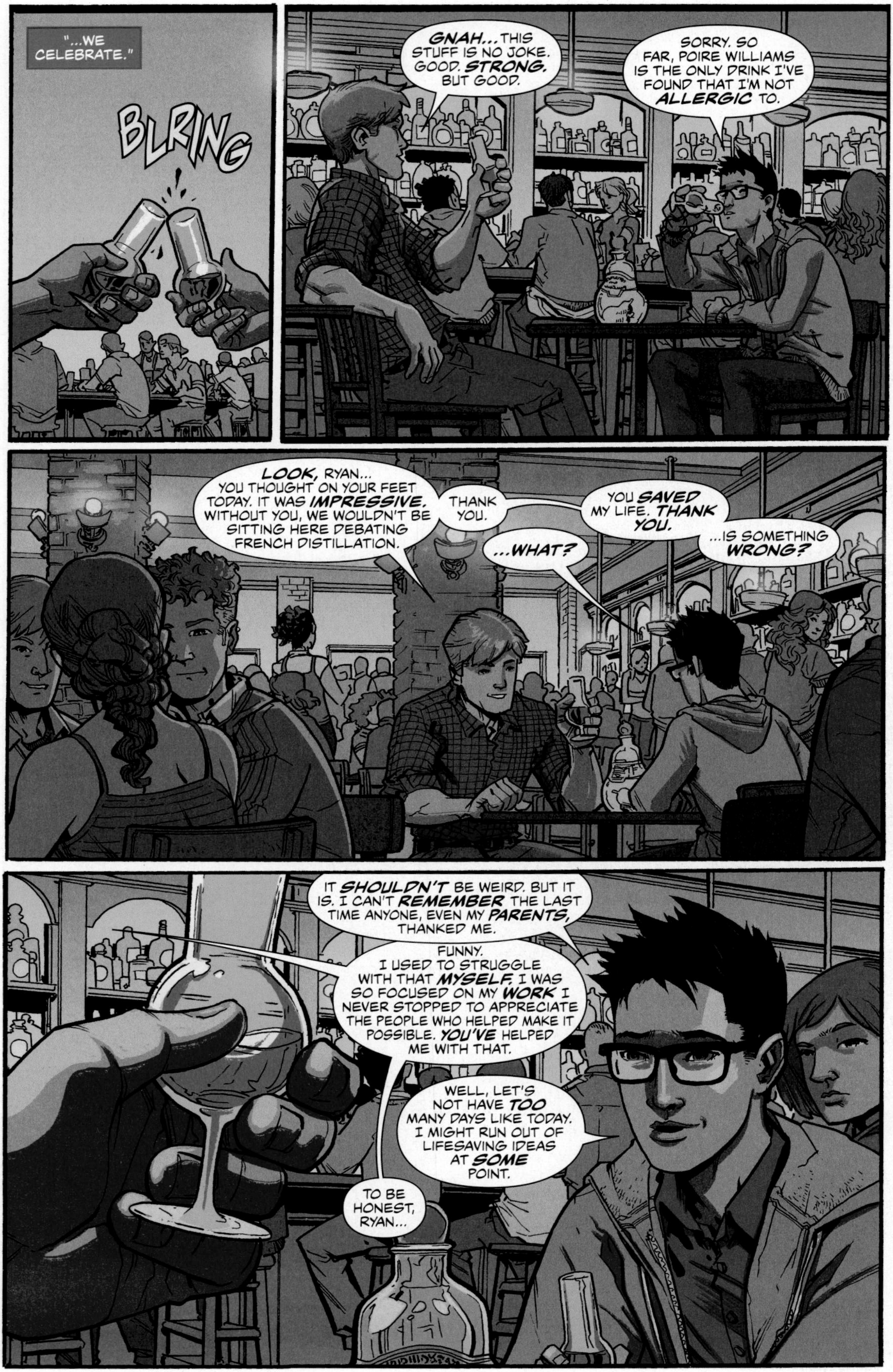
"...WE CELEBRATE."
BLRING
GNAH... THIS STUFF IS NO JOKE. GOOD. STRONG. BUT GOOD.
SORRY. SO FAR, POIRE WILLIAMS IS THE ONLY DRINK I'VE FOUND THAT I'M NOT ALLERGIC TO.
LOOK, RYAN... YOU THOUGHT ON YOUR FEET TODAY. IT WAS IMPRESSIVE. WITHOUT YOU, WE WOULDN'T BE SITTING HERE DEBATING FRENCH DISTILLATION.
THANK YOU.
YOU SAVED MY LIFE. THANK YOU.
...WHAT?
...IS SOMETHING WRONG?
IT SHOULDN'T BE WEIRD. BUT IT IS. I CAN'T REMEMBER THE LAST TIME ANYONE, EVEN MY PARENTS, THANKED ME.
FUNNY. I USED TO STRUGGLE WITH THAT MYSELF. I WAS SO FOCUSED ON MY WORK I NEVER STOPPED TO APPRECIATE THE PEOPLE WHO HELPED MAKE IT POSSIBLE. YOU'VE HELPED ME WITH THAT.
WELL, LET'S NOT HAVE TOO MANY DAYS LIKE TODAY. I MIGHT RUN OUT OF LIFESAVING IDEAS AT SOME POINT.
TO BE HONEST, RYAN...

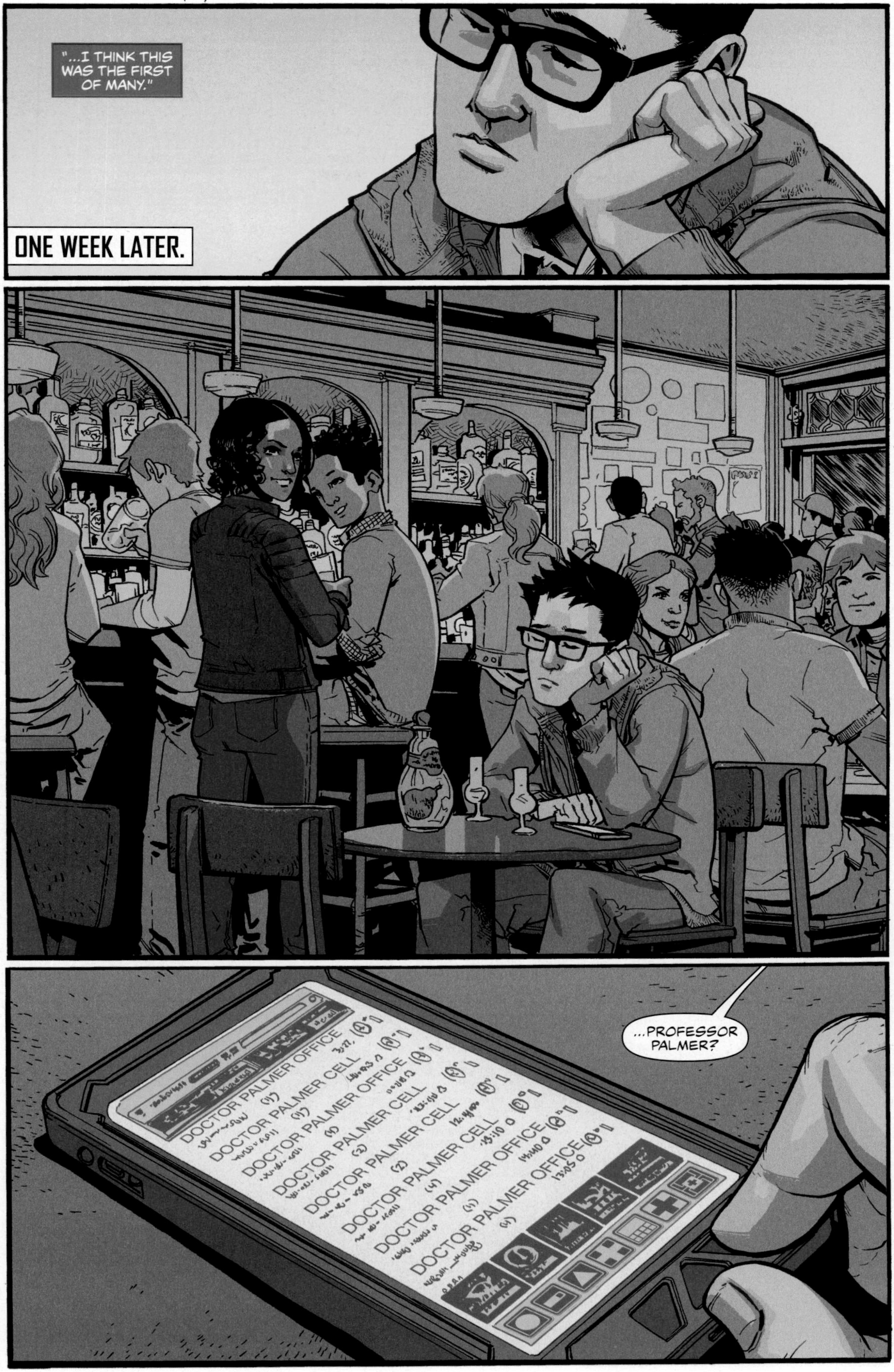
"...I THINK THIS WAS THE FIRST OF MANY."
ONE WEEK LATER.
DOCTOR PALMER OFFICE
DOCTOR PALMER CELL
DOCTOR PALMER OFFICE
DOCTOR PALMER CELL
DOCTOR PALMER CELL
DOCTOR PALMER OFFICE
DOCTOR PALMER OFFICE
...PROFESSOR PALMER?

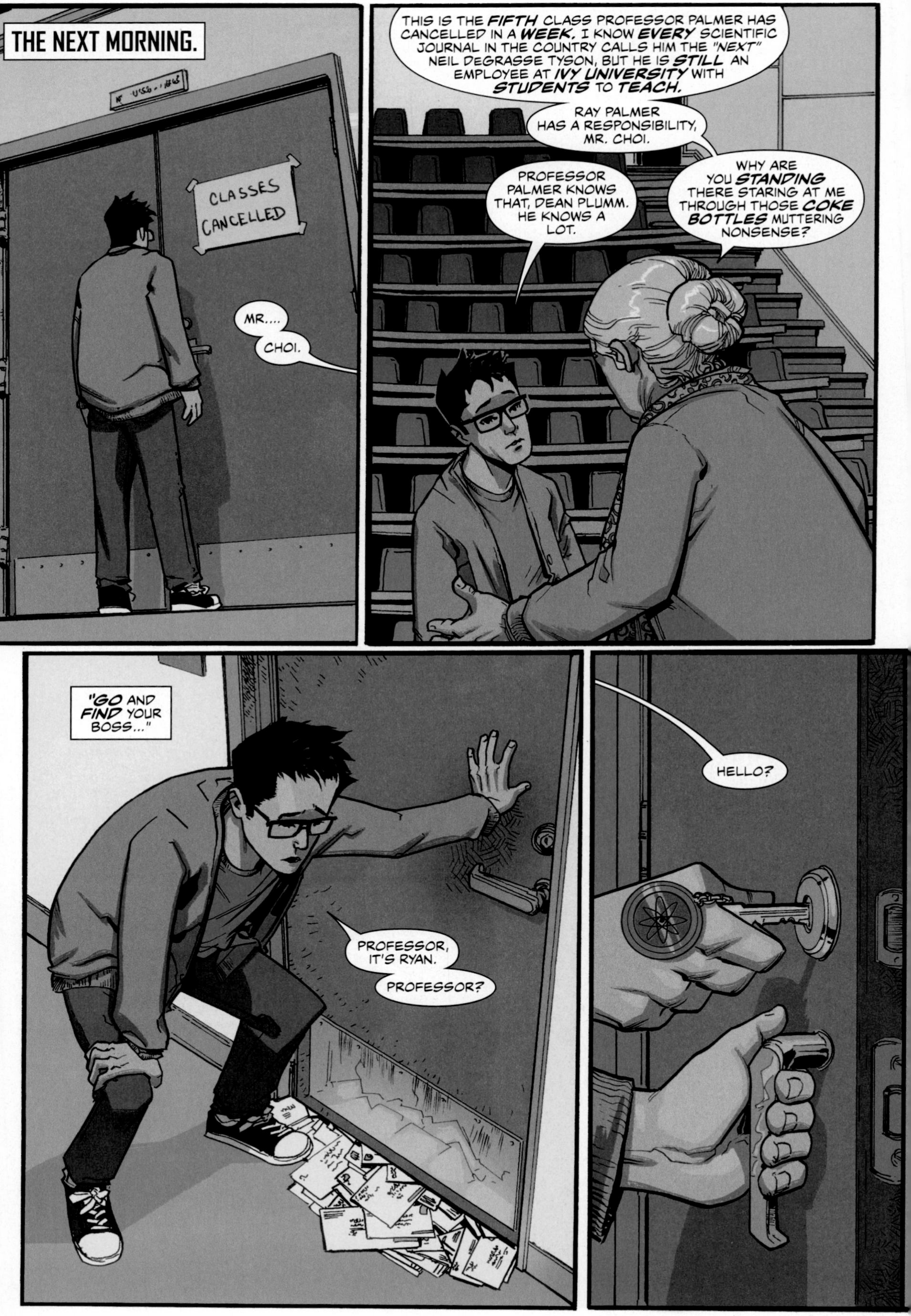
THE NEXT MORNING.
CLASSES CANCELLED
MR.... CHOI.
THIS IS THE FIFTH CLASS PROFESSOR PALMER HAS CANCELLED IN A WEEK. I KNOW EVERY SCIENTIFIC JOURNAL IN THE COUNTRY CALLS HIM THE "NEXT" NEIL DEGRASSE TYSON, BUT HE IS STILL AN EMPLOYEE AT IVY UNIVERSITY WITH STUDENTS TO TEACH.
RAY PALMER HAS A RESPONSIBILITY, MR. CHOI.
PROFESSOR PALMER KNOWS THAT, DEAN PLUMM. HE KNOWS A LOT.
WHY ARE YOU STANDING THERE STARING AT ME THROUGH THOSE COKE BOTTLES MUTTERING NONSENSE?
"GO AND FIND YOUR BOSS..."
PROFESSOR, IT'S RYAN.
PROFESSOR?
HELLO?

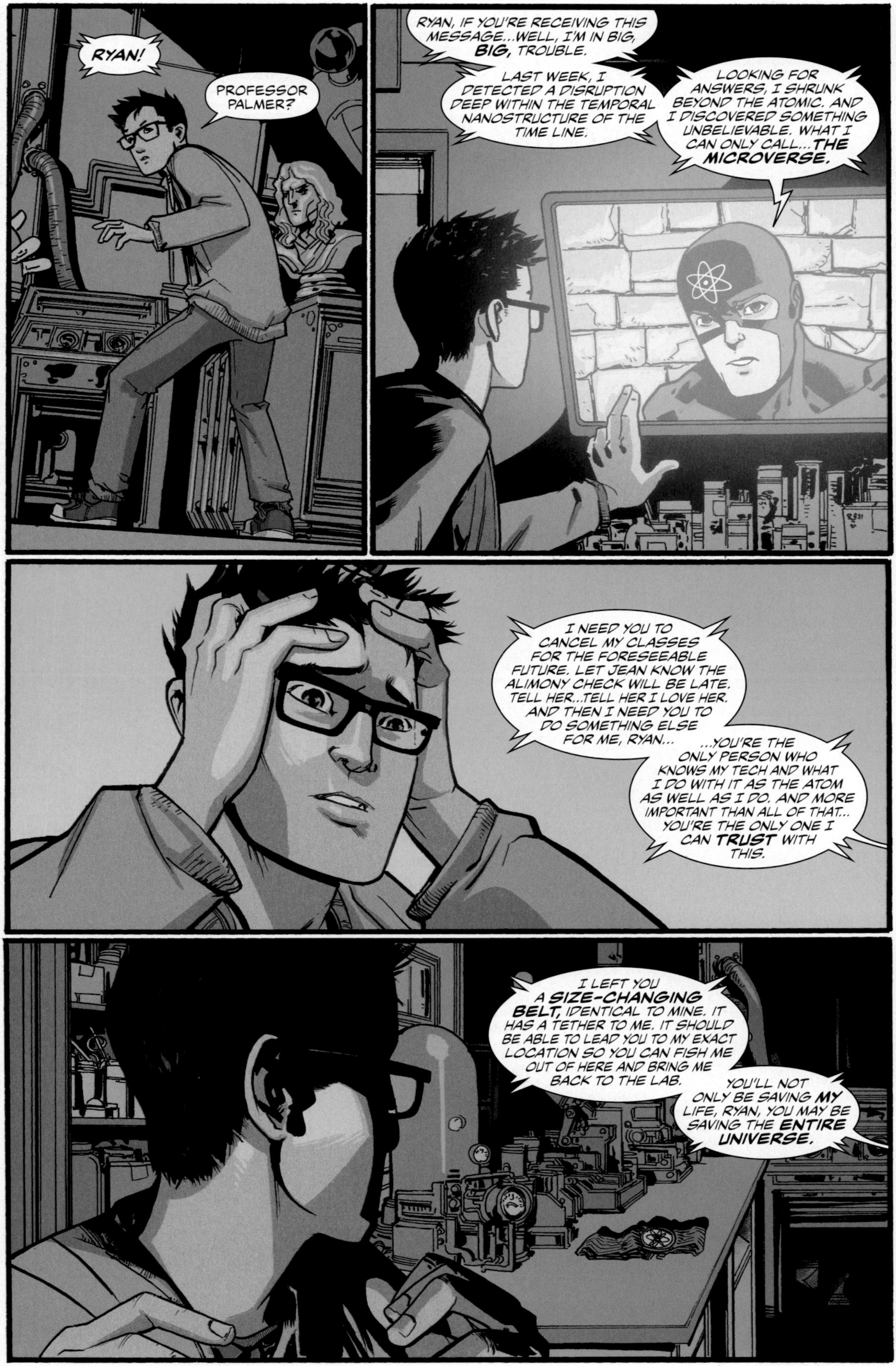
RYAN!
PROFESSOR PALMER?
RYAN, IF YOU'RE RECEIVING THIS MESSAGE...WELL, I'M IN BIG, BIG, TROUBLE.
LAST WEEK, I DETECTED A DISRUPTION DEEP WITHIN THE TEMPORAL NANOSTRUCTURE OF THE TIME LINE.
LOOKING FOR ANSWERS, I SHRUNK BEYOND THE ATOMIC. AND I DISCOVERED SOMETHING UNBELIEVABLE. WHAT I CAN ONLY CALL...THE MICROVERSE.
I NEED YOU TO CANCEL MY CLASSES FOR THE FORESEEABLE FUTURE. LET JEAN KNOW THE ALIMONY CHECK WILL BE LATE. TELL HER...TELL HER I LOVE HER. AND THEN I NEED YOU TO DO SOMETHING ELSE FOR ME, RYAN...
...YOU'RE THE ONLY PERSON WHO KNOWS MY TECH AND WHAT I DO WITH IT AS THE ATOM AS WELL AS I DO. AND MORE IMPORTANT THAN ALL OF THAT... YOU'RE THE ONLY ONE I CAN TRUST WITH THIS.
I LEFT YOU A SIZE-CHANGING BELT, IDENTICAL TO MINE. IT HAS A TETHER TO ME. IT SHOULD BE ABLE TO LEAD YOU TO MY EXACT LOCATION SO YOU CAN FISH ME OUT OF HERE AND BRING ME BACK TO THE LAB.
YOU'LL NOT ONLY BE SAVING MY LIFE, RYAN, YOU MAY BE SAVING THE ENTIRE UNIVERSE.

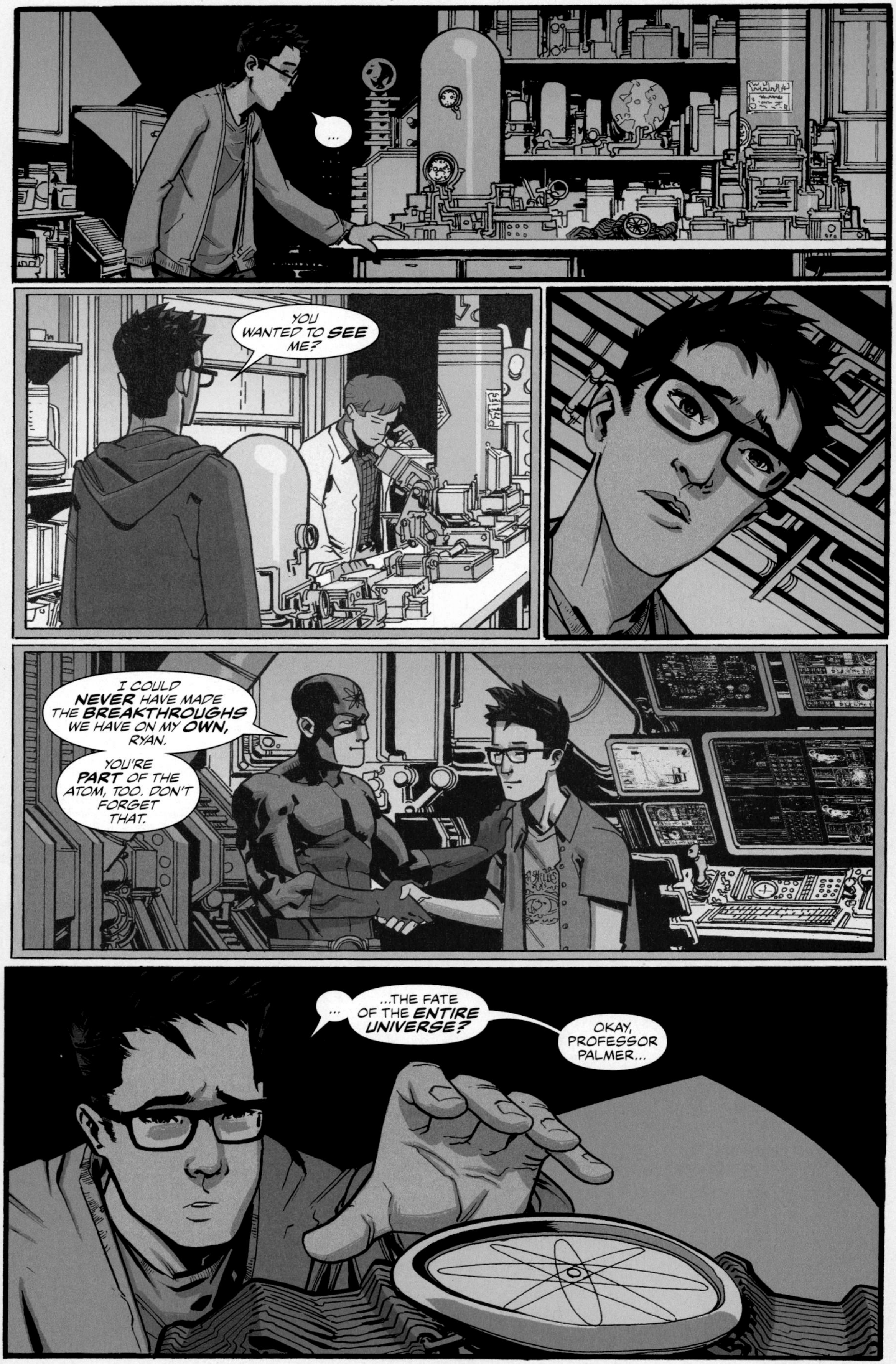
...
YOU WANTED TO SEE ME?
I COULD NEVER HAVE MADE THE BREAKTHROUGHS WE HAVE ON MY OWN, RYAN.
YOU'RE PART OF THE ATOM, TOO. DON'T FORGET THAT.
...
...THE FATE OF THE ENTIRE UNIVERSE?
OKAY, PROFESSOR PALMER...

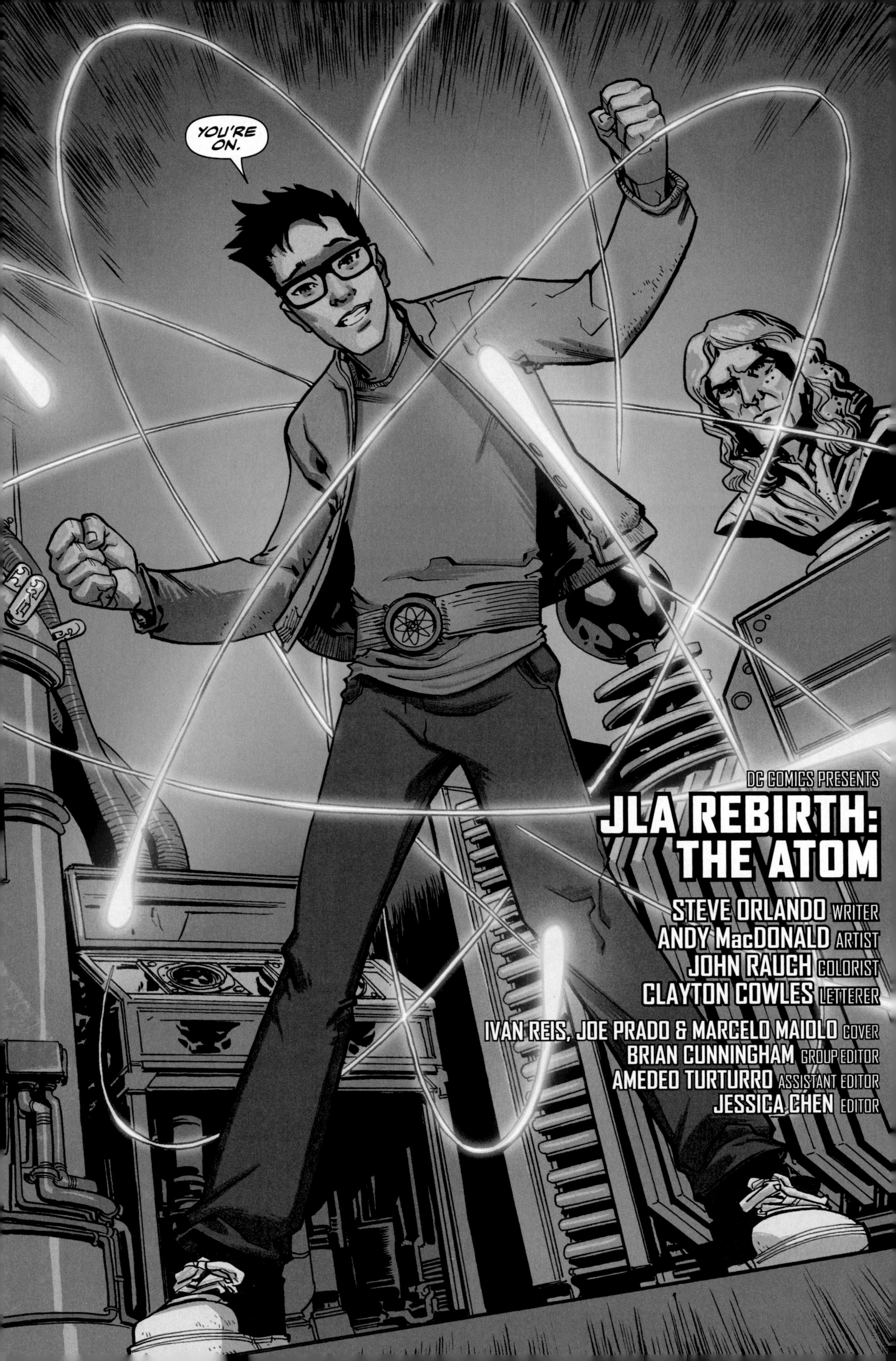

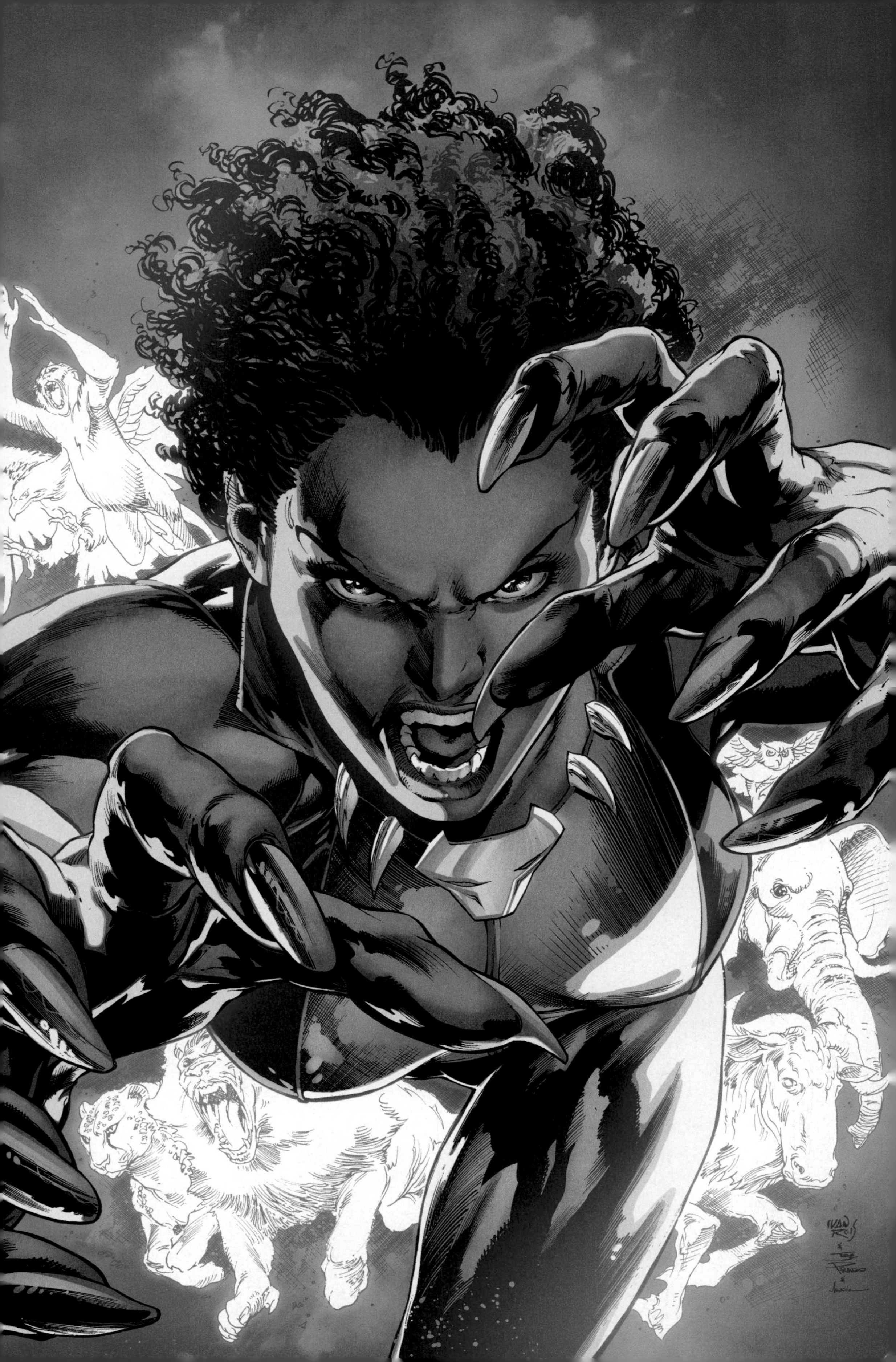

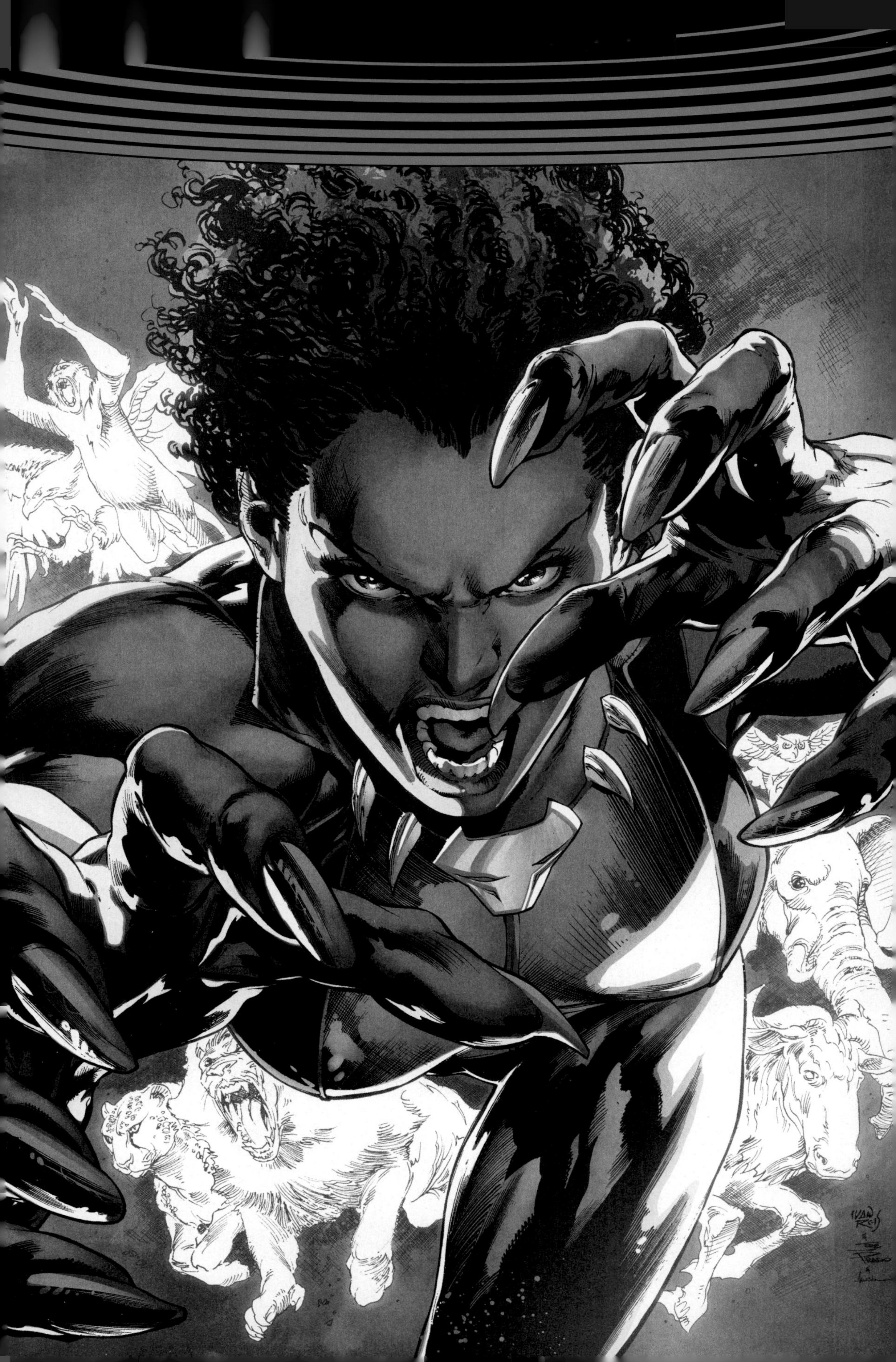

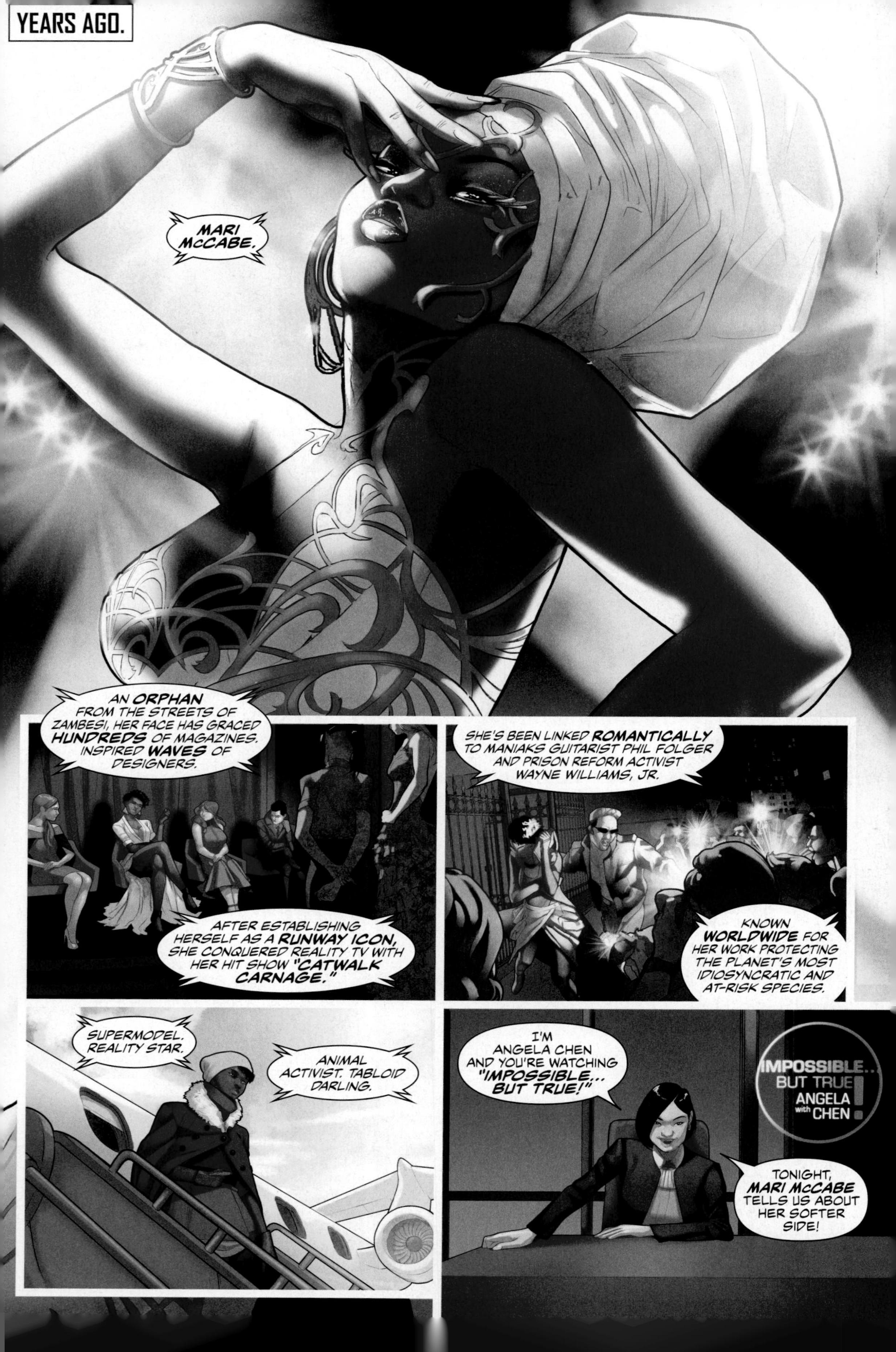
YEARS AGO.
MARI McCABE.
AN ORPHAN FROM THE STREETS OF ZAMBESI, HER FACE HAS GRACED HUNDREDS OF MAGAZINES. INSPIRED WAVES OF DESIGNERS.
AFTER ESTABLISHING HERSELF AS A RUNWAY ICON, SHE CONQUERED REALITY TV WITH HER HIT SHOW "CATWALK CARNAGE."
SHE'S BEEN LINKED ROMANTICALLY TO MANIAKS GUITARIST PHIL FOLGER AND PRISON REFORM ACTIVIST WAYNE WILLIAMS, JR.
KNOWN WORLDWIDE FOR HER WORK PROTECTING THE PLANET'S MOST IDIOSYNCRATIC AND AT-RISK SPECIES.
SUPERMODEL. REALITY STAR.
ANIMAL ACTIVIST. TABLOID DARLING.
I'M ANGELA CHEN AND YOU'RE WATCHING "IMPOSSIBLE... BUT TRUE!"
IMPOSSIBLE... BUT TRUE! with ANGELA CHEN
TONIGHT, MARI McCABE TELLS US ABOUT HER SOFTER SIDE!

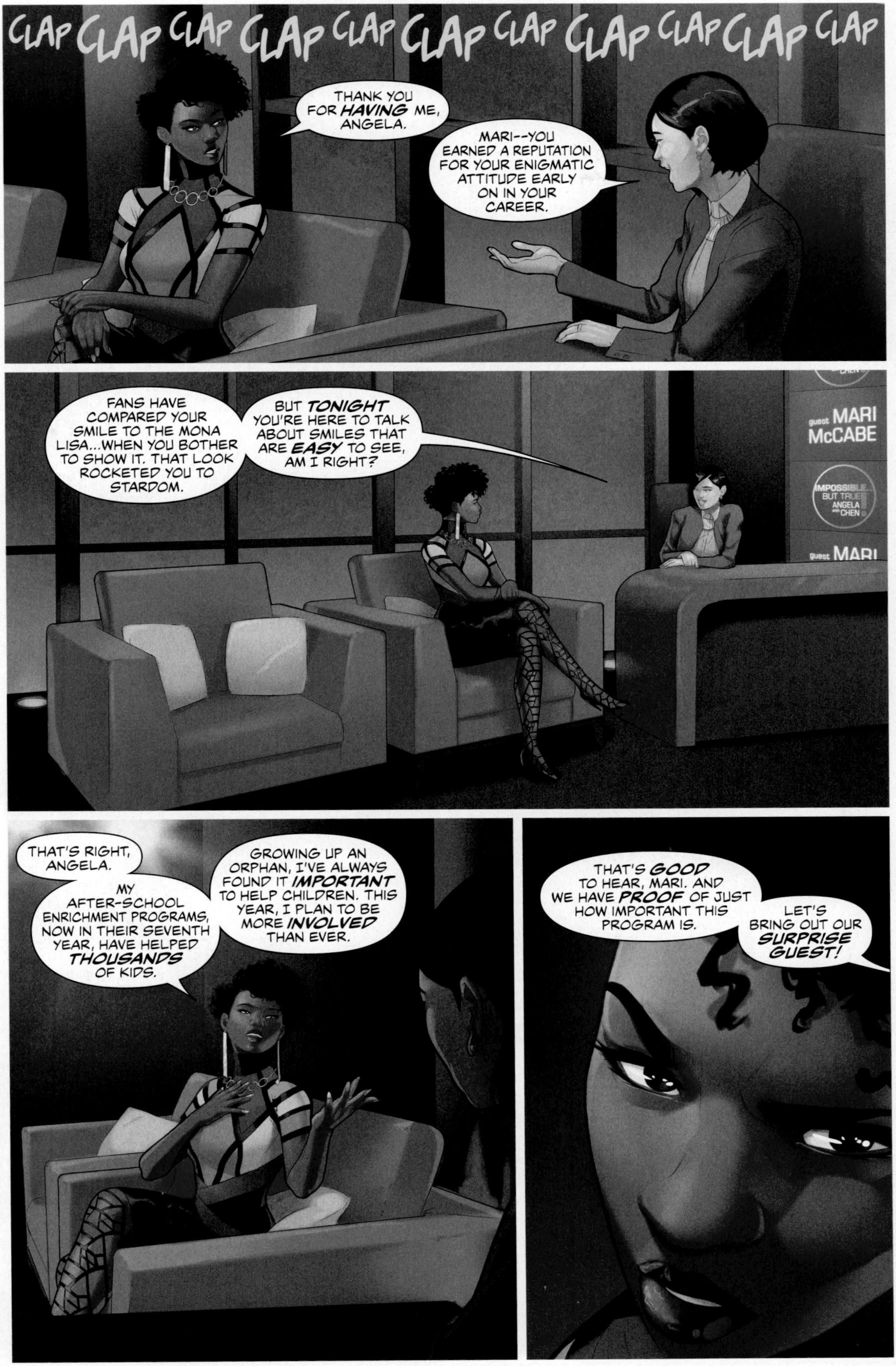
CLAP CLAP CLAP CLAP CLAP CLAP CLAP CLAP CLAP CLAP CLAP
THANK YOU FOR HAVING ME, ANGELA.
MARI--YOU EARNED A REPUTATION FOR YOUR ENIGMATIC ATTITUDE EARLY ON IN YOUR CAREER.
FANS HAVE COMPARED YOUR SMILE TO THE MONA LISA...WHEN YOU BOTHER TO SHOW IT. THAT LOOK ROCKETED YOU TO STARDOM.
BUT TONIGHT YOU'RE HERE TO TALK ABOUT SMILES THAT ARE EASY TO SEE, AM I RIGHT?
guest MARI McCABE
IMPOSSIBLE... BUT TRUE! ANGELA with CHEN
guest MARI
THAT'S RIGHT, ANGELA.
MY AFTER-SCHOOL ENRICHMENT PROGRAMS, NOW IN THEIR SEVENTH YEAR, HAVE HELPED THOUSANDS OF KIDS.
GROWING UP AN ORPHAN, I'VE ALWAYS FOUND IT IMPORTANT TO HELP CHILDREN. THIS YEAR, I PLAN TO BE MORE INVOLVED THAN EVER.
THAT'S GOOD TO HEAR, MARI. AND WE HAVE PROOF OF JUST HOW IMPORTANT THIS PROGRAM IS.
LET'S BRING OUT OUR SURPRISE GUEST!

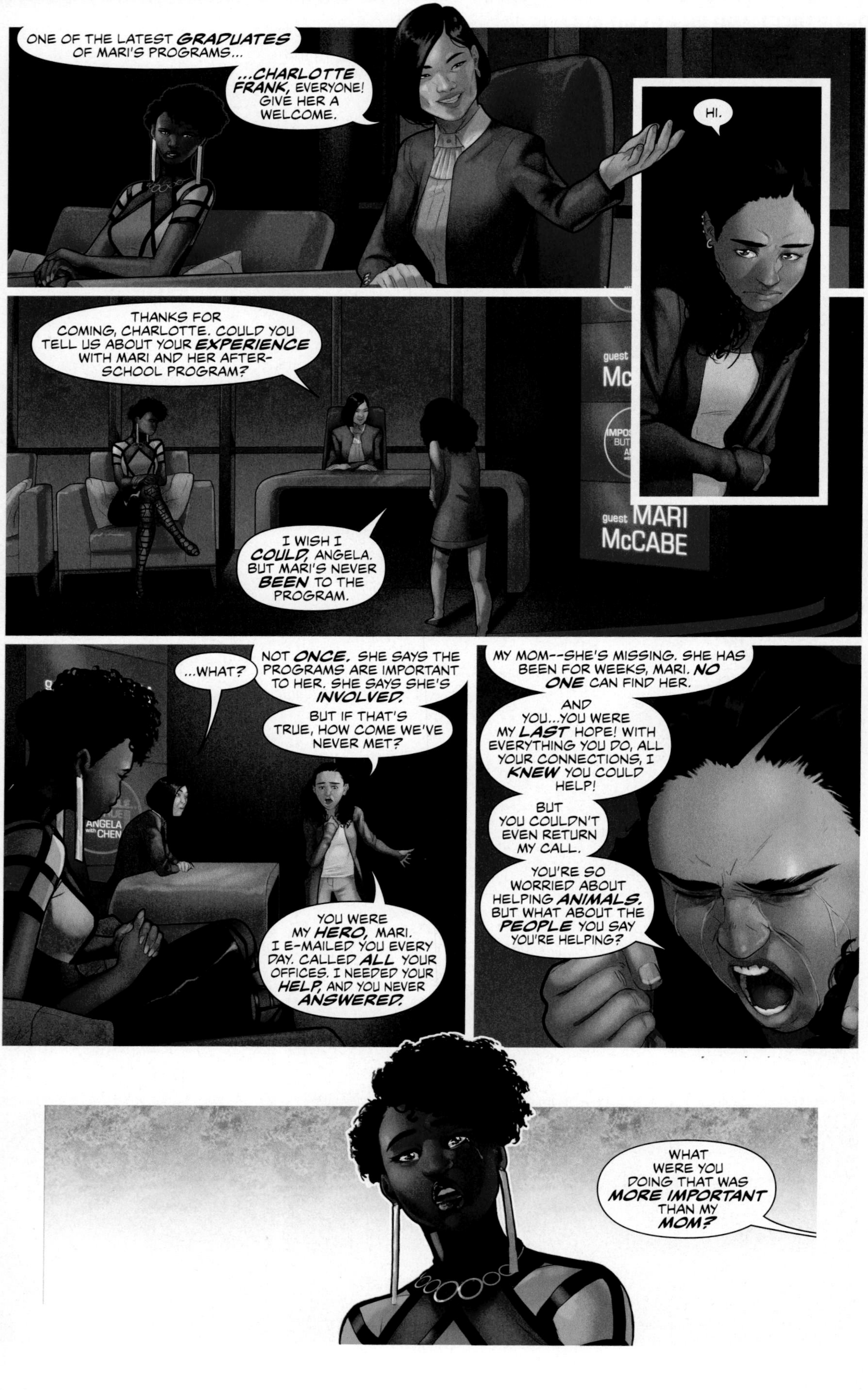
ONE OF THE LATEST GRADUATES OF MARI'S PROGRAMS...
...CHARLOTTE FRANK, EVERYONE! GIVE HER A WELCOME.
HI.
THANKS FOR COMING, CHARLOTTE. COULD YOU TELL US ABOUT YOUR EXPERIENCE WITH MARI AND HER AFTER-SCHOOL PROGRAM?
guest MARI McCABE
I WISH I COULD, ANGELA. BUT MARI'S NEVER BEEN TO THE PROGRAM.
...WHAT?
NOT ONCE. SHE SAYS THE PROGRAMS ARE IMPORTANT TO HER. SHE SAYS SHE'S INVOLVED.
BUT IF THAT'S TRUE, HOW COME WE'VE NEVER MET?
YOU WERE MY HERO, MARI. I E-MAILED YOU EVERY DAY. CALLED ALL YOUR OFFICES. I NEEDED YOUR HELP, AND YOU NEVER ANSWERED.
MY MOM--SHE'S MISSING. SHE HAS BEEN FOR WEEKS, MARI. NO ONE CAN FIND HER.
AND YOU...YOU WERE MY LAST HOPE! WITH EVERYTHING YOU DO, ALL YOUR CONNECTIONS, I KNEW YOU COULD HELP!
BUT YOU COULDN'T EVEN RETURN MY CALL.
YOU'RE SO WORRIED ABOUT HELPING ANIMALS. BUT WHAT ABOUT THE PEOPLE YOU SAY YOU'RE HELPING?
WHAT WERE YOU DOING THAT WAS MORE IMPORTANT THAN MY MOM?

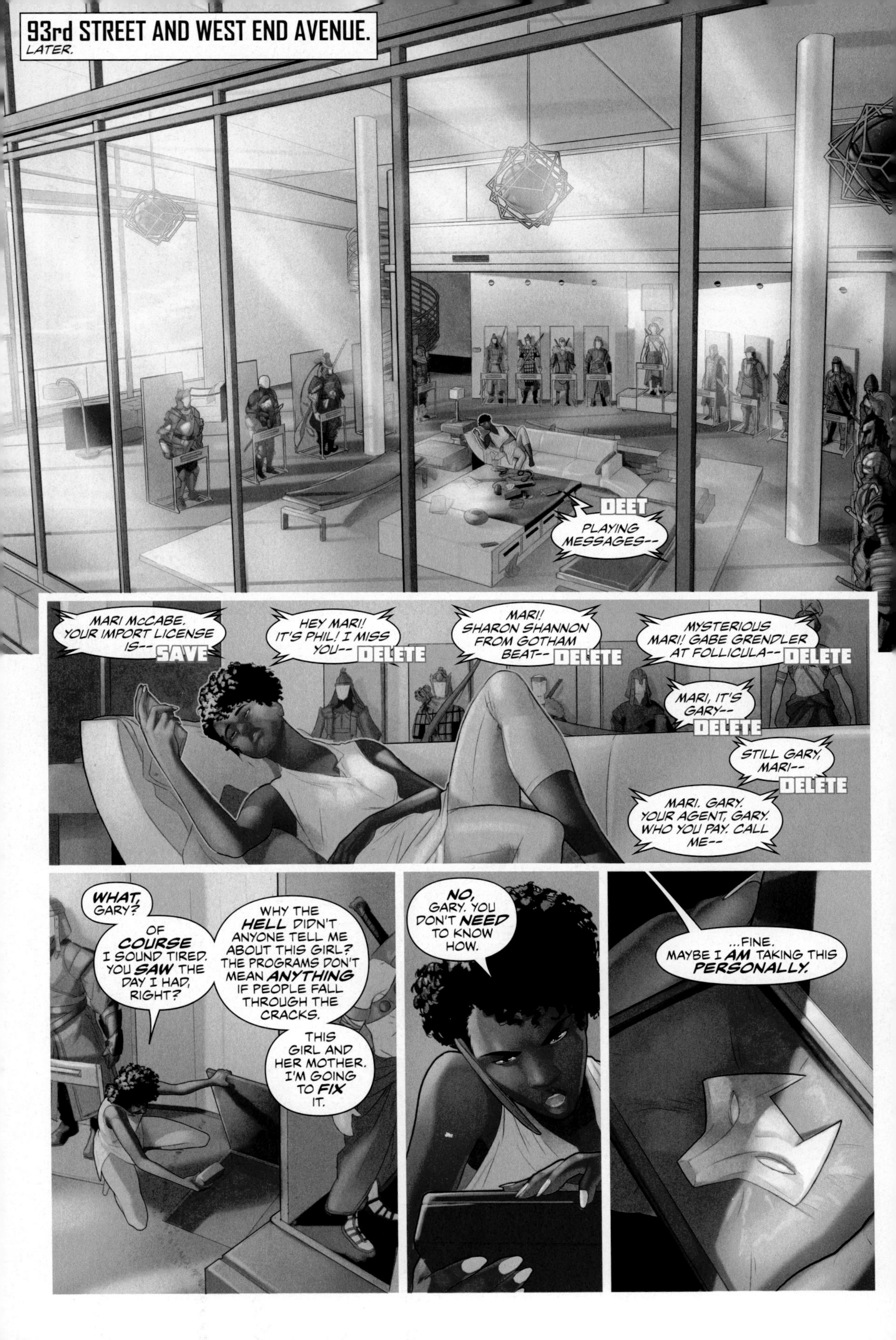
93rd STREET AND WEST END AVENUE.
LATER.
DEET
PLAYING MESSAGES--
MARI McCABE. YOUR IMPORT LICENSE IS-- SAVE
HEY MARI! IT'S PHIL! I MISS YOU-- DELETE
MARI! SHARON SHANNON FROM GOTHAM BEAT-- DELETE
MYSTERIOUS MARI! GABE GRENDLER AT FOLLICULA-- DELETE
MARI, IT'S GARY-- DELETE
STILL GARY, MARI-- DELETE
MARI. GARY. YOUR AGENT, GARY. WHO YOU PAY. CALL ME--
WHAT, GARY?
OF COURSE I SOUND TIRED. YOU SAW THE DAY I HAD, RIGHT?
WHY THE HELL DIDN'T ANYONE TELL ME ABOUT THIS GIRL? THE PROGRAMS DON'T MEAN ANYTHING IF PEOPLE FALL THROUGH THE CRACKS.
THIS GIRL AND HER MOTHER. I'M GOING TO FIX IT.
NO, GARY. YOU DON'T NEED TO KNOW HOW.
...FINE. MAYBE I AM TAKING THIS PERSONALLY.

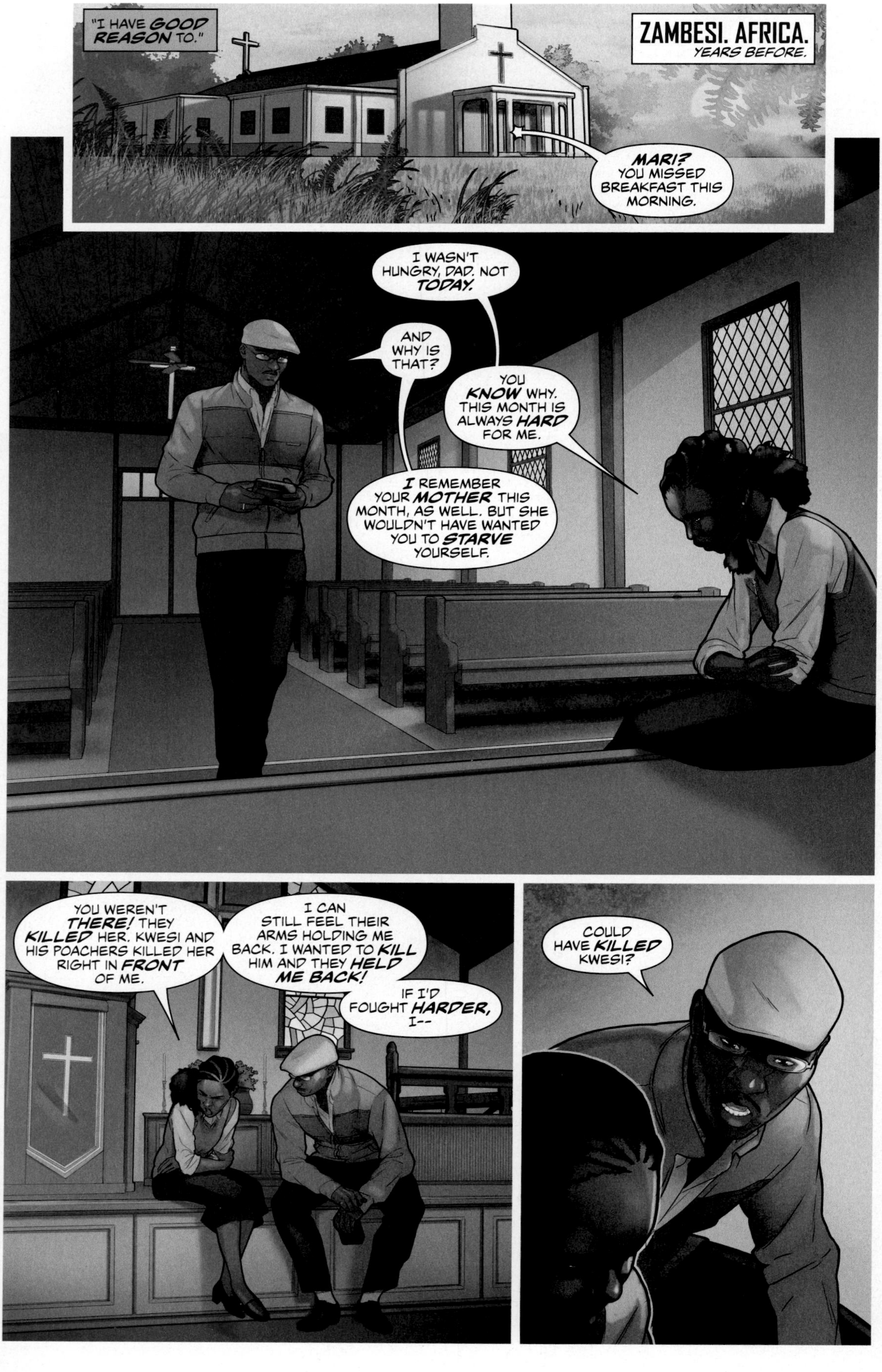
"I HAVE GOOD REASON TO."
ZAMBESI. AFRICA. YEARS BEFORE.
MARI? YOU MISSED BREAKFAST THIS MORNING.
I WASN'T HUNGRY, DAD. NOT TODAY.
AND WHY IS THAT?
YOU KNOW WHY. THIS MONTH IS ALWAYS HARD FOR ME.
I REMEMBER YOUR MOTHER THIS MONTH, AS WELL. BUT SHE WOULDN'T HAVE WANTED YOU TO STARVE YOURSELF.
YOU WEREN'T THERE! THEY KILLED HER. KWESI AND HIS POACHERS KILLED HER RIGHT IN FRONT OF ME.
I CAN STILL FEEL THEIR ARMS HOLDING ME BACK. I WANTED TO KILL HIM AND THEY HELD ME BACK!
IF I'D FOUGHT HARDER, I--
COULD HAVE KILLED KWESI?

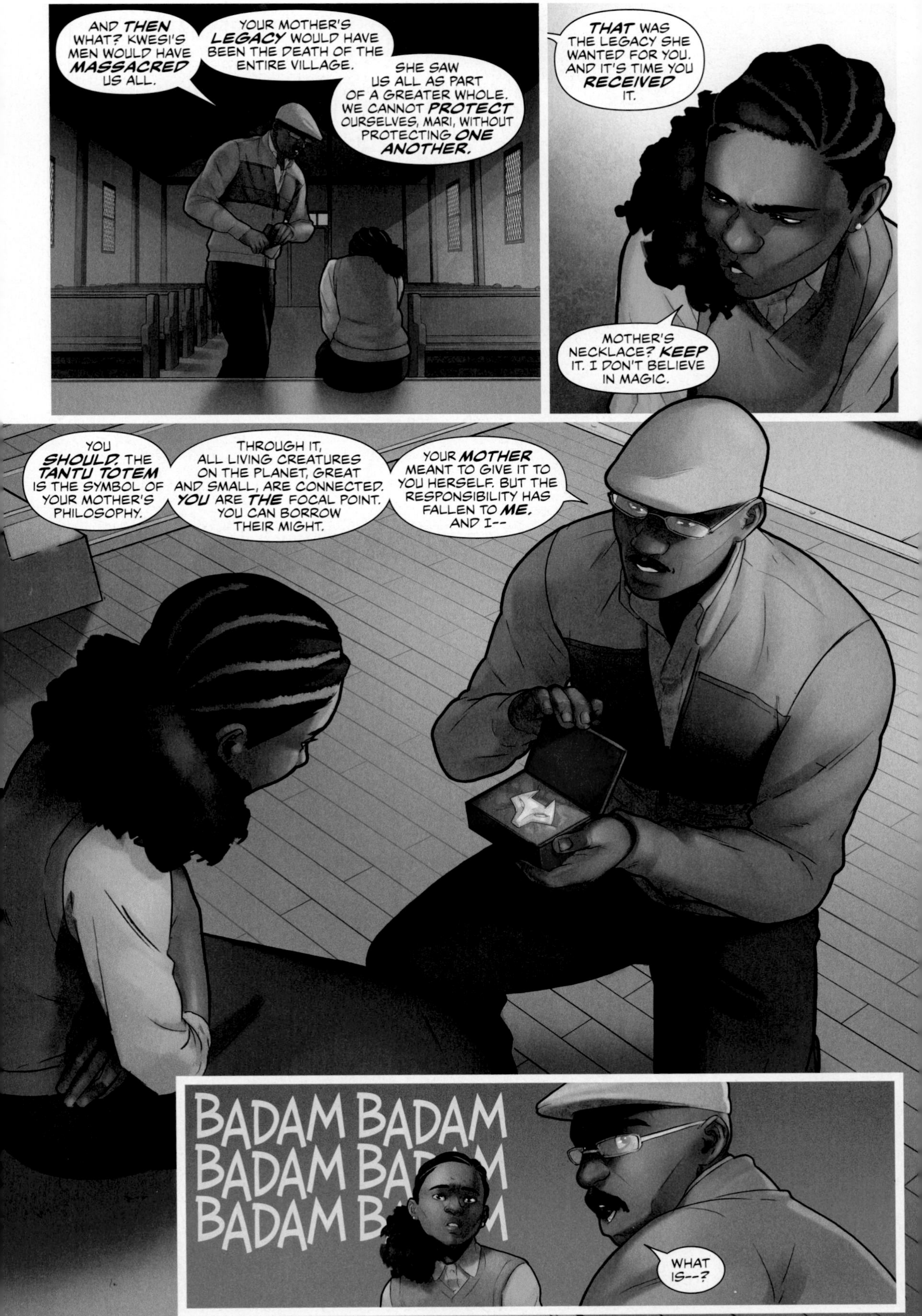
AND THEN WHAT? KWESI'S MEN WOULD HAVE MASSACRED US ALL.
YOUR MOTHER'S LEGACY WOULD HAVE BEEN THE DEATH OF THE ENTIRE VILLAGE.
SHE SAW US ALL AS PART OF A GREATER WHOLE. WE CANNOT PROTECT OURSELVES, MARI, WITHOUT PROTECTING ONE ANOTHER.
THAT WAS THE LEGACY SHE WANTED FOR YOU. AND IT'S TIME YOU RECEIVED IT.
MOTHER'S NECKLACE? KEEP IT. I DON'T BELIEVE IN MAGIC.
YOU SHOULD. THE TANTU TOTEM IS THE SYMBOL OF YOUR MOTHER'S PHILOSOPHY.
THROUGH IT, ALL LIVING CREATURES ON THE PLANET, GREAT AND SMALL, ARE CONNECTED. YOU ARE THE FOCAL POINT. YOU CAN BORROW THEIR MIGHT.
YOUR MOTHER MEANT TO GIVE IT TO YOU HERSELF. BUT THE RESPONSIBILITY HAS FALLEN TO ME. AND I--
BADAM BADAM
BADAM BADAM
BADAM BADAM
WHAT IS--?

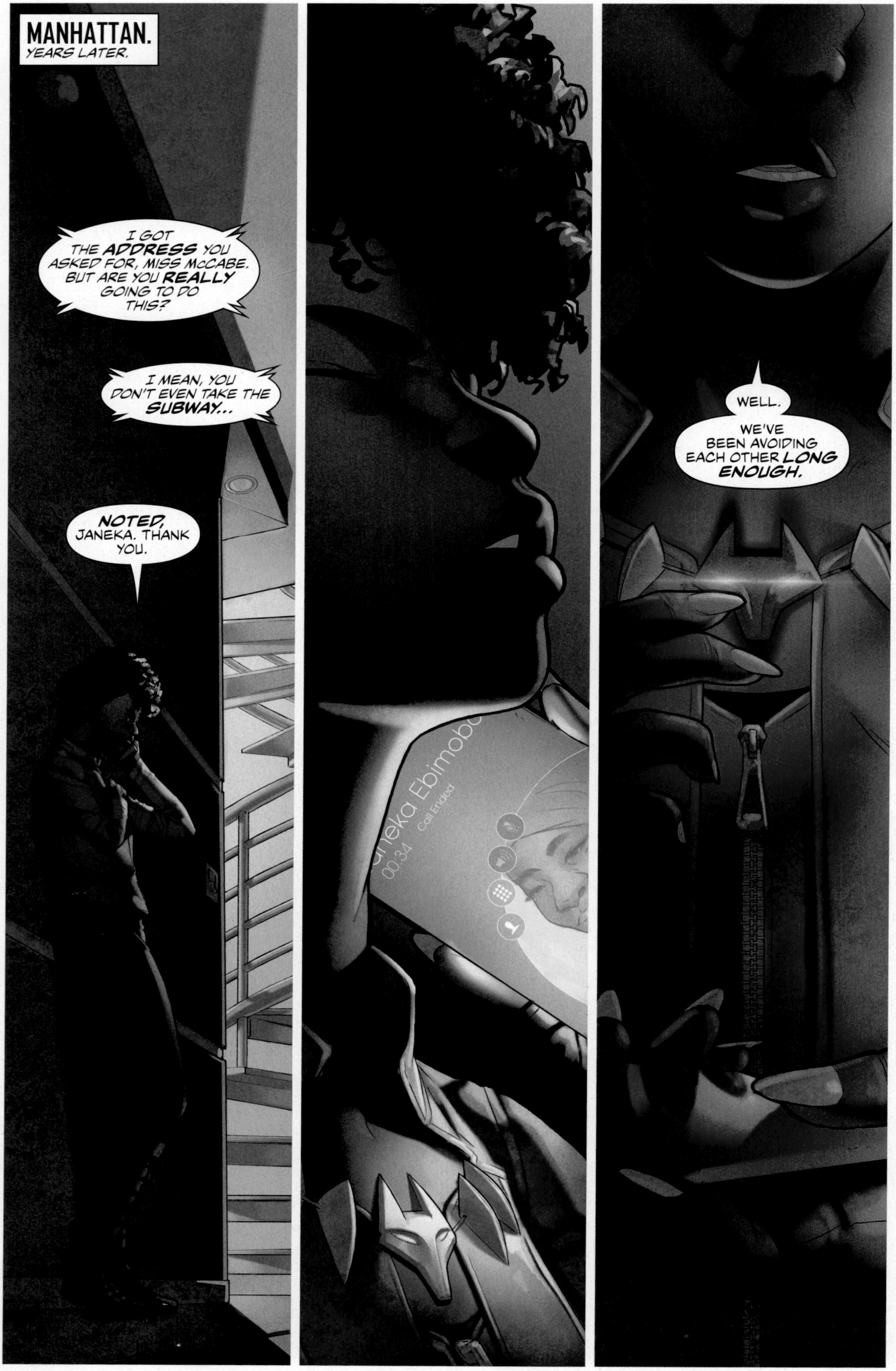
MANHATTAN.
YEARS LATER.
I GOT THE ADDRESS YOU ASKED FOR, MISS McCABE. BUT ARE YOU REALLY GOING TO DO THIS?
I MEAN, YOU DON'T EVEN TAKE THE SUBWAY...
NOTED, JANEKA. THANK YOU.
00:34 Call Ended
WELL.
WE'VE BEEN AVOIDING EACH OTHER LONG ENOUGH.

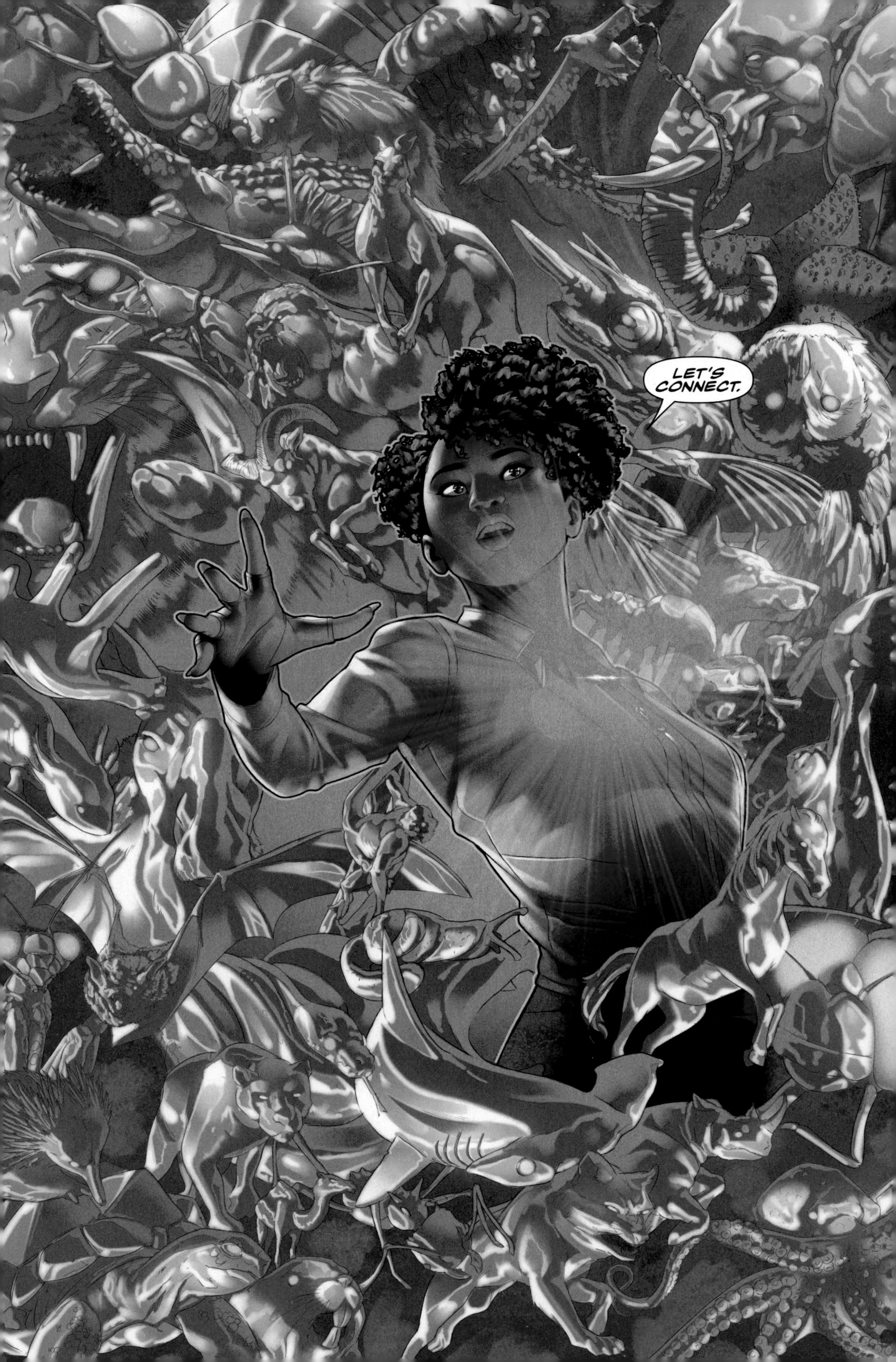
LET'S CONNECT.

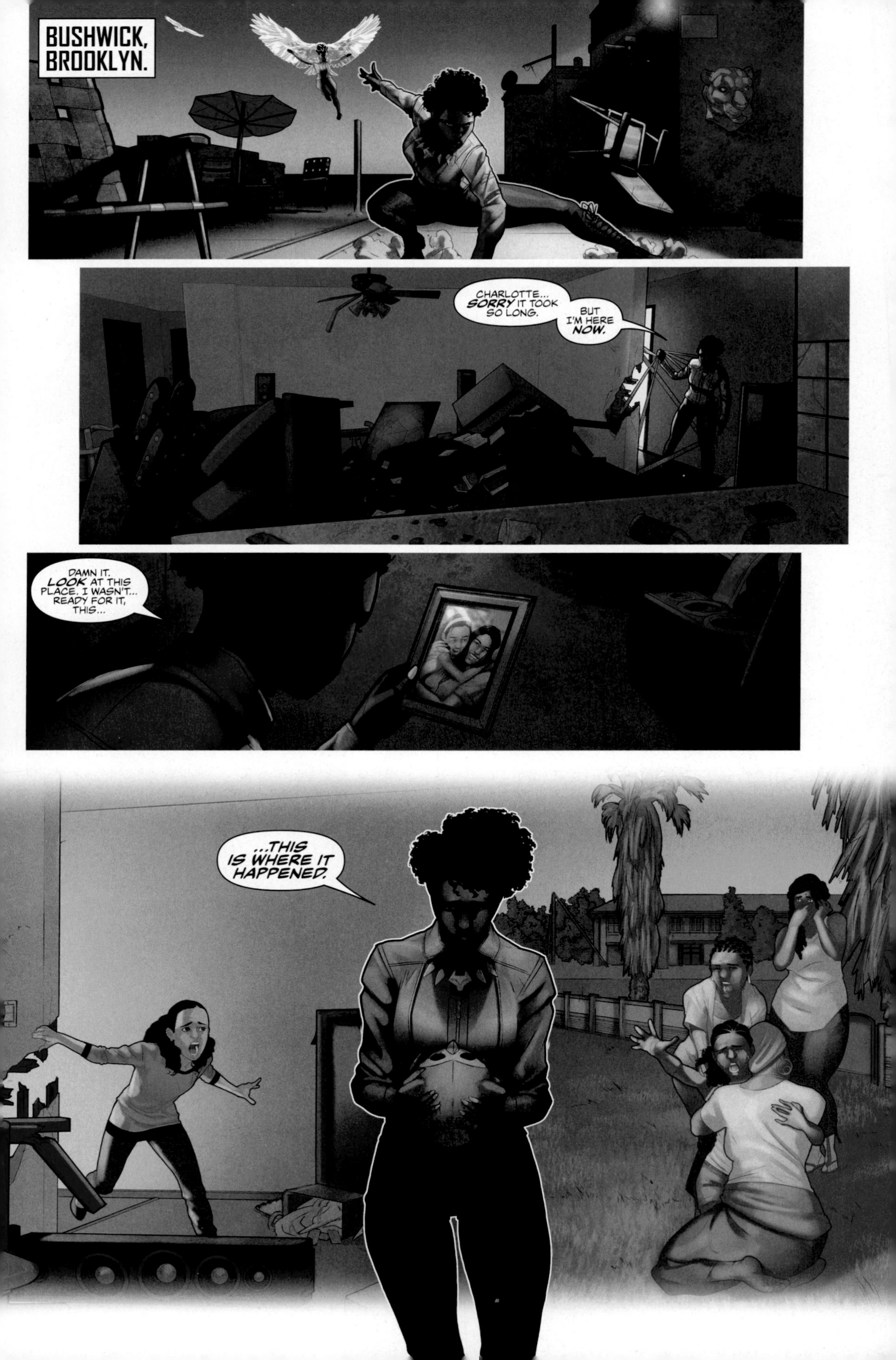
BUSHWICK, BROOKLYN.
CHARLOTTE... SORRY IT TOOK SO LONG.
BUT I'M HERE NOW.
DAMN IT. LOOK AT THIS PLACE. I WASN'T... READY FOR IT, THIS...
...THIS IS WHERE IT HAPPENED.

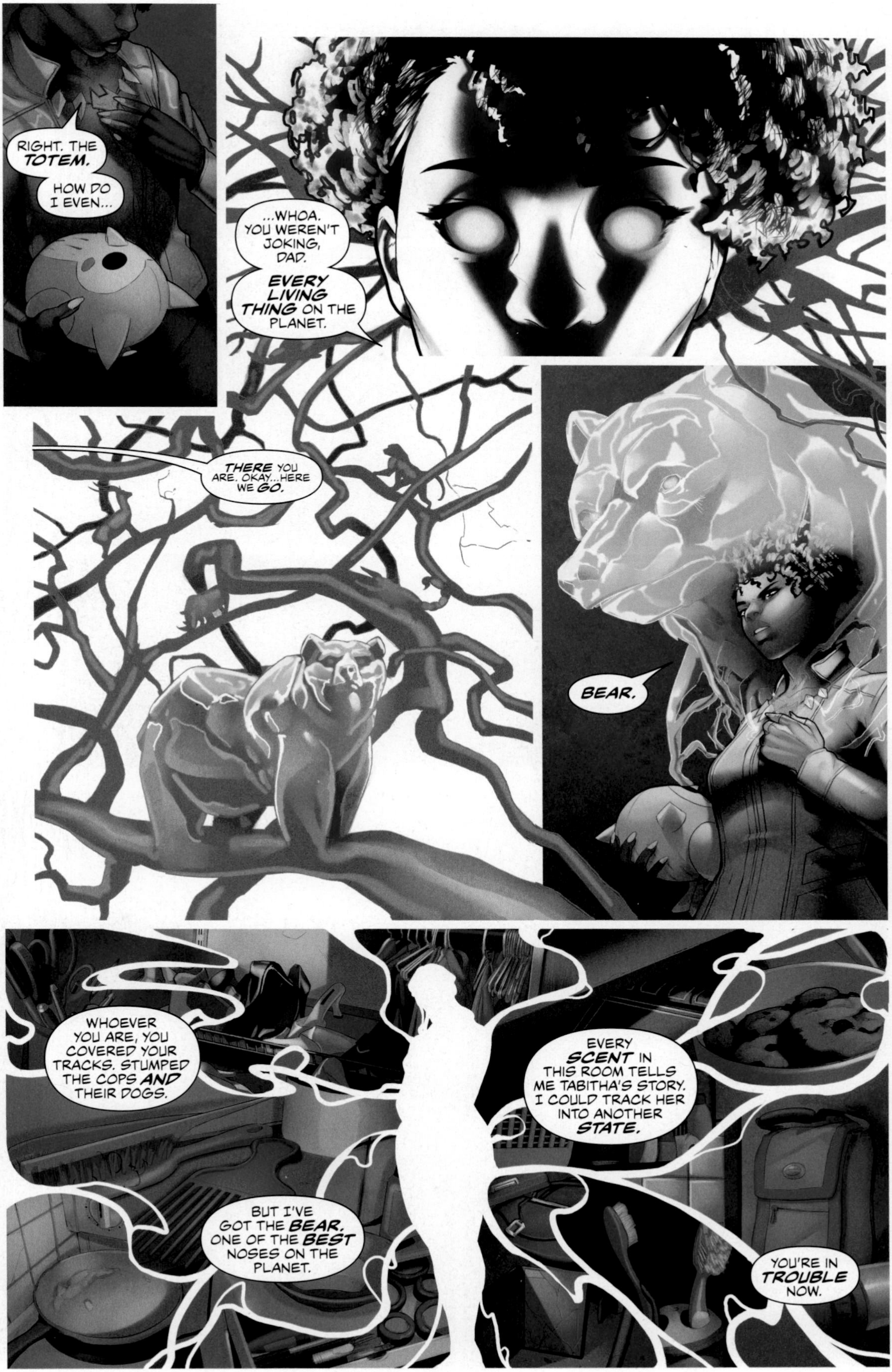
RIGHT. THE TOTEM.
HOW DO I EVEN...
...WHOA. YOU WEREN'T JOKING, DAD.
EVERY LIVING THING ON THE PLANET.
THERE YOU ARE. OKAY...HERE WE GO.
BEAR.
WHOEVER YOU ARE, YOU COVERED YOUR TRACKS. STUMPED THE COPS AND THEIR DOGS.
EVERY SCENT IN THIS ROOM TELLS ME TABITHA'S STORY. I COULD TRACK HER INTO ANOTHER STATE.
BUT I'VE GOT THE BEAR. ONE OF THE BEST NOSES ON THE PLANET.
YOU'RE IN TROUBLE NOW.

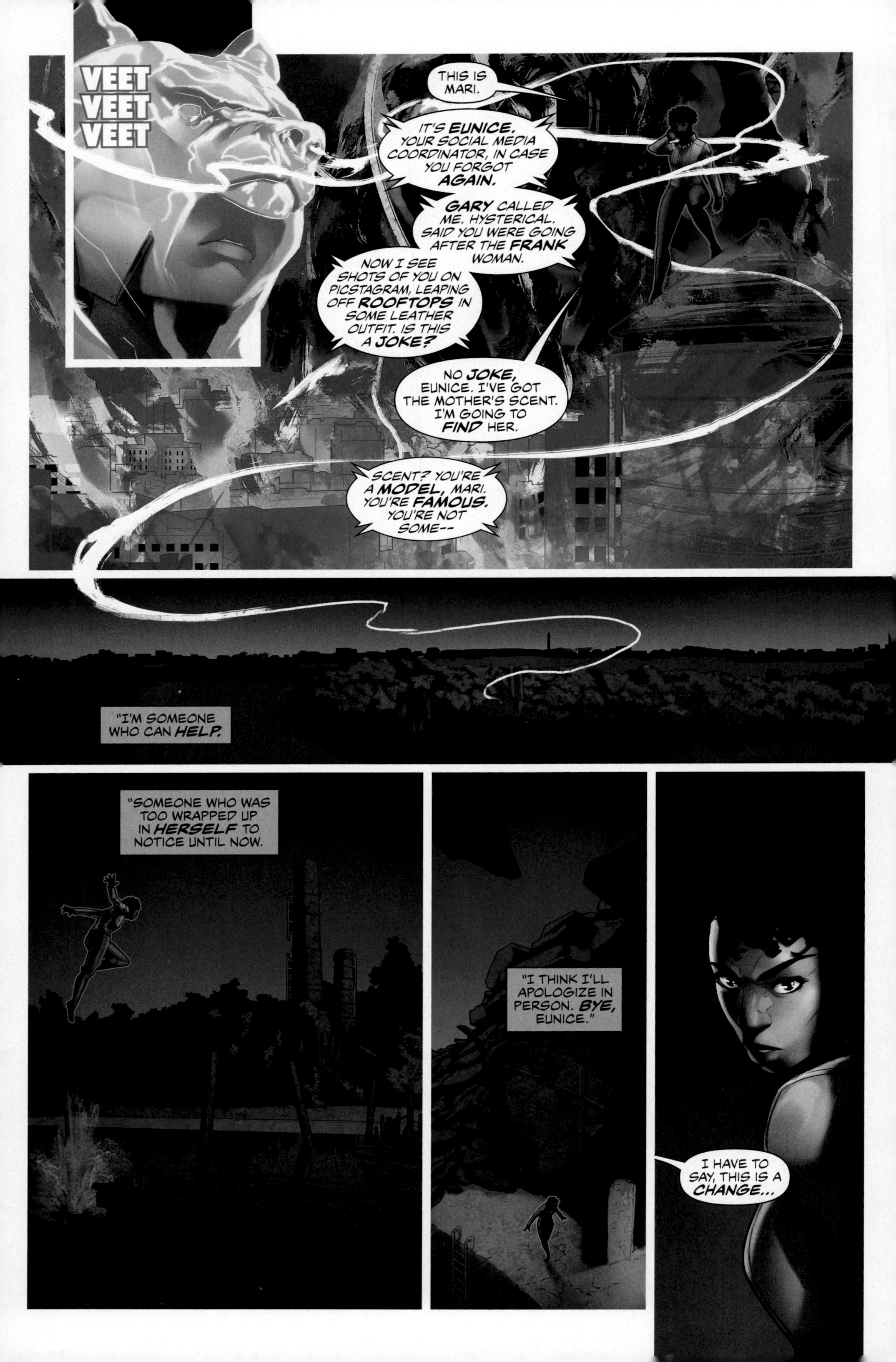
VEET
VEET
VEET
THIS IS MARI.
IT'S EUNICE. YOUR SOCIAL MEDIA COORDINATOR, IN CASE YOU FORGOT AGAIN.
GARY CALLED ME. HYSTERICAL. SAID YOU WERE GOING AFTER THE FRANK WOMAN.
NOW I SEE SHOTS OF YOU ON PICSTAGRAM, LEAPING OFF ROOFTOPS IN SOME LEATHER OUTFIT. IS THIS A JOKE?
NO JOKE, EUNICE. I'VE GOT THE MOTHER'S SCENT. I'M GOING TO FIND HER.
SCENT? YOU'RE A MODEL, MARI. YOU'RE FAMOUS. YOU'RE NOT SOME--
"I'M SOMEONE WHO CAN HELP.
"SOMEONE WHO WAS TOO WRAPPED UP IN HERSELF TO NOTICE UNTIL NOW.
"I THINK I'LL APOLOGIZE IN PERSON. BYE, EUNICE."
I HAVE TO SAY, THIS IS A CHANGE...

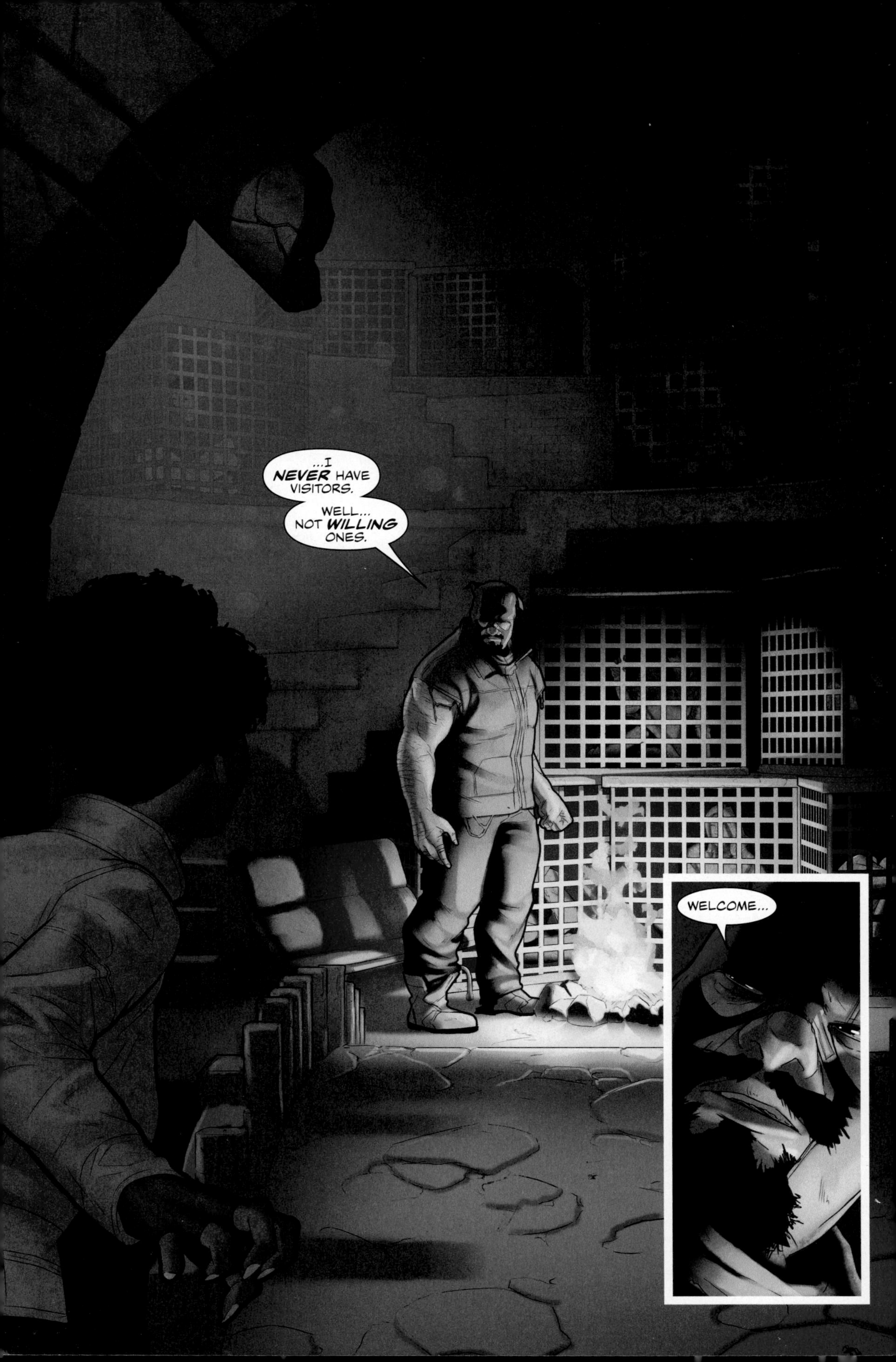
...I **NEVER** HAVE VISITORS.
WELL... NOT **WILLING** ONES.
WELCOME...

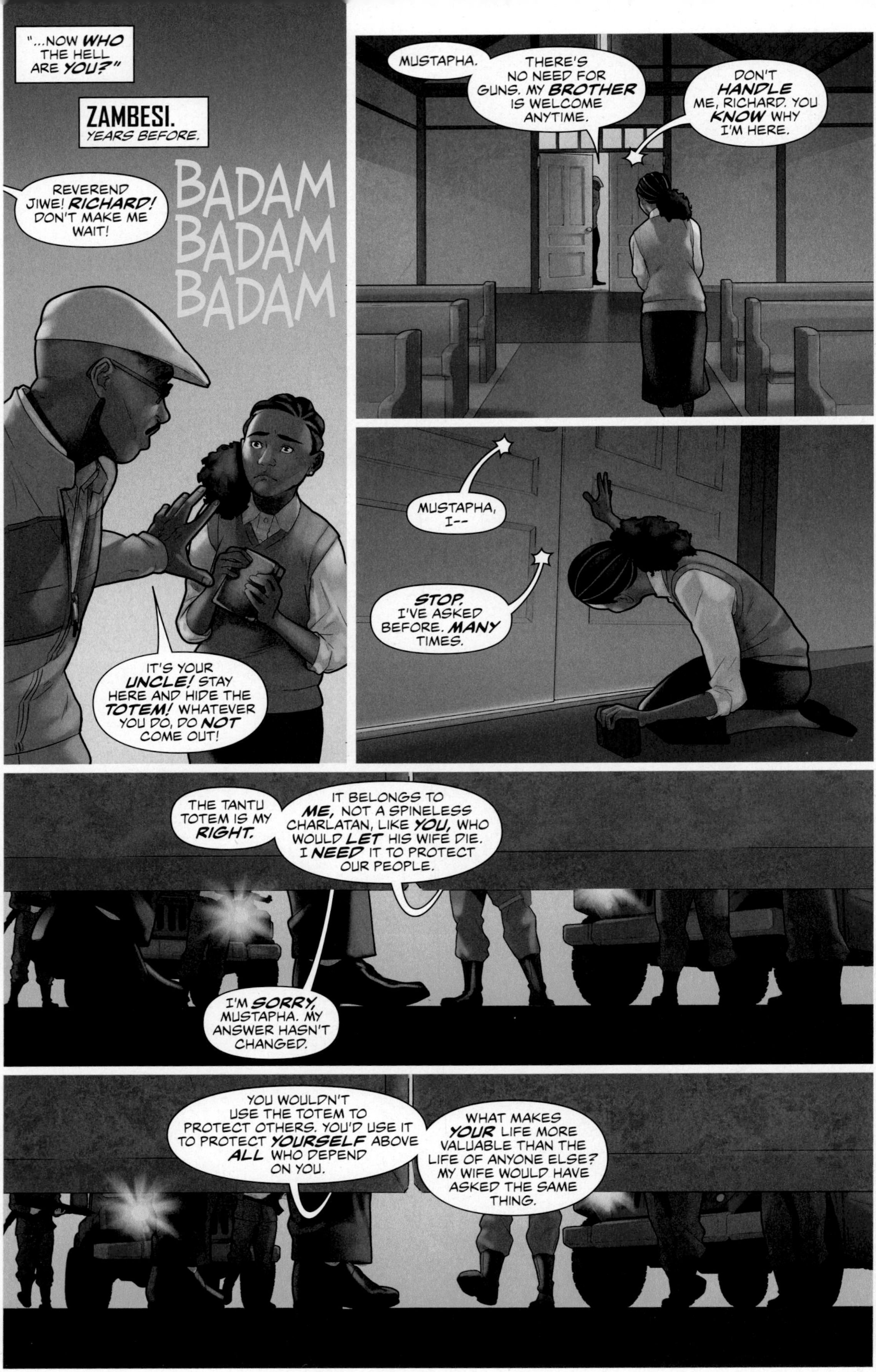
"...NOW WHO THE HELL ARE YOU?"
ZAMBESI. YEARS BEFORE.
REVEREND JIWE! RICHARD! DON'T MAKE ME WAIT!
BADAM BADAM BADAM
IT'S YOUR UNCLE! STAY HERE AND HIDE THE TOTEM! WHATEVER YOU DO, DO NOT COME OUT!
MUSTAPHA.
THERE'S NO NEED FOR GUNS. MY BROTHER IS WELCOME ANYTIME.
DON'T HANDLE ME, RICHARD. YOU KNOW WHY I'M HERE.
MUSTAPHA, I--
STOP. I'VE ASKED BEFORE. MANY TIMES.
THE TANTU TOTEM IS MY RIGHT.
IT BELONGS TO ME, NOT A SPINELESS CHARLATAN, LIKE YOU, WHO WOULD LET HIS WIFE DIE. I NEED IT TO PROTECT OUR PEOPLE.
I'M SORRY, MUSTAPHA. MY ANSWER HASN'T CHANGED.
YOU WOULDN'T USE THE TOTEM TO PROTECT OTHERS. YOU'D USE IT TO PROTECT YOURSELF ABOVE ALL WHO DEPEND ON YOU.
WHAT MAKES YOUR LIFE MORE VALUABLE THAN THE LIFE OF ANYONE ELSE? MY WIFE WOULD HAVE ASKED THE SAME THING.

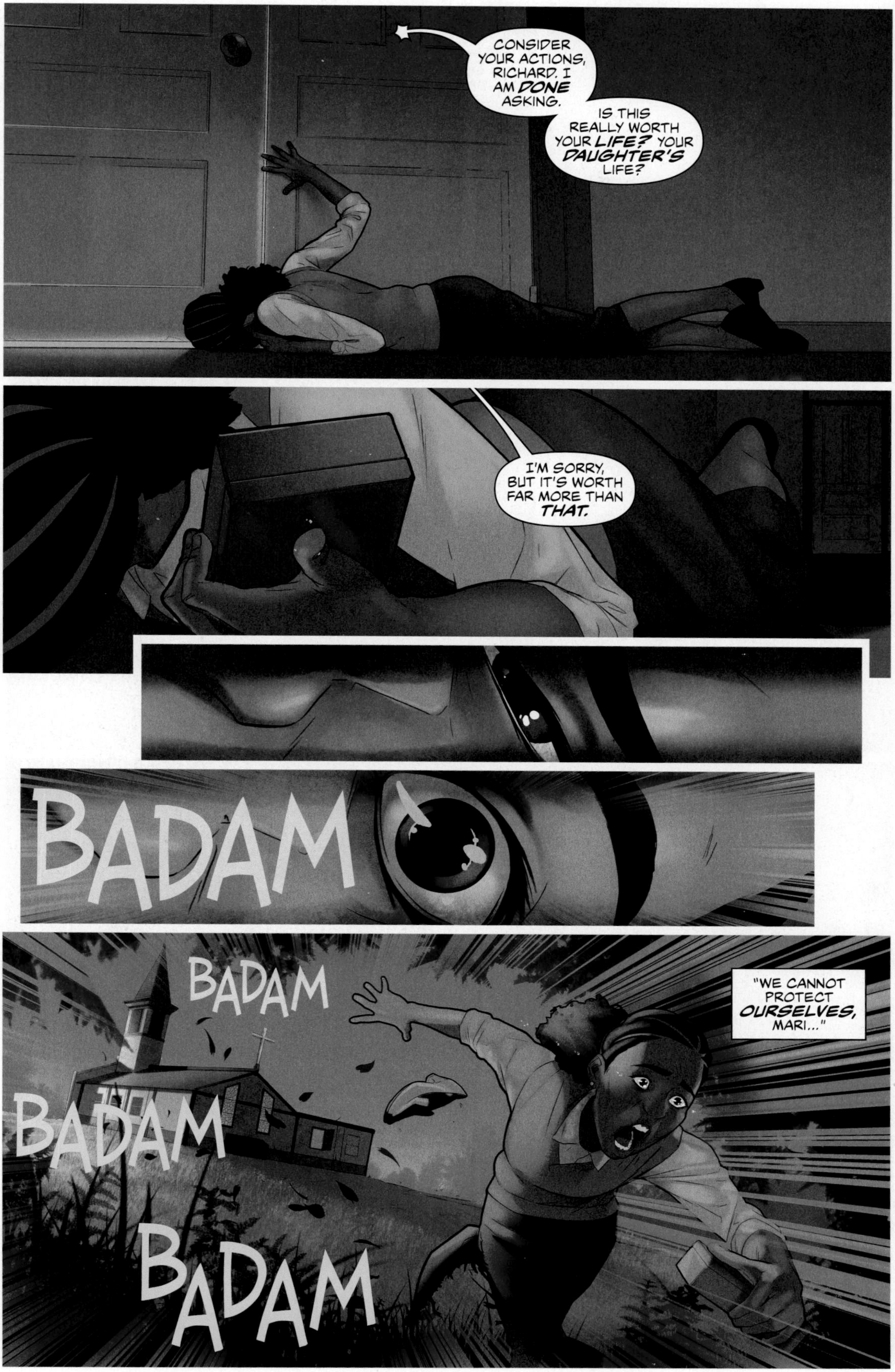
CONSIDER YOUR ACTIONS, RICHARD. I AM DONE ASKING.
IS THIS REALLY WORTH YOUR LIFE? YOUR DAUGHTER'S LIFE?
I'M SORRY, BUT IT'S WORTH FAR MORE THAN THAT.
BADAM
BADAM
"WE CANNOT PROTECT OURSELVES, MARI..."
BADAM
BADAM

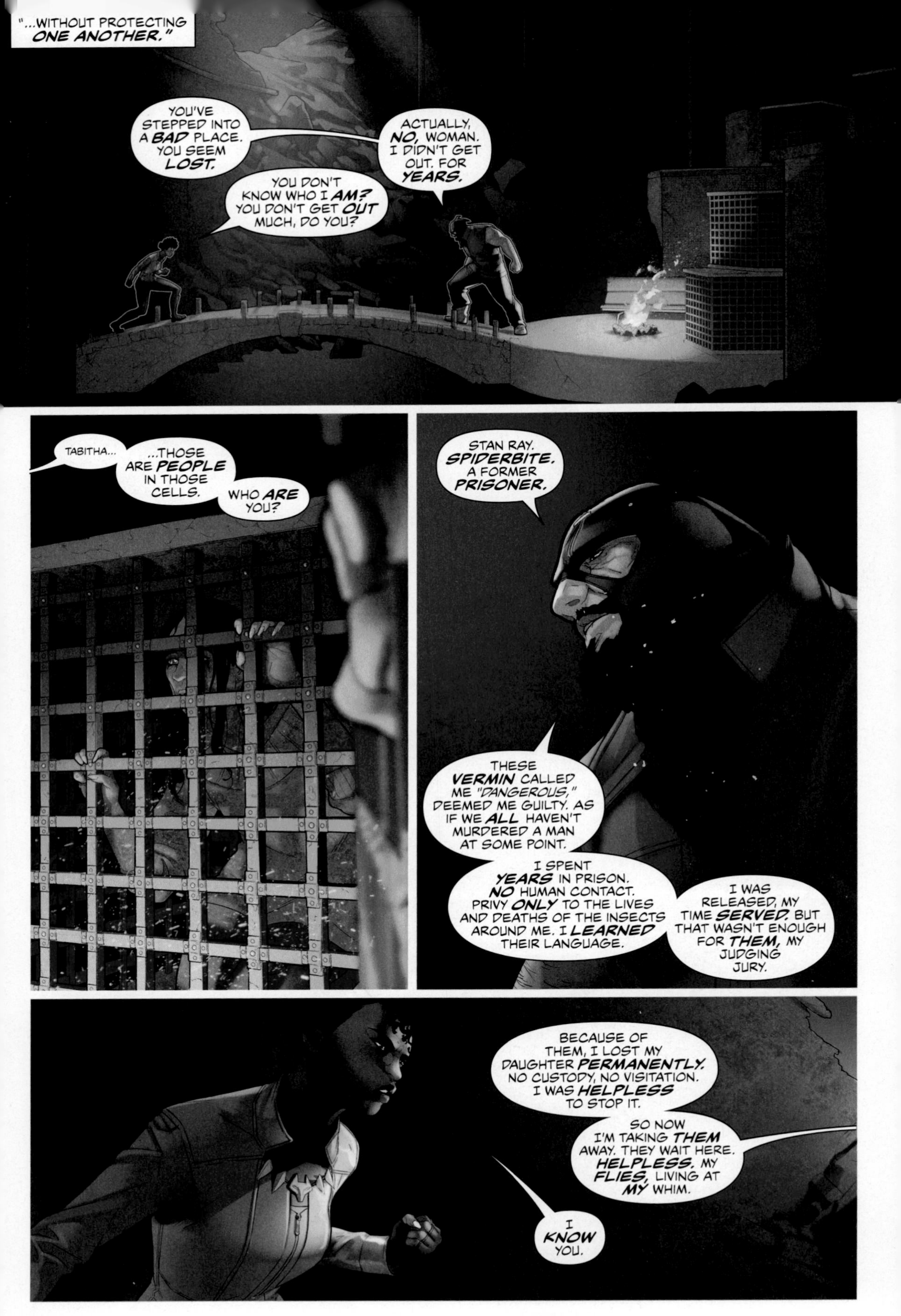

"...WITHOUT PROTECTING ONE ANOTHER."
YOU'VE STEPPED INTO A BAD PLACE. YOU SEEM LOST.
ACTUALLY, NO, WOMAN. I DIDN'T GET OUT. FOR YEARS.
YOU DON'T KNOW WHO I AM? YOU DON'T GET OUT MUCH, DO YOU?
TABITHA...
...THOSE ARE PEOPLE IN THOSE CELLS.
WHO ARE YOU?
STAN RAY. SPIDERBITE. A FORMER PRISONER.
THESE VERMIN CALLED ME "DANGEROUS," DEEMED ME GUILTY. AS IF WE ALL HAVEN'T MURDERED A MAN AT SOME POINT.
I SPENT YEARS IN PRISON. NO HUMAN CONTACT. PRIVY ONLY TO THE LIVES AND DEATHS OF THE INSECTS AROUND ME. I LEARNED THEIR LANGUAGE.
I WAS RELEASED, MY TIME SERVED. BUT THAT WASN'T ENOUGH FOR THEM, MY JUDGING JURY.
BECAUSE OF THEM, I LOST MY DAUGHTER PERMANENTLY. NO CUSTODY, NO VISITATION. I WAS HELPLESS TO STOP IT.
SO NOW I'M TAKING THEM AWAY. THEY WAIT HERE. HELPLESS. MY FLIES, LIVING AT MY WHIM.
I KNOW YOU.

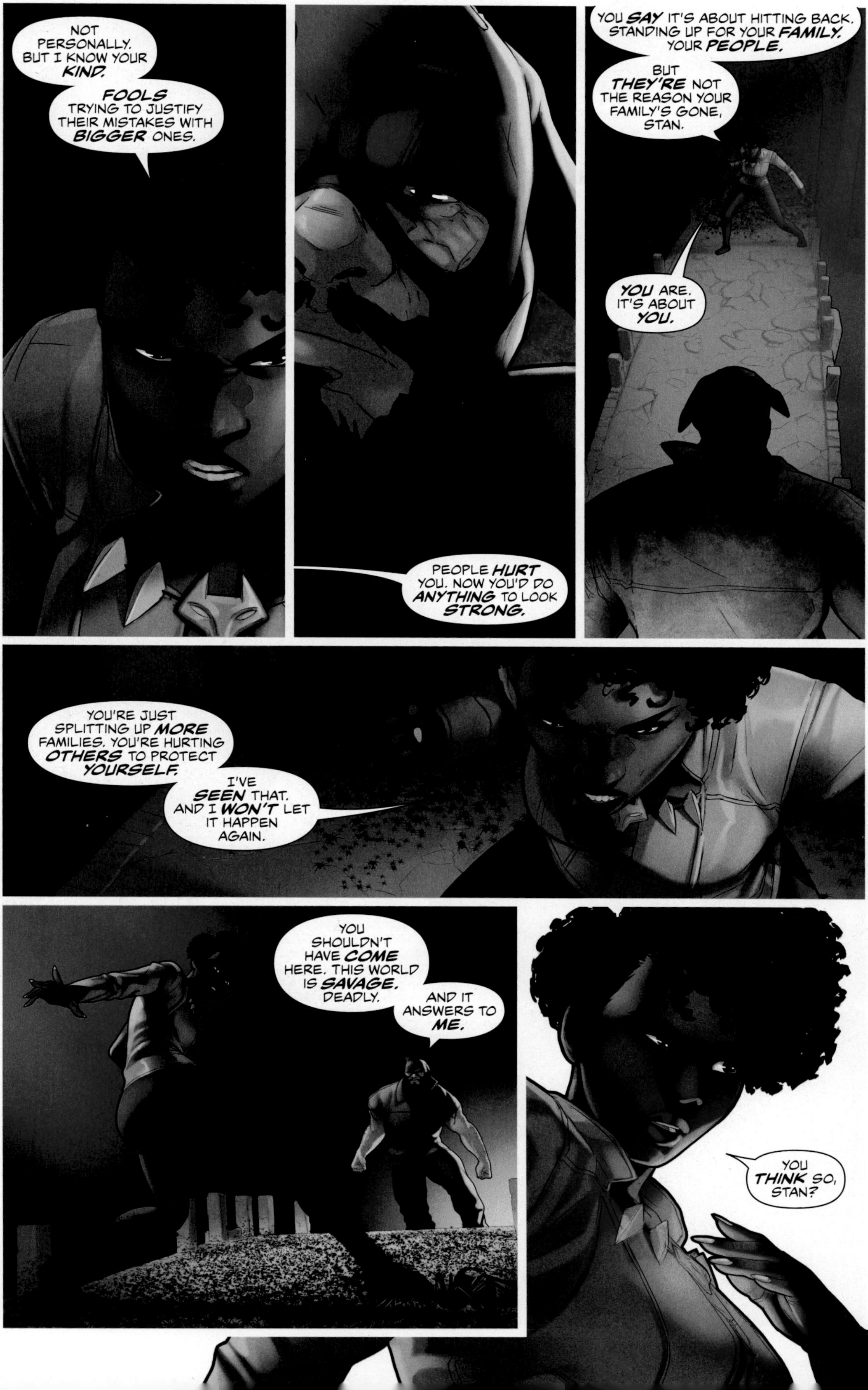
NOT PERSONALLY. BUT I KNOW YOUR KIND.
FOOLS TRYING TO JUSTIFY THEIR MISTAKES WITH BIGGER ONES.
PEOPLE HURT YOU. NOW YOU'D DO ANYTHING TO LOOK STRONG.
YOU SAY IT'S ABOUT HITTING BACK. STANDING UP FOR YOUR FAMILY. YOUR PEOPLE.
BUT THEY'RE NOT THE REASON YOUR FAMILY'S GONE, STAN.
YOU ARE. IT'S ABOUT YOU.
YOU'RE JUST SPLITTING UP MORE FAMILIES. YOU'RE HURTING OTHERS TO PROTECT YOURSELF.
I'VE SEEN THAT. AND I WON'T LET IT HAPPEN AGAIN.
YOU SHOULDN'T HAVE COME HERE. THIS WORLD IS SAVAGE. DEADLY.
AND IT ANSWERS TO ME.
YOU THINK SO, STAN?

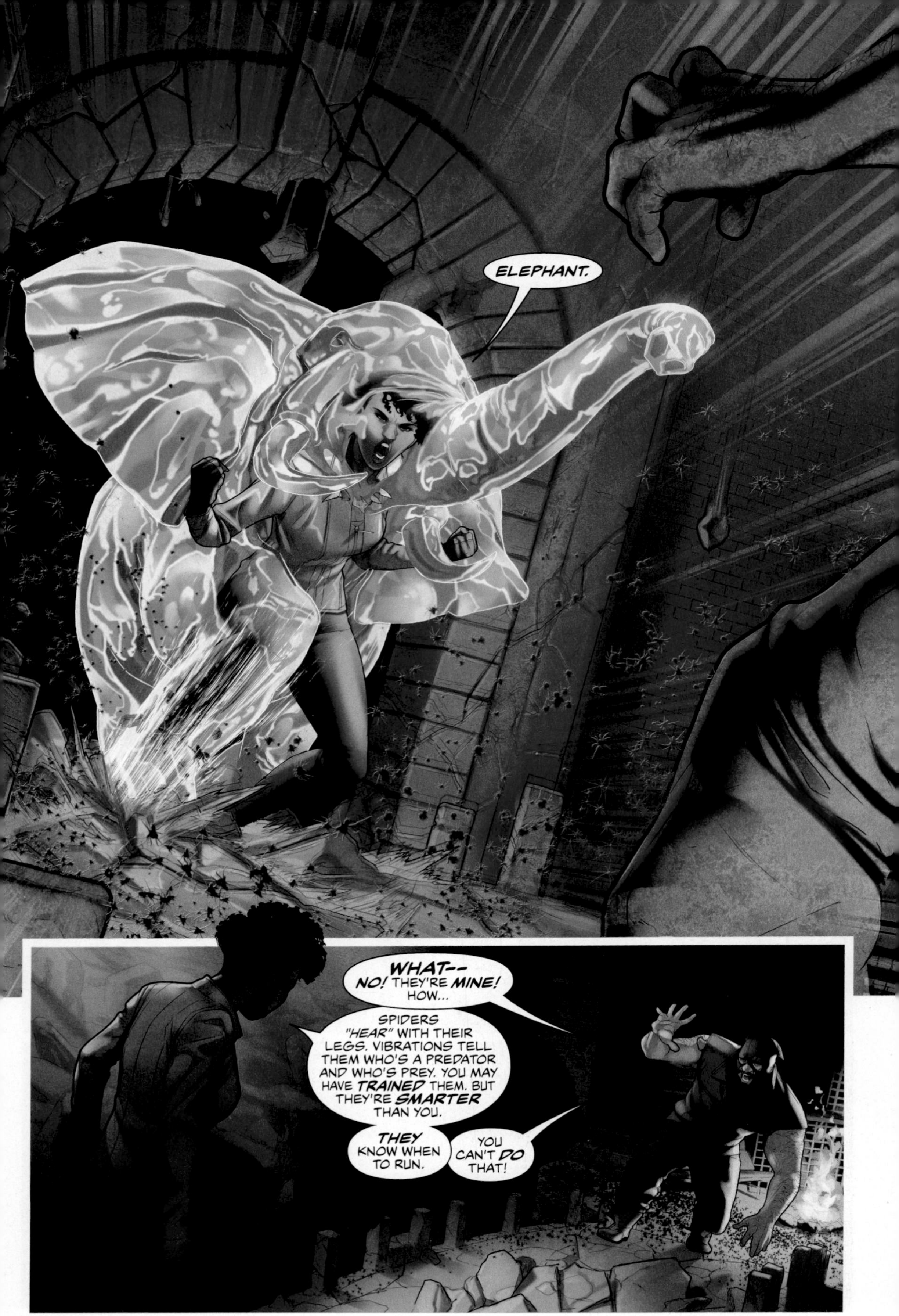
ELEPHANT.
WHAT-- NO! THEY'RE MINE! HOW...
SPIDERS "HEAR" WITH THEIR LEGS. VIBRATIONS TELL THEM WHO'S A PREDATOR AND WHO'S PREY. YOU MAY HAVE TRAINED THEM. BUT THEY'RE SMARTER THAN YOU.
THEY KNOW WHEN TO RUN.
YOU CAN'T DO THAT!

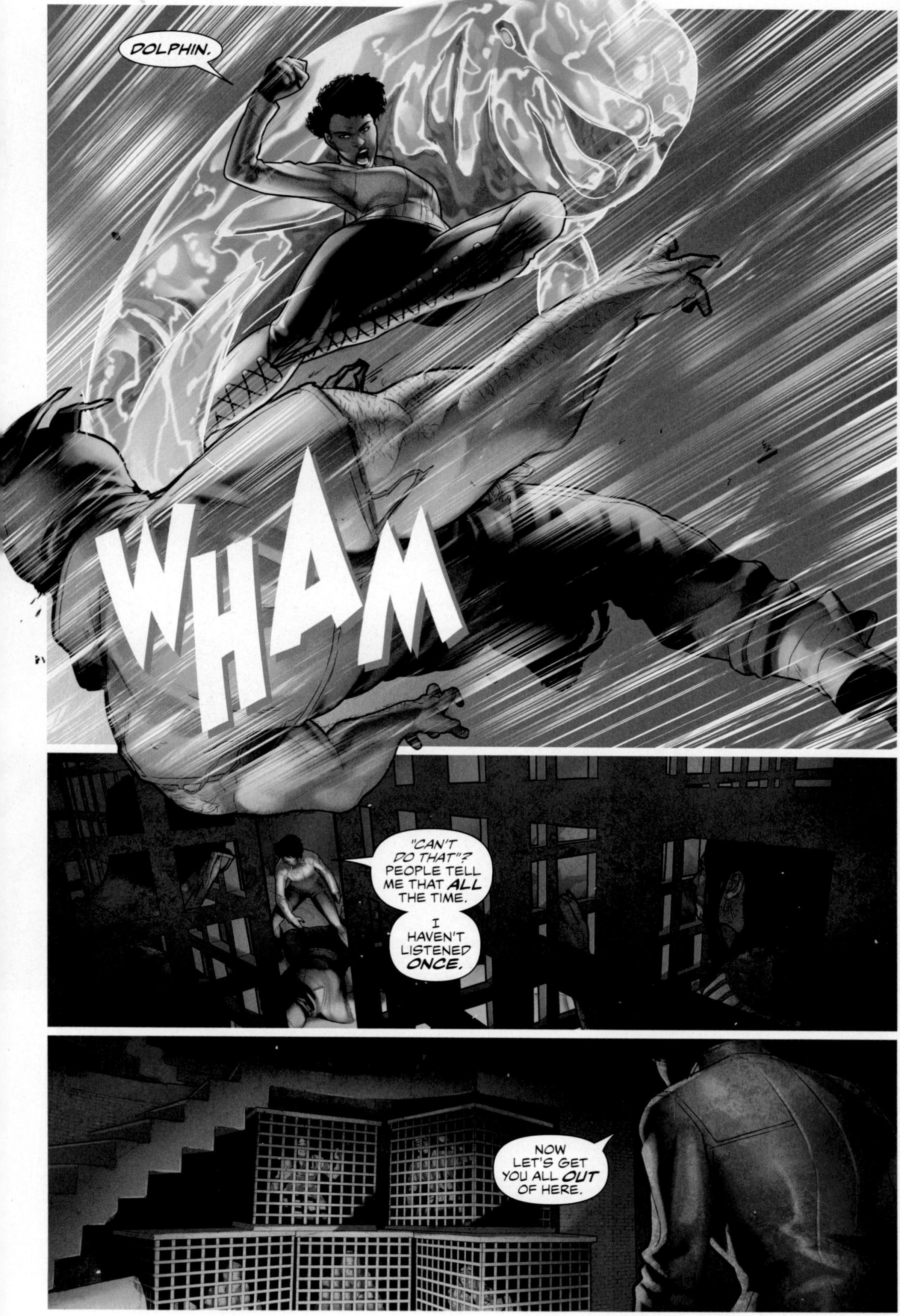
DOLPHIN.
WHAM
"CAN'T DO THAT"? PEOPLE TELL ME THAT ALL THE TIME.
I HAVEN'T LISTENED ONCE.
NOW LET'S GET YOU ALL OUT OF HERE.

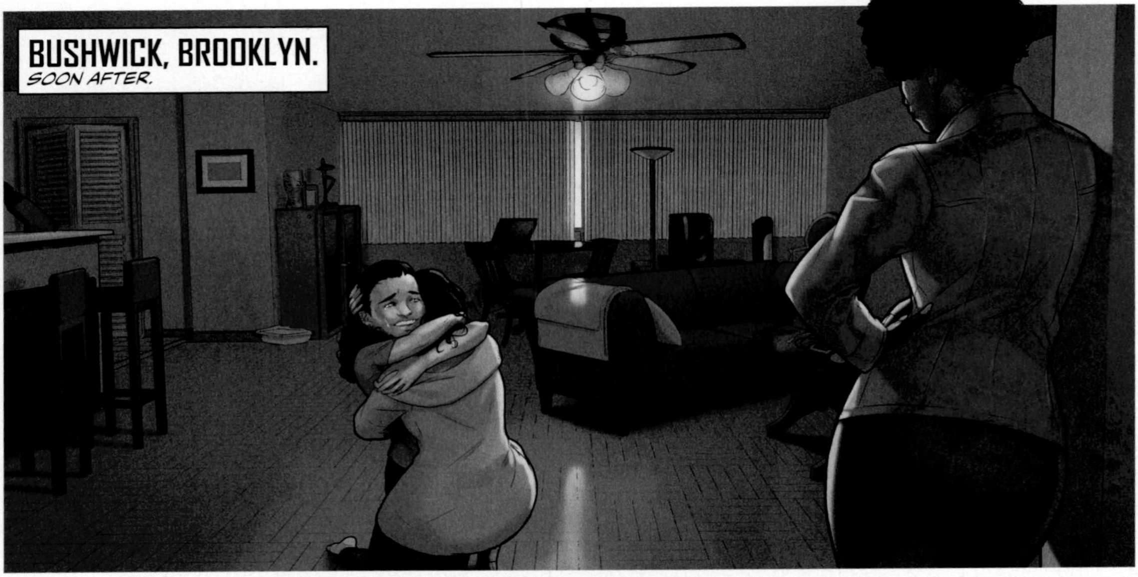
BUSHWICK, BROOKLYN.
SOON AFTER.

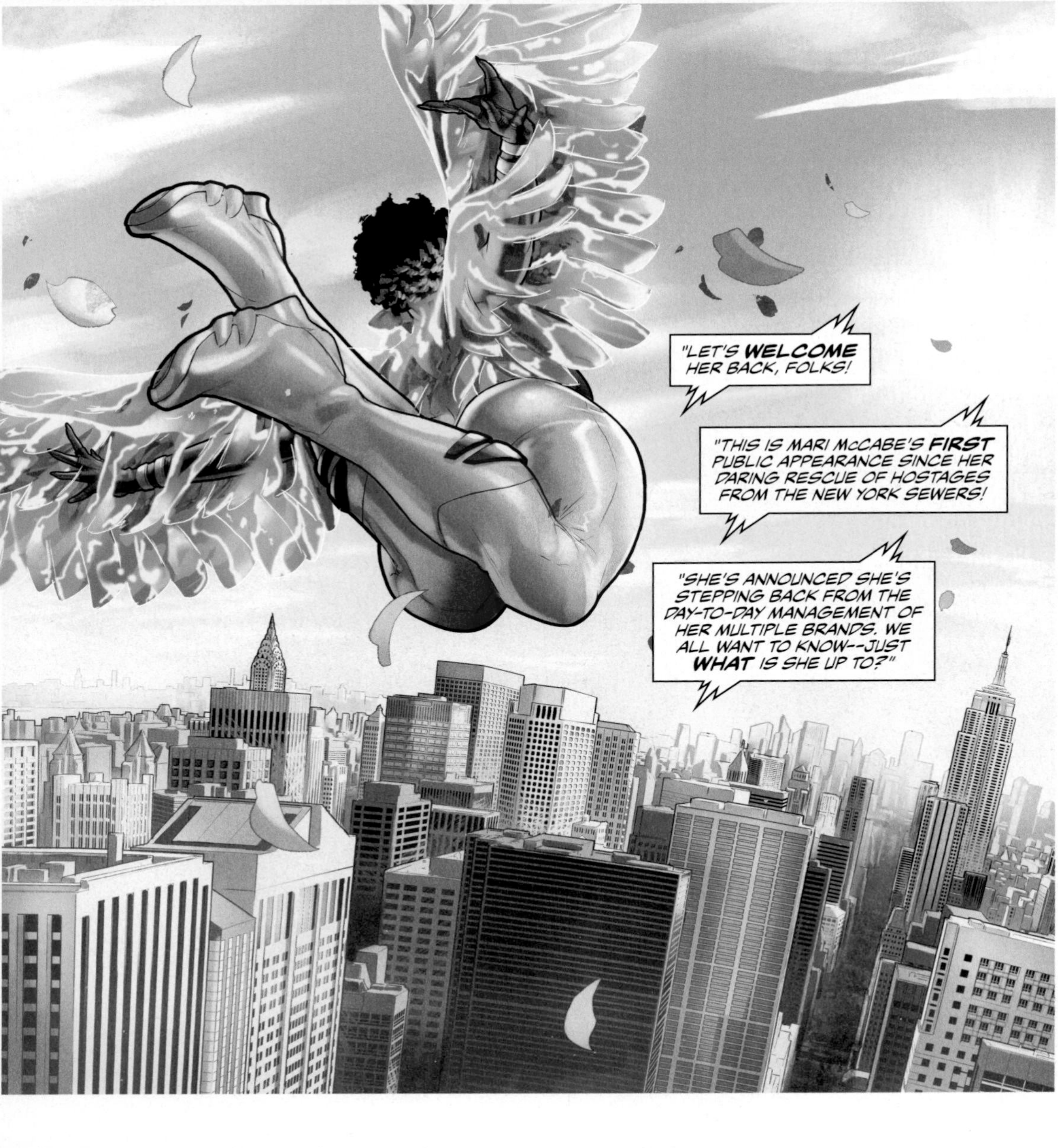
"LET'S WELCOME HER BACK, FOLKS!
"THIS IS MARI McCABE'S FIRST PUBLIC APPEARANCE SINCE HER DARING RESCUE OF HOSTAGES FROM THE NEW YORK SEWERS!
"SHE'S ANNOUNCED SHE'S STEPPING BACK FROM THE DAY-TO-DAY MANAGEMENT OF HER MULTIPLE BRANDS. WE ALL WANT TO KNOW--JUST WHAT IS SHE UP TO?"

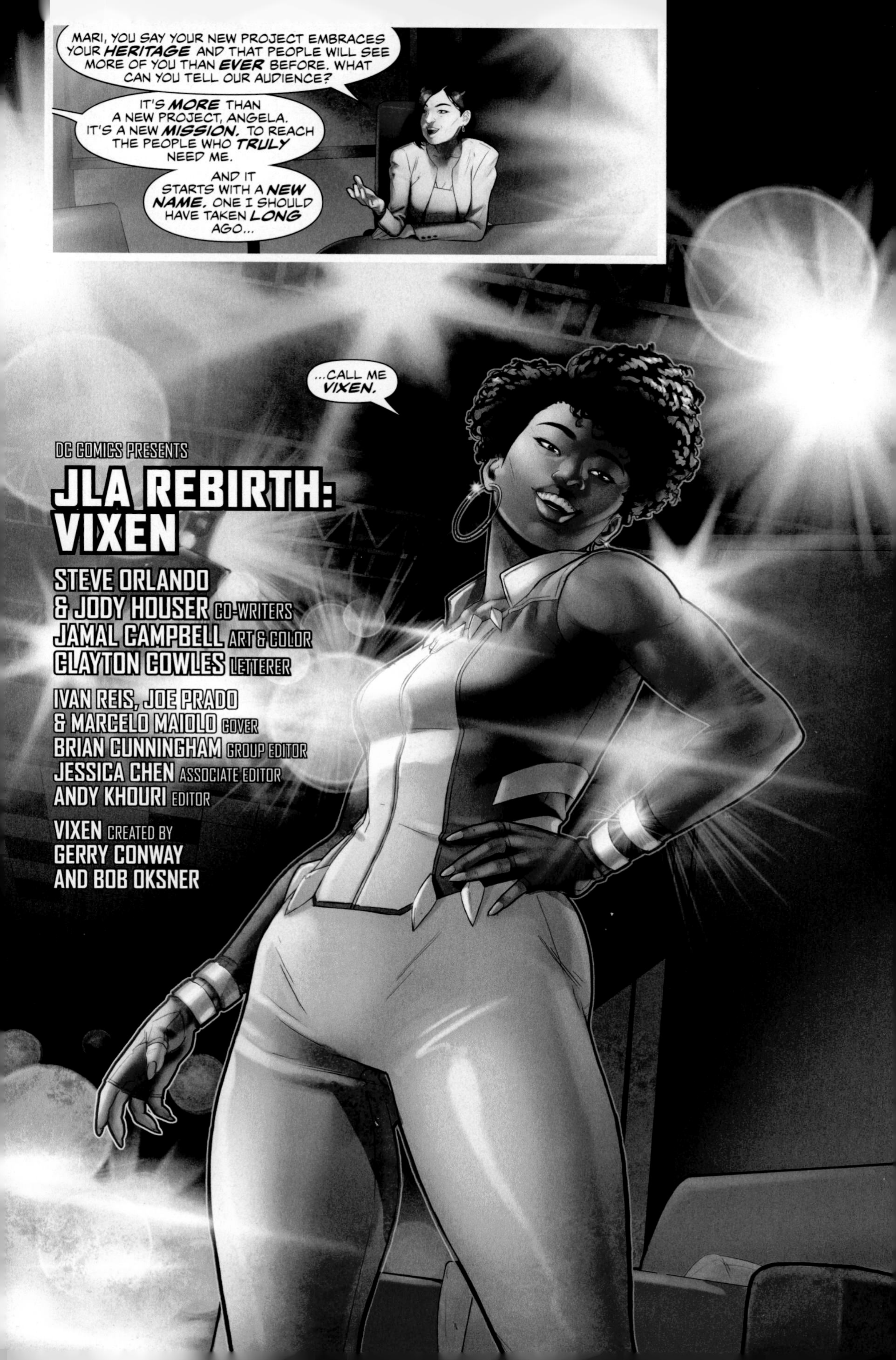

MARI, YOU SAY YOUR NEW PROJECT EMBRACES YOUR HERITAGE AND THAT PEOPLE WILL SEE MORE OF YOU THAN EVER BEFORE. WHAT CAN YOU TELL OUR AUDIENCE?
IT'S MORE THAN A NEW PROJECT, ANGELA. IT'S A NEW MISSION. TO REACH THE PEOPLE WHO TRULY NEED ME.
AND IT STARTS WITH A NEW NAME. ONE I SHOULD HAVE TAKEN LONG AGO...
...CALL ME VIXEN.
DC COMICS PRESENTS
JLA REBIRTH: VIXEN
STEVE ORLANDO
& JODY HOUSER CO-WRITERS
JAMAL CAMPBELL ART & COLOR
CLAYTON COWLES LETTERER
IVAN REIS, JOE PRADO
& MARCELO MAIOLO COVER
BRIAN CUNNINGHAM GROUP EDITOR
JESSICA CHEN ASSOCIATE EDITOR
ANDY KHOURI EDITOR
VIXEN CREATED BY
GERRY CONWAY
AND BOB OKSNER

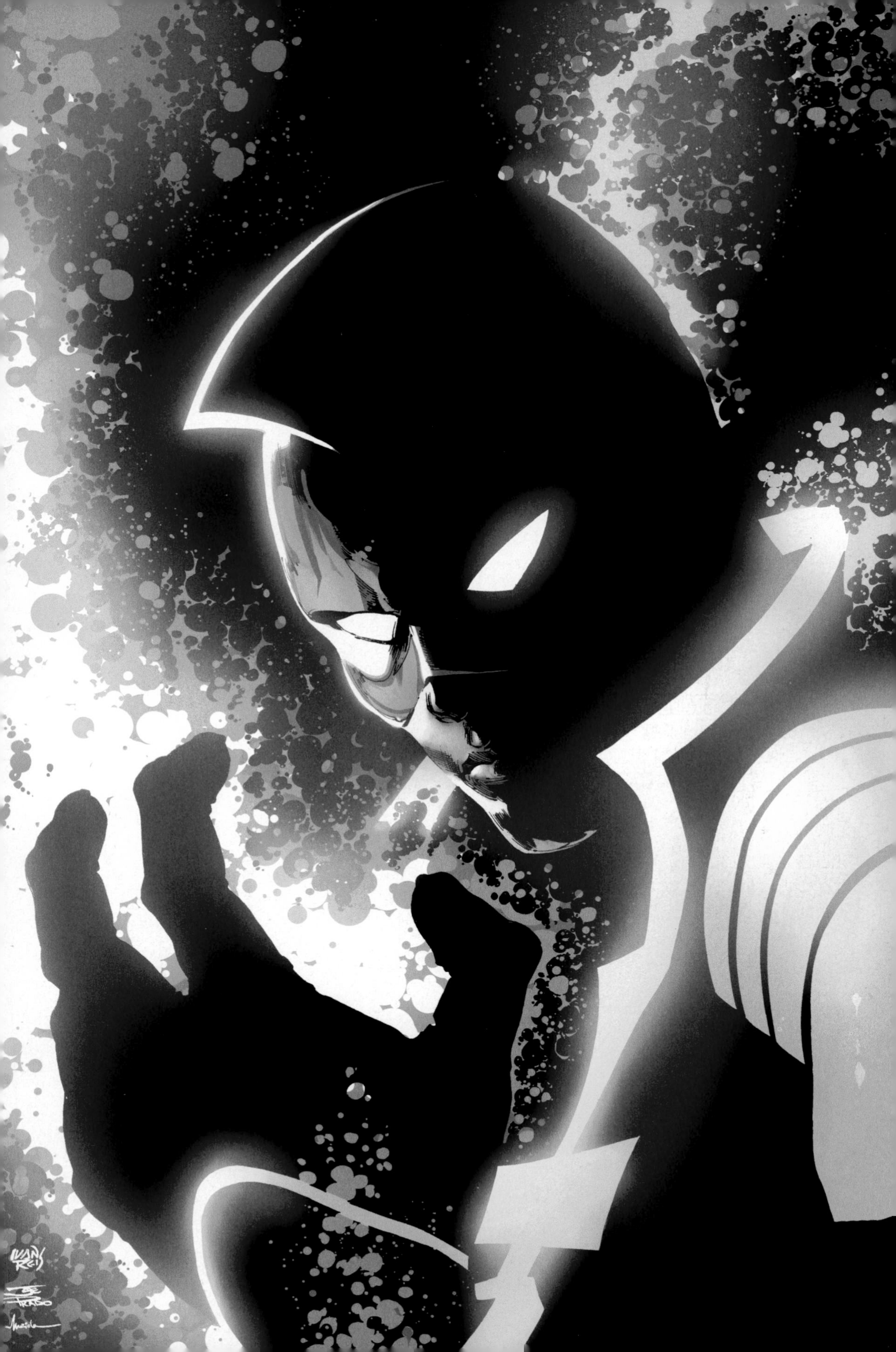

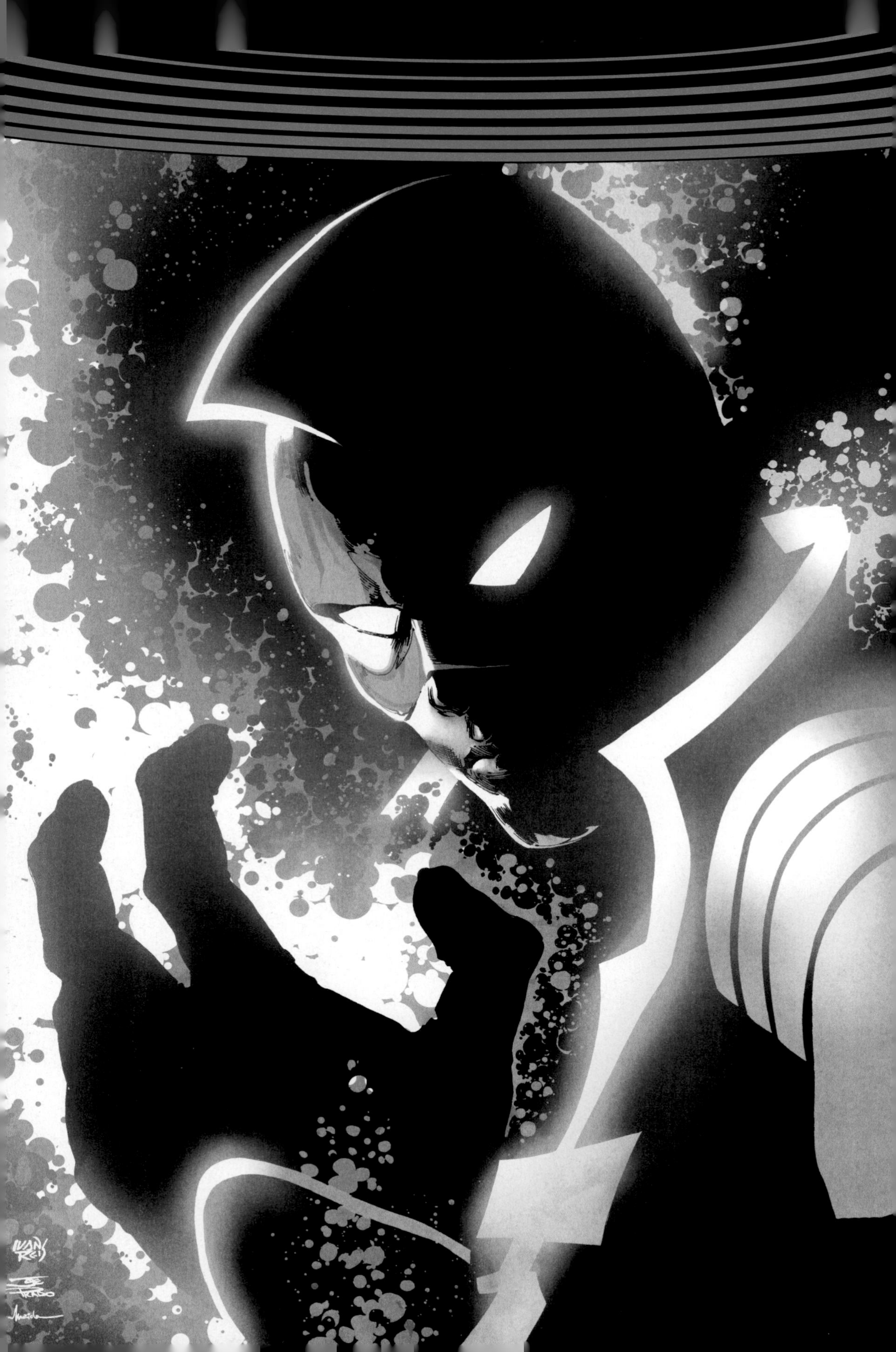

DC COMICS PRESENTS

JLA REBIRTH: THE RAY

STEVE ORLANDO WRITER STEPHEN BYRNE ART & COLOR CLAYTON COWLES LETTERER
IVAN REIS, JOE PRADO & MARCELO MAIOLO COVER
BRIAN CUNNINGHAM GROUP EDITOR JESSICA CHEN ASSOCIATE EDITOR ANDY KHOURI EDITOR

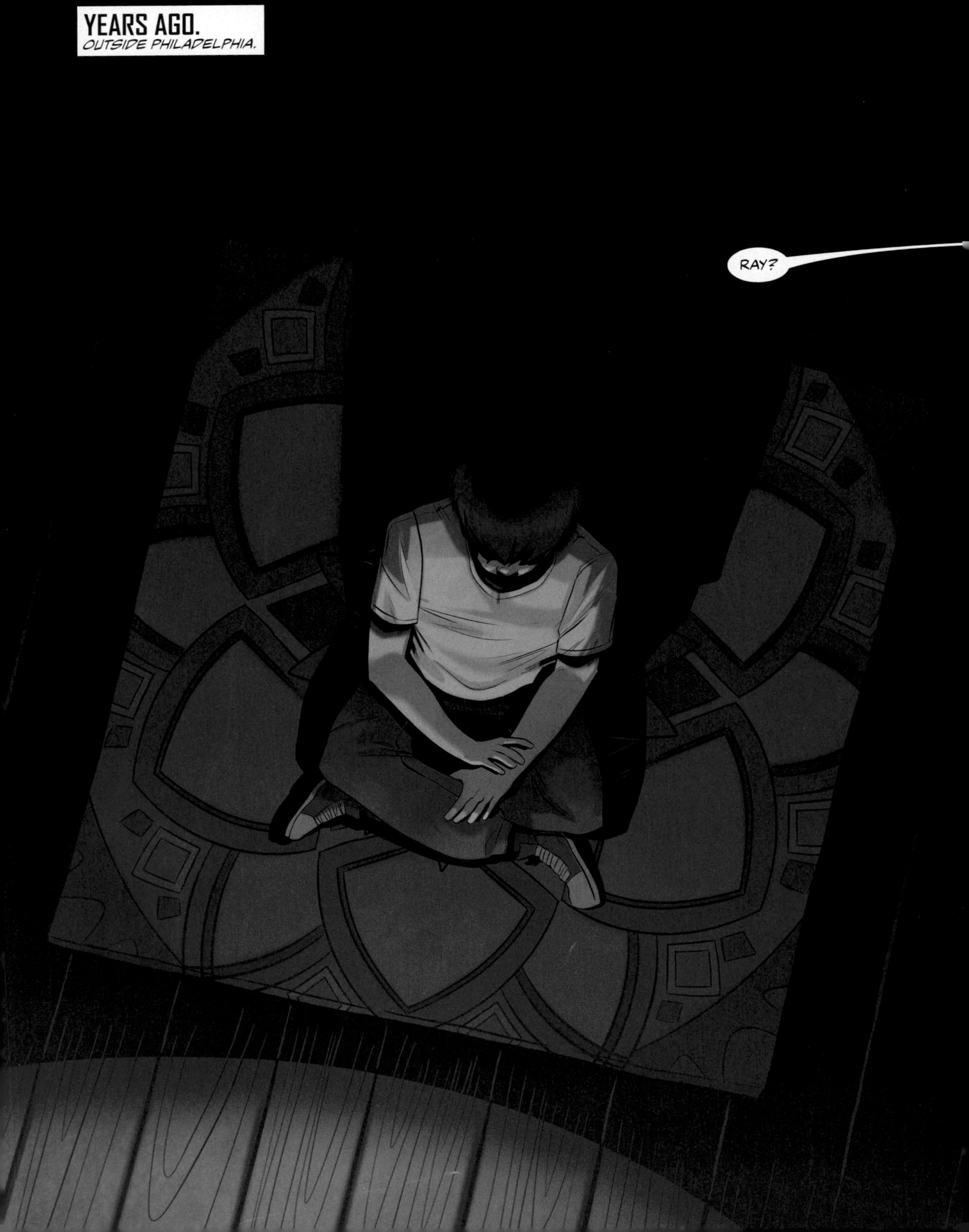

YEARS AGO.
OUTSIDE PHILADELPHIA.
RAY?

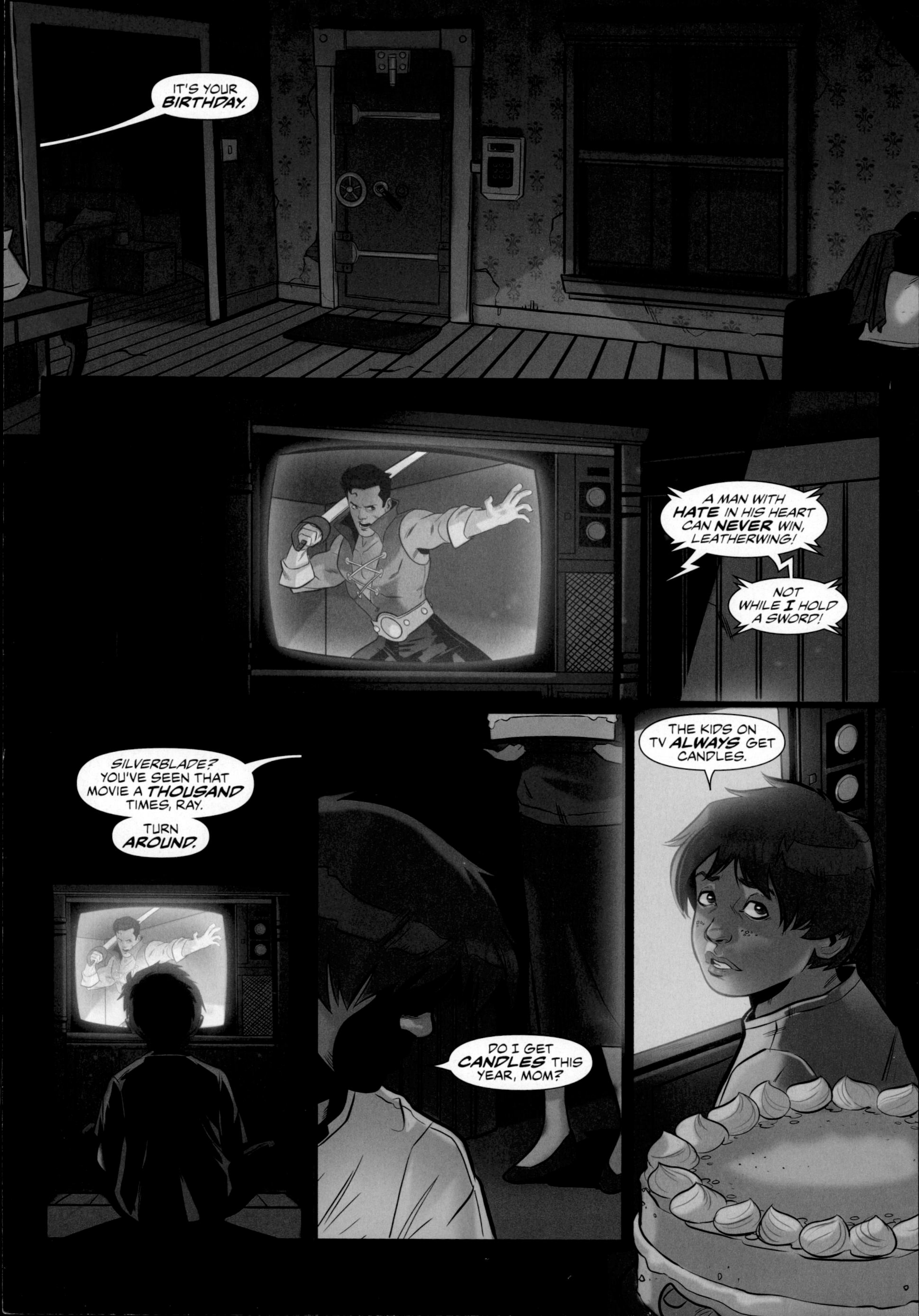
IT'S YOUR BIRTHDAY.
A MAN WITH HATE IN HIS HEART CAN NEVER WIN, LEATHERWING!
NOT WHILE I HOLD A SWORD!
SILVERBLADE? YOU'VE SEEN THAT MOVIE A THOUSAND TIMES, RAY.
TURN AROUND.
DO I GET CANDLES THIS YEAR, MOM?
THE KIDS ON TV ALWAYS GET CANDLES.

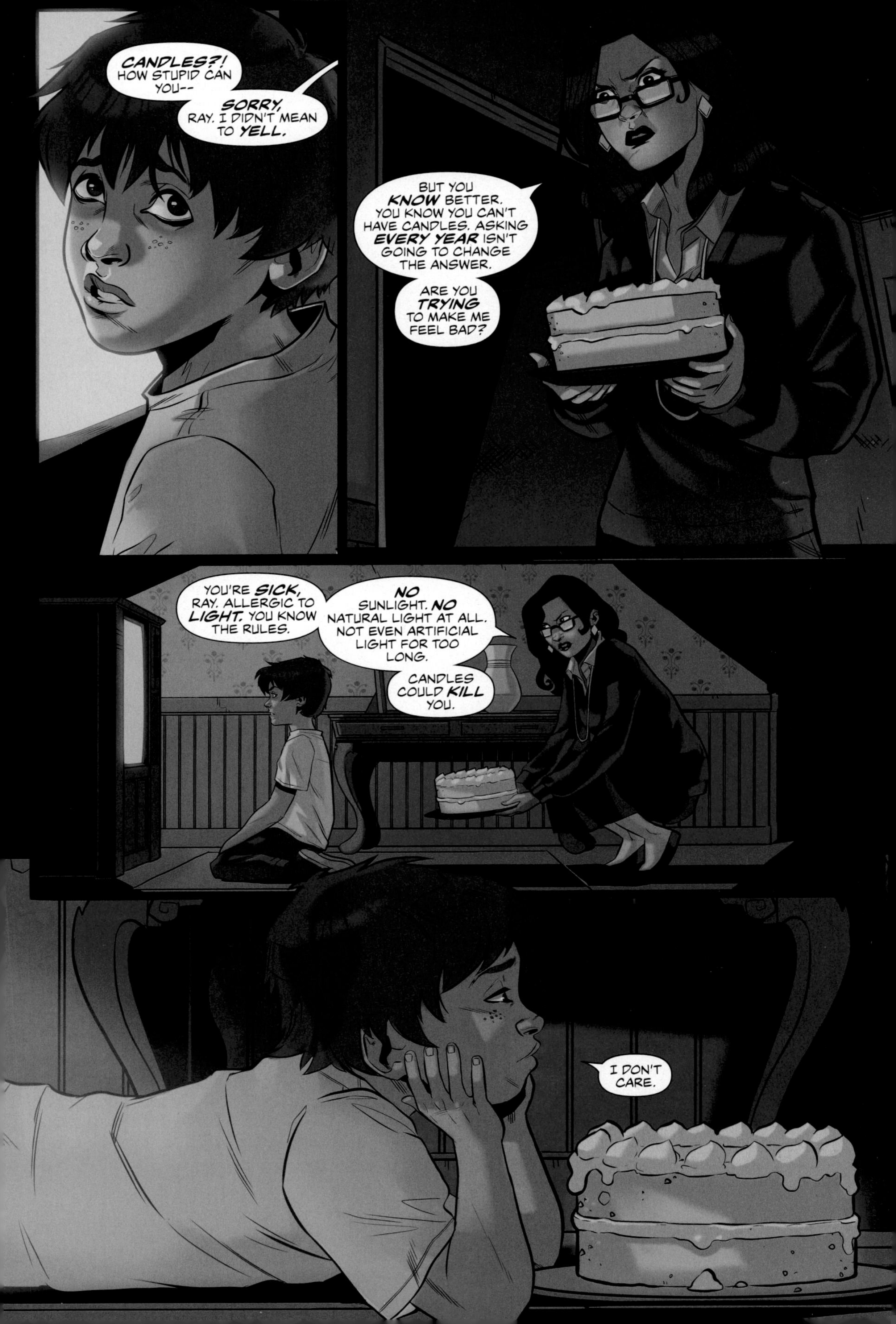

CANDLES?! HOW STUPID CAN YOU--
SORRY, RAY. I DIDN'T MEAN TO YELL.
BUT YOU KNOW BETTER. YOU KNOW YOU CAN'T HAVE CANDLES. ASKING EVERY YEAR ISN'T GOING TO CHANGE THE ANSWER.
ARE YOU TRYING TO MAKE ME FEEL BAD?
YOU'RE SICK, RAY. ALLERGIC TO LIGHT. YOU KNOW THE RULES.
NO SUNLIGHT. NO NATURAL LIGHT AT ALL. NOT EVEN ARTIFICIAL LIGHT FOR TOO LONG.
CANDLES COULD KILL YOU.
I DON'T CARE.

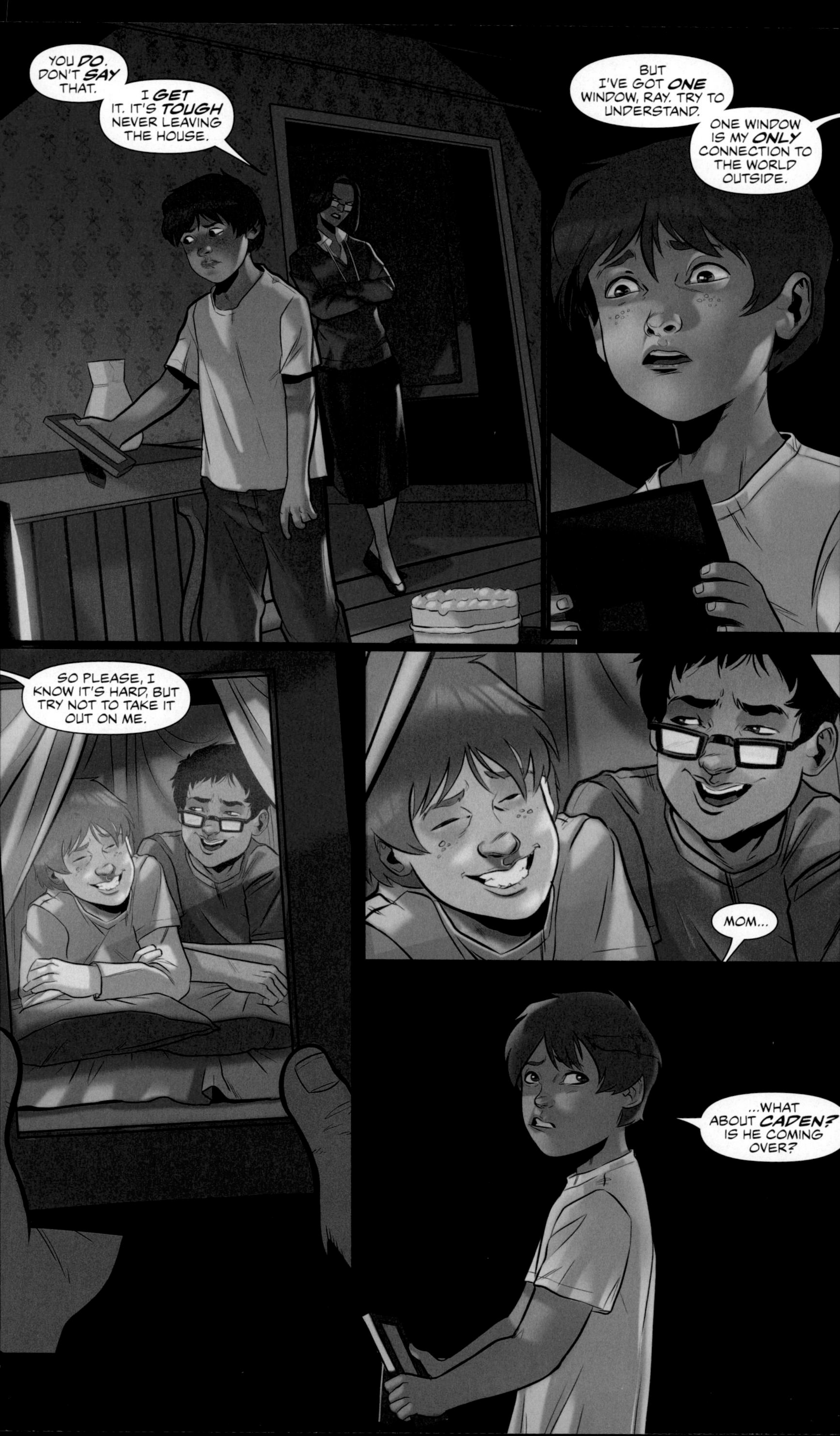
YOU DO. DON'T SAY THAT.
I GET IT. IT'S TOUGH NEVER LEAVING THE HOUSE.
BUT I'VE GOT ONE WINDOW, RAY. TRY TO UNDERSTAND.
ONE WINDOW IS MY ONLY CONNECTION TO THE WORLD OUTSIDE.
SO PLEASE, I KNOW IT'S HARD, BUT TRY NOT TO TAKE IT OUT ON ME.
MOM...
...WHAT ABOUT CADEN? IS HE COMING OVER?

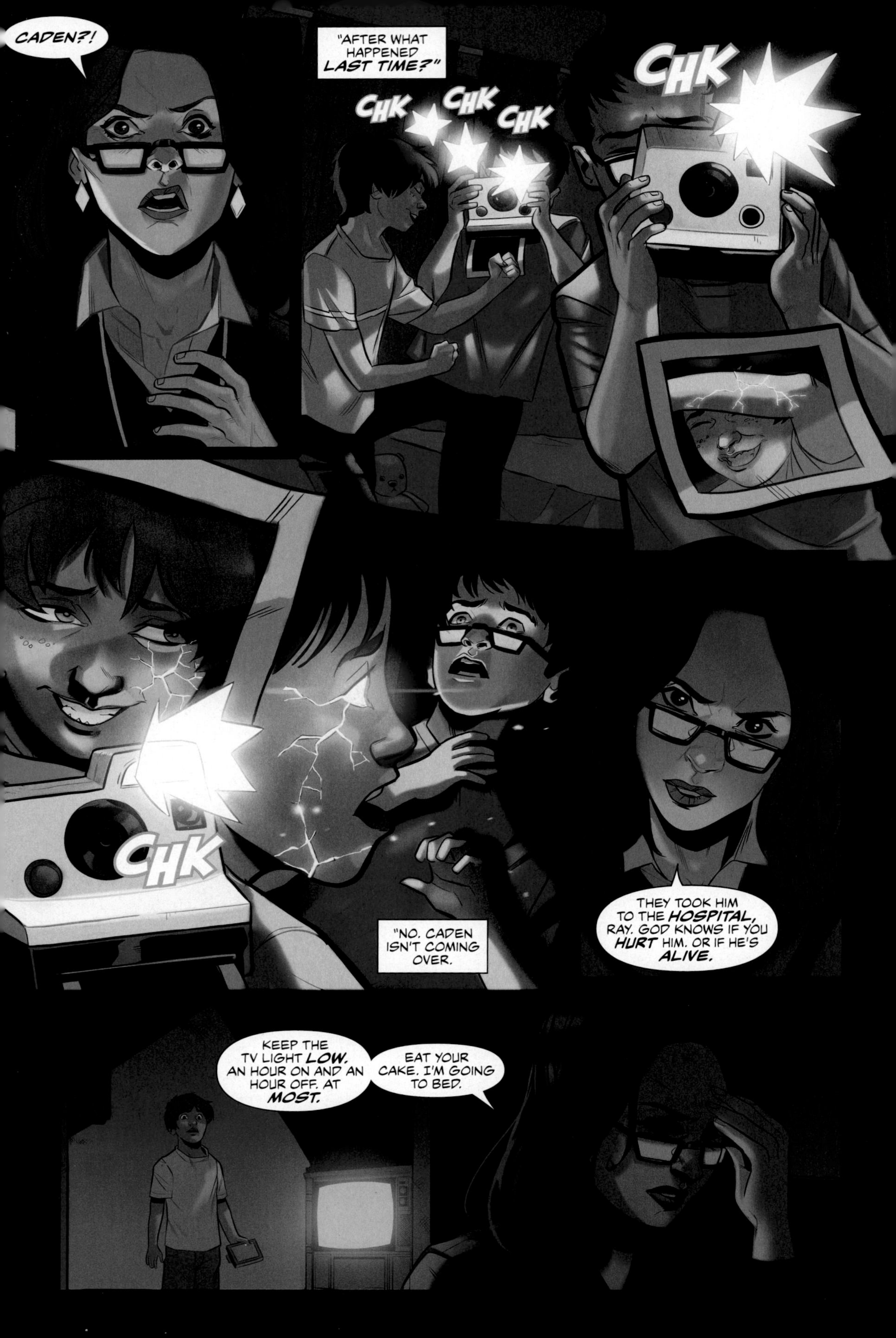
CADEN?!
"AFTER WHAT HAPPENED LAST TIME?"
CHK CHK CHK
CHK
CHK
"NO. CADEN ISN'T COMING OVER.
THEY TOOK HIM TO THE HOSPITAL, RAY. GOD KNOWS IF YOU HURT HIM. OR IF HE'S ALIVE.
KEEP THE TV LIGHT LOW. AN HOUR ON AND AN HOUR OFF. AT MOST.
EAT YOUR CAKE. I'M GOING TO BED.

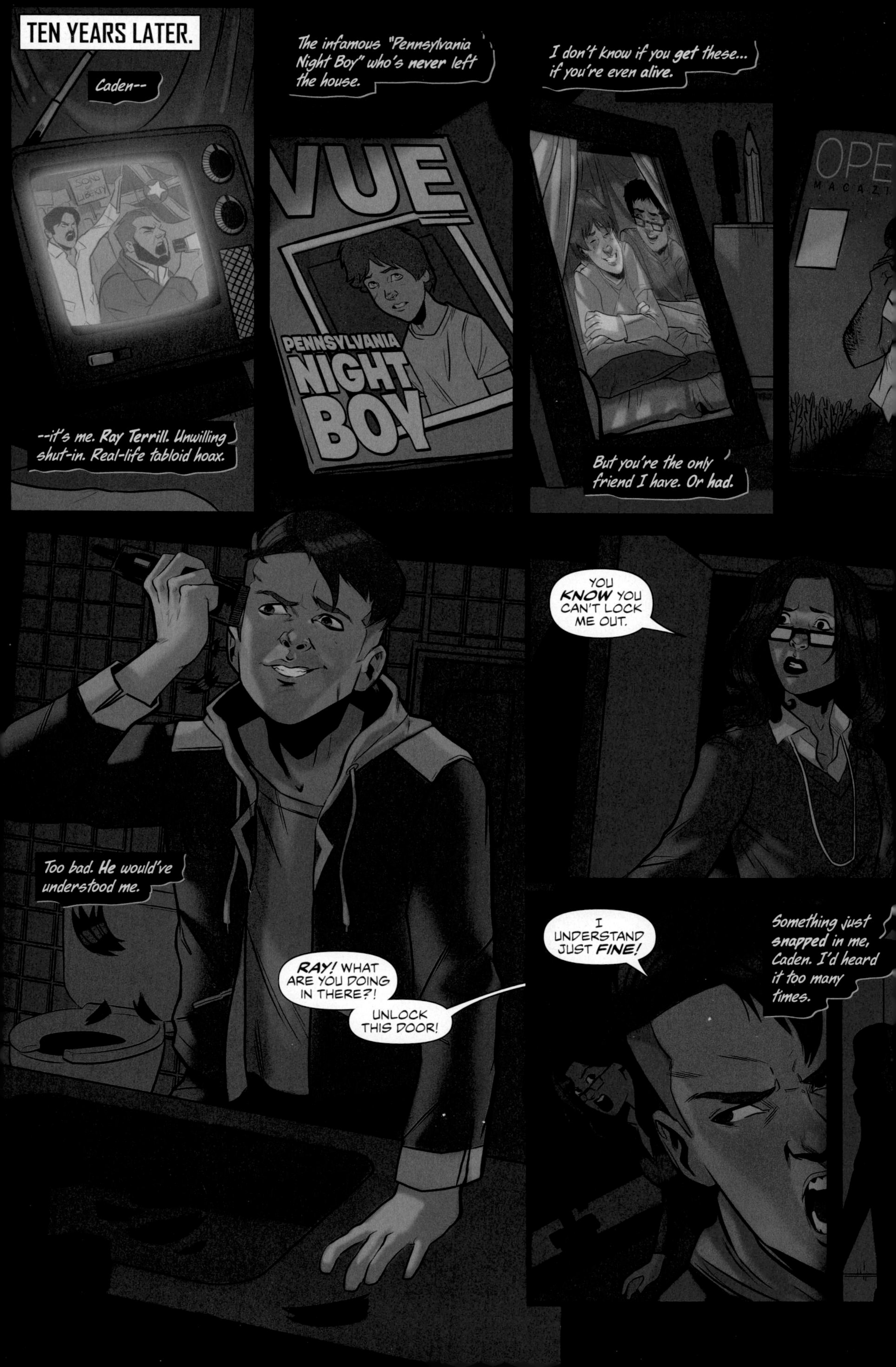
TEN YEARS LATER.
Caden--
--it's me. Ray Terrill. Unwilling shut-in. Real-life tabloid hoax.
The infamous "Pennsylvania Night Boy" who's never left the house.
VUE
PENNSYLVANIA NIGHT BOY
I don't know if you get these... if you're even alive.
But you're the only friend I have. Or had.
Too bad. He would've understood me.
RAY! WHAT ARE YOU DOING IN THERE?!
UNLOCK THIS DOOR!
YOU KNOW YOU CAN'T LOCK ME OUT.
I UNDERSTAND JUST FINE!
Something just snapped in me, Caden. I'd heard it too many times.

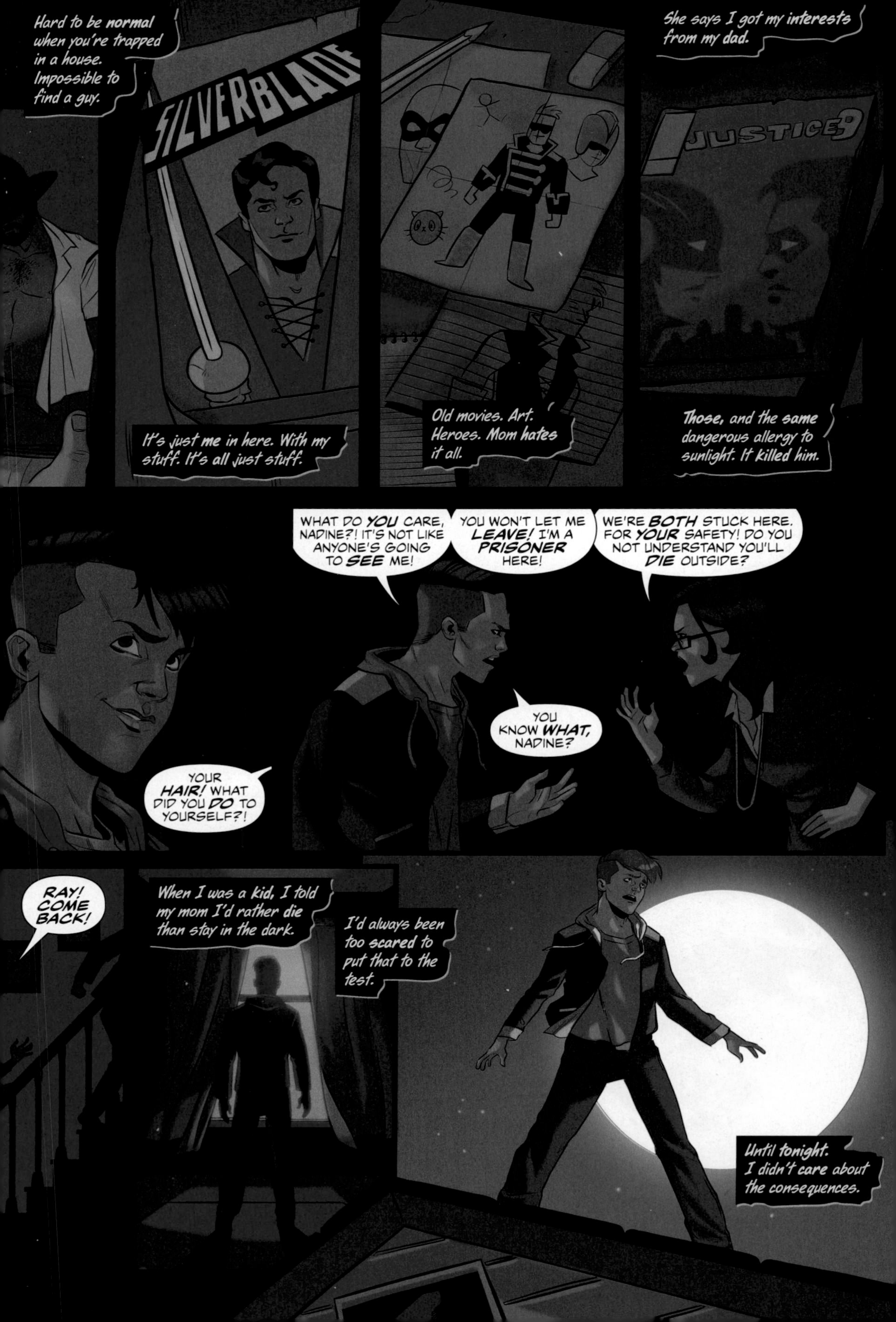
Hard to be normal when you're trapped in a house. Impossible to find a guy.
SILVERBLADE
It's just me in here. With my stuff. It's all just stuff.
Old movies. Art. Heroes. Mom hates it all.
She says I got my interests from my dad.
JUSTICE 9
Those, and the same dangerous allergy to sunlight. It killed him.
YOUR HAIR! WHAT DID YOU DO TO YOURSELF?!
WHAT DO YOU CARE, NADINE?! IT'S NOT LIKE ANYONE'S GOING TO SEE ME!
YOU WON'T LET ME LEAVE! I'M A PRISONER HERE!
WE'RE BOTH STUCK HERE. FOR YOUR SAFETY! DO YOU NOT UNDERSTAND YOU'LL DIE OUTSIDE?
YOU KNOW WHAT, NADINE?
RAY! COME BACK!
When I was a kid, I told my mom I'd rather die than stay in the dark.
I'd always been too scared to put that to the test.
Until tonight. I didn't care about the consequences.

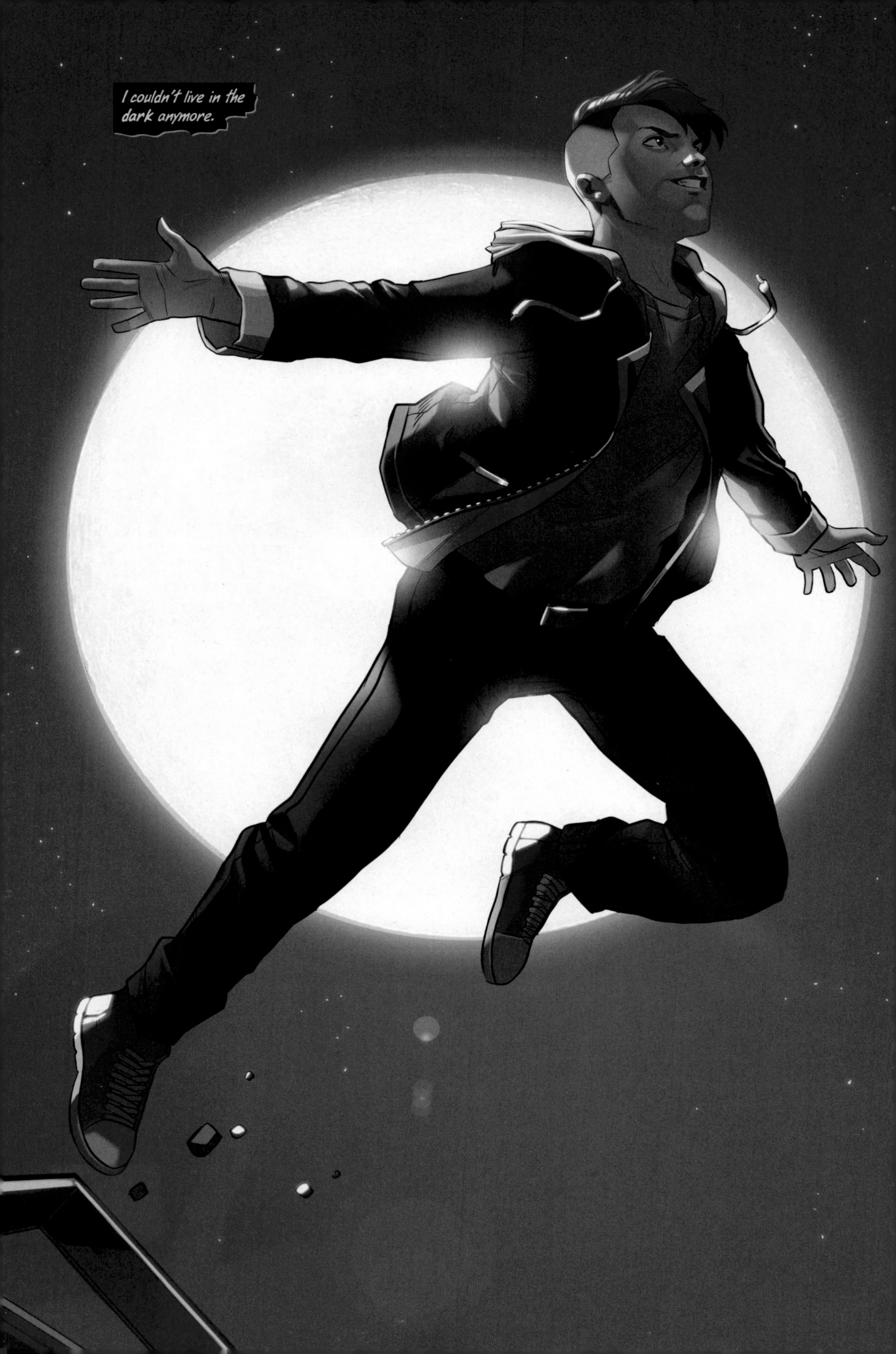
I couldn't live in the dark anymore.

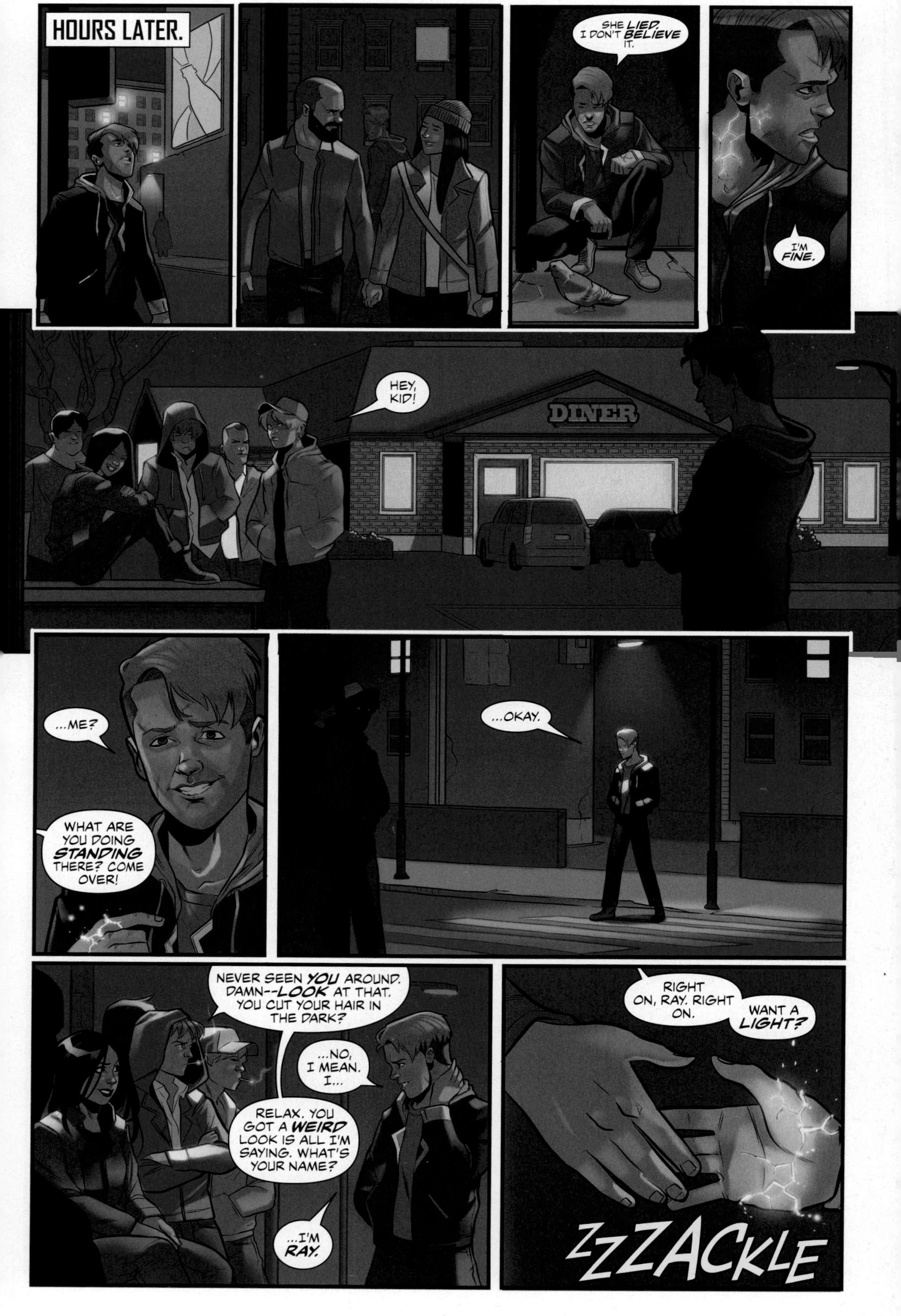
HOURS LATER.
SHE LIED. I DON'T BELIEVE IT.
I'M FINE.
HEY, KID!
DINER
...ME?
WHAT ARE YOU DOING STANDING THERE? COME OVER!
...OKAY.
NEVER SEEN YOU AROUND. DAMN--LOOK AT THAT. YOU CUT YOUR HAIR IN THE DARK?
...NO, I MEAN. I...
RELAX. YOU GOT A WEIRD LOOK IS ALL I'M SAYING. WHAT'S YOUR NAME?
...I'M RAY.
RIGHT ON, RAY. RIGHT ON.
WANT A LIGHT?
ZZZACKLE

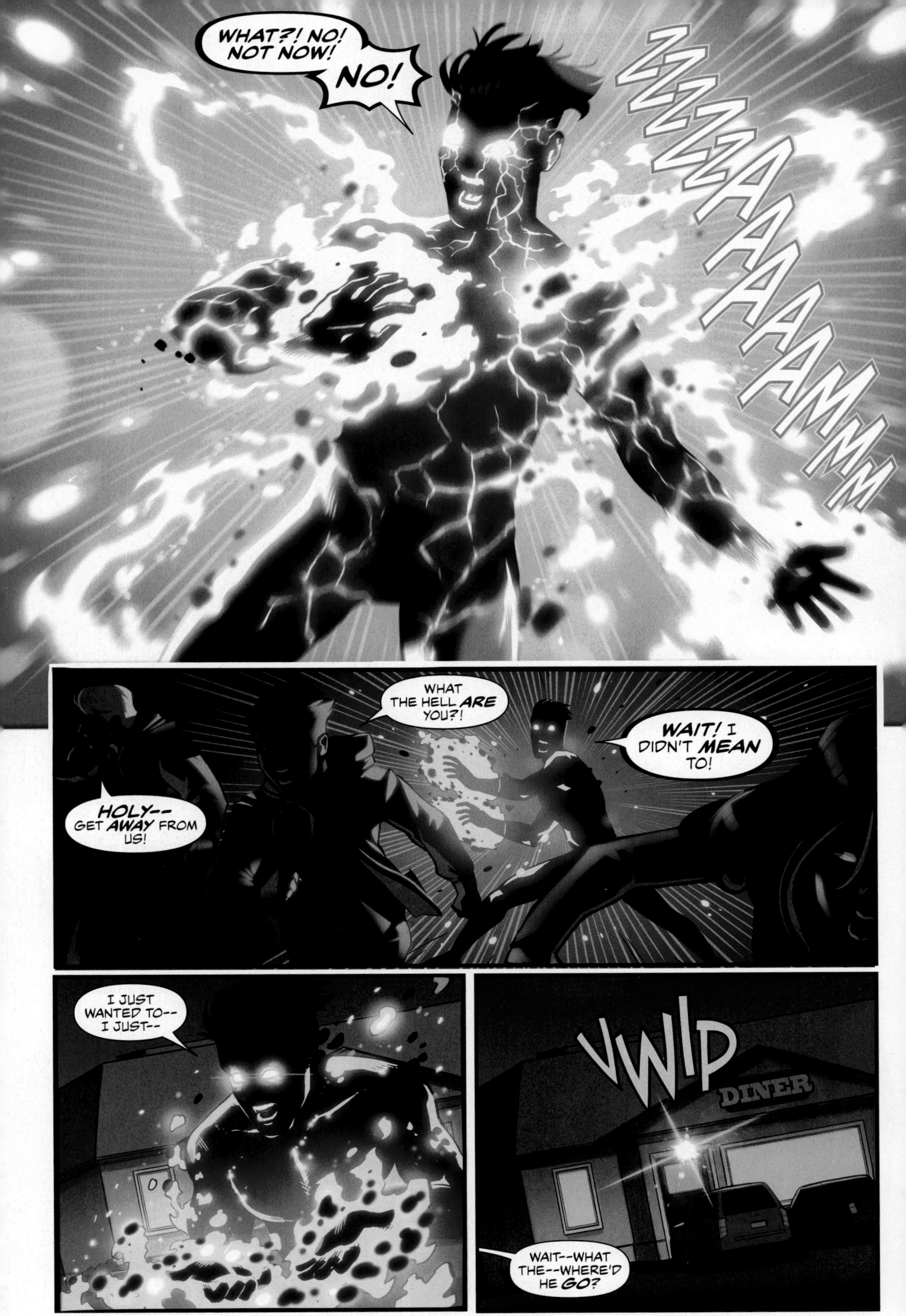
WHAT?! NO! NOT NOW!
NO!
ZZZZZAAAAAMMMM
WHAT THE HELL ARE YOU?!
WAIT! I DIDN'T MEAN TO!
HOLY-- GET AWAY FROM US!
I JUST WANTED TO-- I JUST--
VWIP
DINER
WAIT--WHAT THE--WHERE'D HE GO?

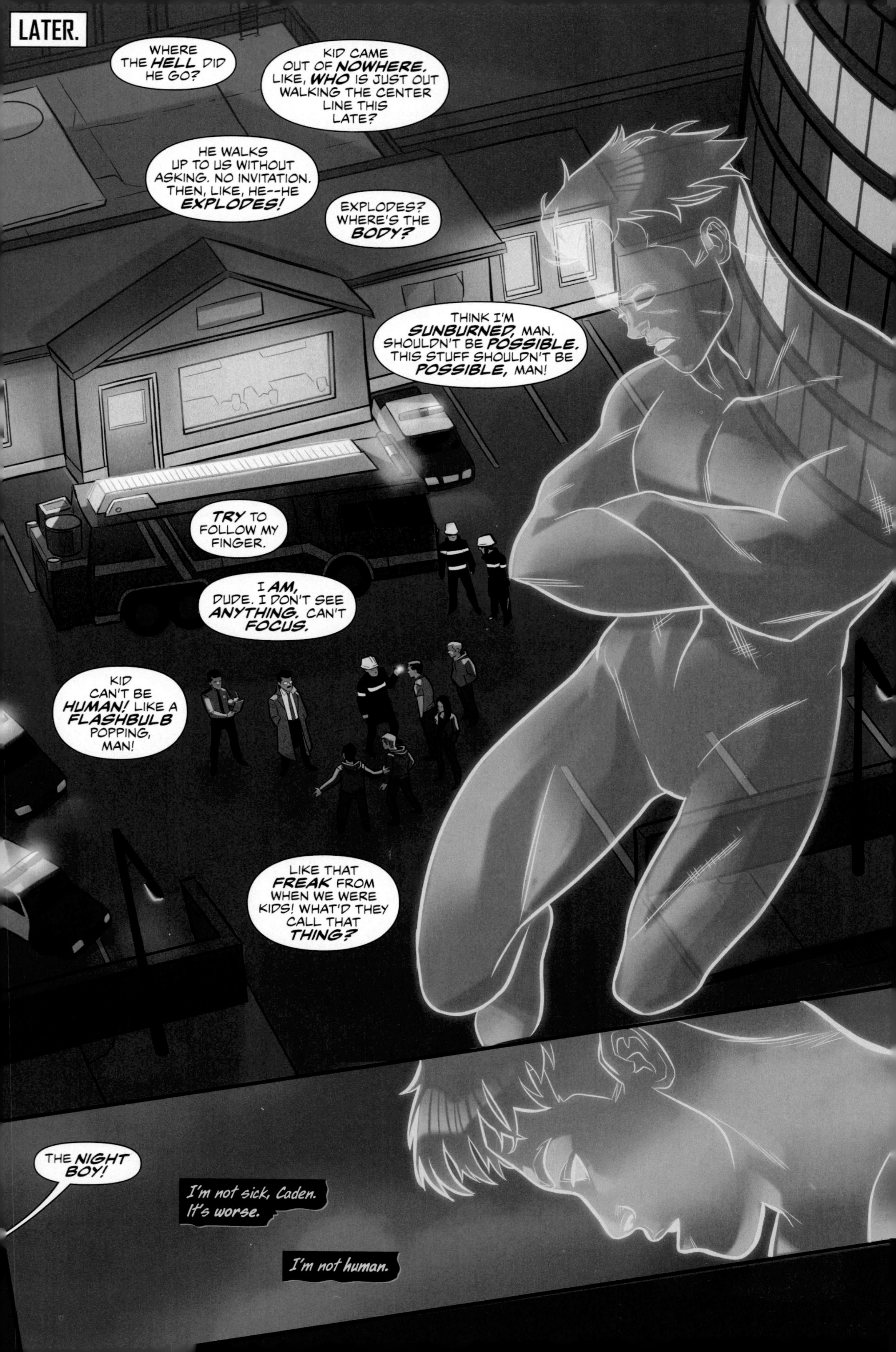
LATER.
WHERE THE HELL DID HE GO?
KID CAME OUT OF NOWHERE. LIKE, WHO IS JUST OUT WALKING THE CENTER LINE THIS LATE?
HE WALKS UP TO US WITHOUT ASKING. NO INVITATION. THEN, LIKE, HE--HE EXPLODES!
EXPLODES? WHERE'S THE BODY?
THINK I'M SUNBURNED, MAN. SHOULDN'T BE POSSIBLE. THIS STUFF SHOULDN'T BE POSSIBLE, MAN!
TRY TO FOLLOW MY FINGER.
I AM, DUDE. I DON'T SEE ANYTHING. CAN'T FOCUS.
KID CAN'T BE HUMAN! LIKE A FLASHBULB POPPING, MAN!
LIKE THAT FREAK FROM WHEN WE WERE KIDS! WHAT'D THEY CALL THAT THING?
THE NIGHT BOY!
I'm not sick, Caden. It's worse.
I'm not human.

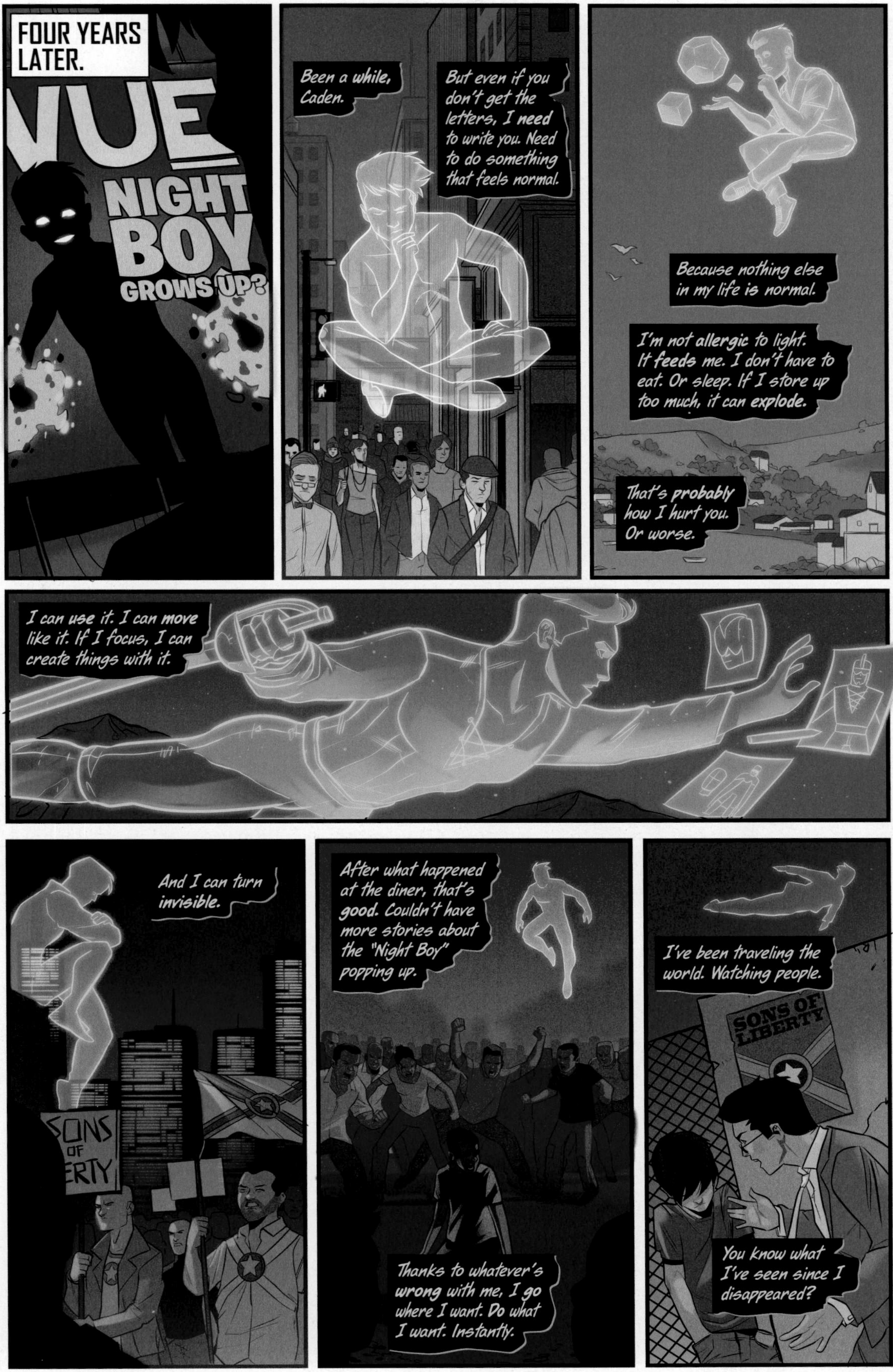
FOUR YEARS LATER.
VUE
NIGHT BOY GROWS UP?
Been a while, Caden.
But even if you don't get the letters, I need to write you. Need to do something that feels normal.
Because nothing else in my life is normal.
I'm not allergic to light. It feeds me. I don't have to eat. Or sleep. If I store up too much, it can explode.
That's probably how I hurt you. Or worse.
I can use it. I can move like it. If I focus, I can create things with it.
And I can turn invisible.
SONS OF ...ERTY
After what happened at the diner, that's good. Couldn't have more stories about the "Night Boy" popping up.
Thanks to whatever's wrong with me, I go where I want. Do what I want. Instantly.
I've been traveling the world. Watching people.
SONS OF LIBERTY
You know what I've seen since I disappeared?

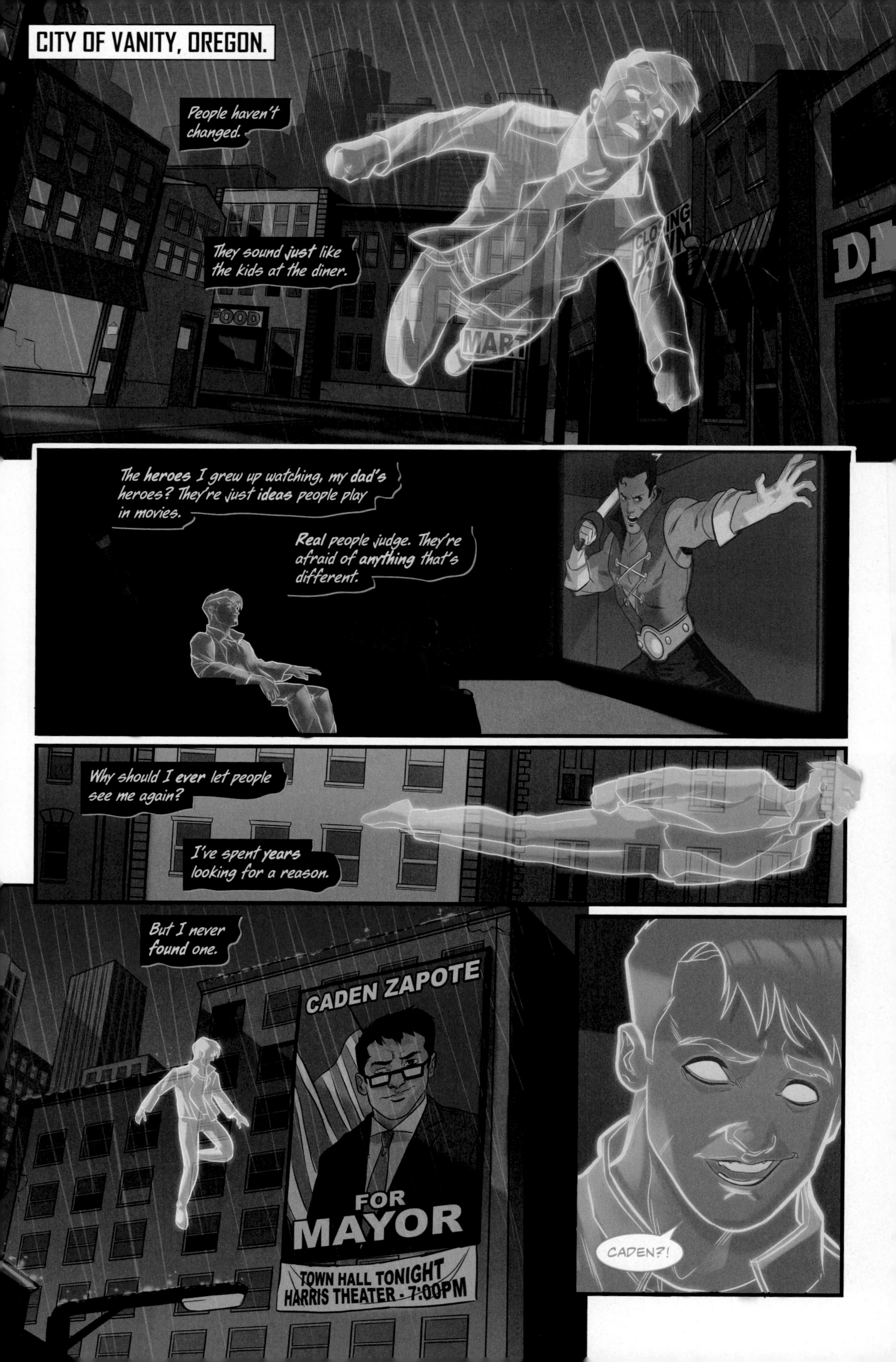
CITY OF VANITY, OREGON.
People haven't changed.
They sound just like the kids at the diner.
CLOSING DOWN
FOOD
MART
The heroes I grew up watching, my dad's heroes? They're just ideas people play in movies.
Real people judge. They're afraid of anything that's different.
Why should I ever let people see me again?
I've spent years looking for a reason.
But I never found one.
CADEN ZAPOTE
FOR MAYOR
TOWN HALL TONIGHT
HARRIS THEATER - 7:00PM
CADEN?!

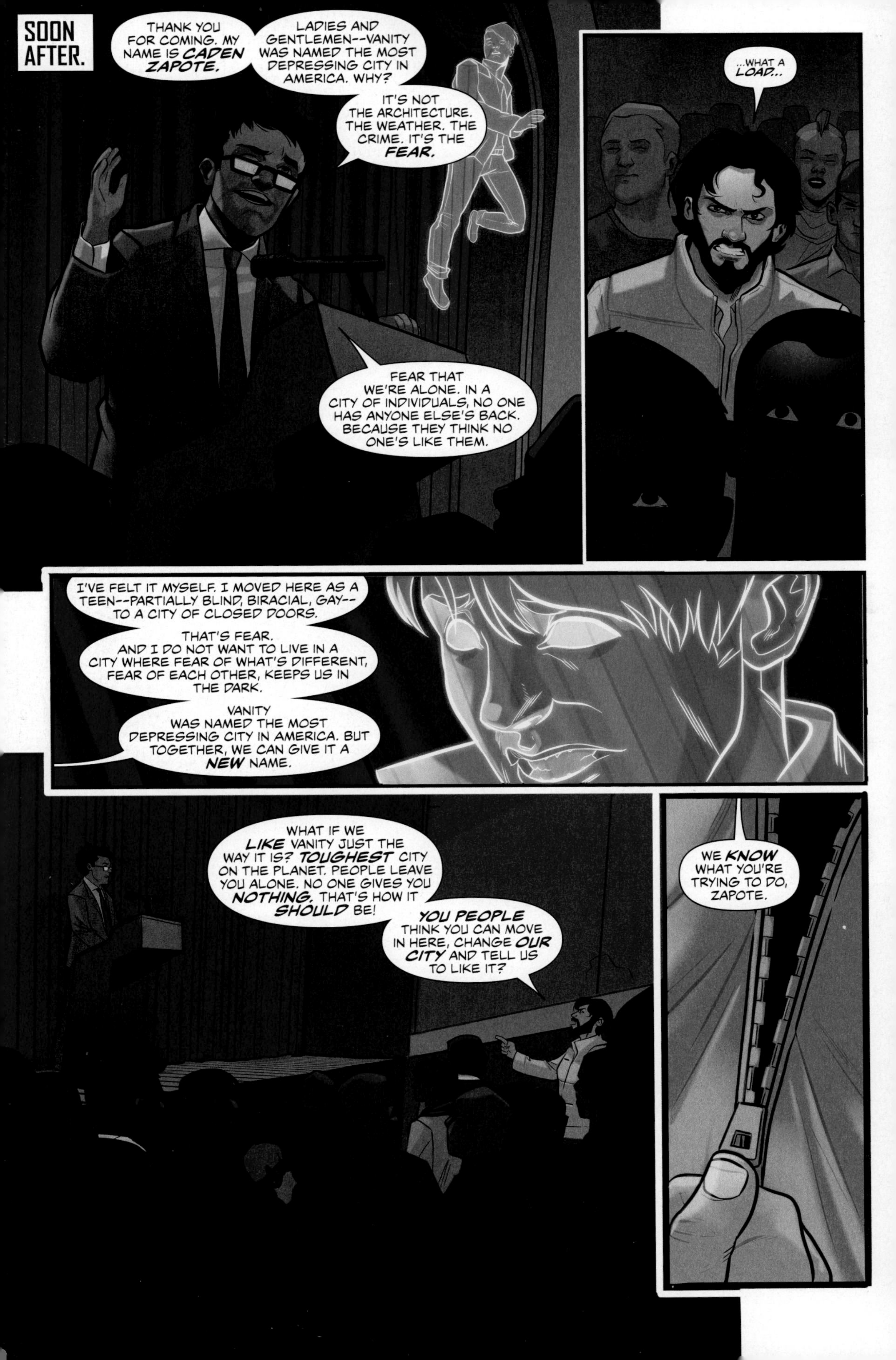
SOON AFTER.
THANK YOU FOR COMING. MY NAME IS CADEN ZAPOTE.
LADIES AND GENTLEMEN--VANITY WAS NAMED THE MOST DEPRESSING CITY IN AMERICA. WHY?
IT'S NOT THE ARCHITECTURE. THE WEATHER. THE CRIME. IT'S THE FEAR.
FEAR THAT WE'RE ALONE. IN A CITY OF INDIVIDUALS, NO ONE HAS ANYONE ELSE'S BACK. BECAUSE THEY THINK NO ONE'S LIKE THEM.
...WHAT A LOAD...
I'VE FELT IT MYSELF. I MOVED HERE AS A TEEN--PARTIALLY BLIND, BIRACIAL, GAY--TO A CITY OF CLOSED DOORS.
THAT'S FEAR. AND I DO NOT WANT TO LIVE IN A CITY WHERE FEAR OF WHAT'S DIFFERENT, FEAR OF EACH OTHER, KEEPS US IN THE DARK.
VANITY WAS NAMED THE MOST DEPRESSING CITY IN AMERICA. BUT TOGETHER, WE CAN GIVE IT A NEW NAME.
WHAT IF WE LIKE VANITY JUST THE WAY IT IS? TOUGHEST CITY ON THE PLANET. PEOPLE LEAVE YOU ALONE. NO ONE GIVES YOU NOTHING. THAT'S HOW IT SHOULD BE!
YOU PEOPLE THINK YOU CAN MOVE IN HERE, CHANGE OUR CITY AND TELL US TO LIKE IT?
WE KNOW WHAT YOU'RE TRYING TO DO, ZAPOTE.

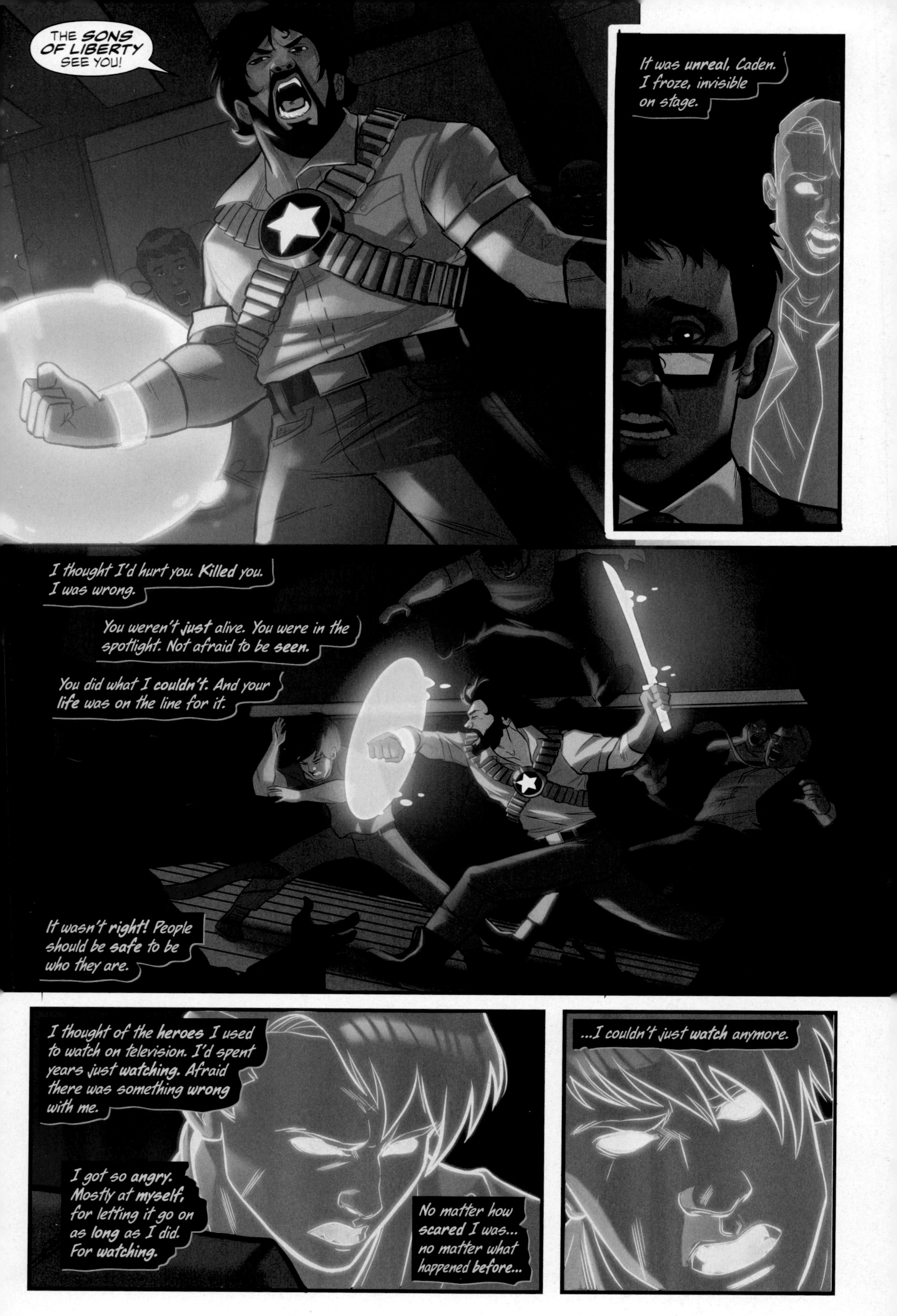
THE SONS OF LIBERTY SEE YOU!
It was unreal, Caden. I froze, invisible on stage.
I thought I'd hurt you. Killed you. I was wrong.
You weren't just alive. You were in the spotlight. Not afraid to be seen.
You did what I couldn't. And your life was on the line for it.
It wasn't right! People should be safe to be who they are.
I thought of the heroes I used to watch on television. I'd spent years just watching. Afraid there was something wrong with me.
I got so angry. Mostly at myself, for letting it go on as long as I did. For watching.
No matter how scared I was... no matter what happened before...
...I couldn't just watch anymore.

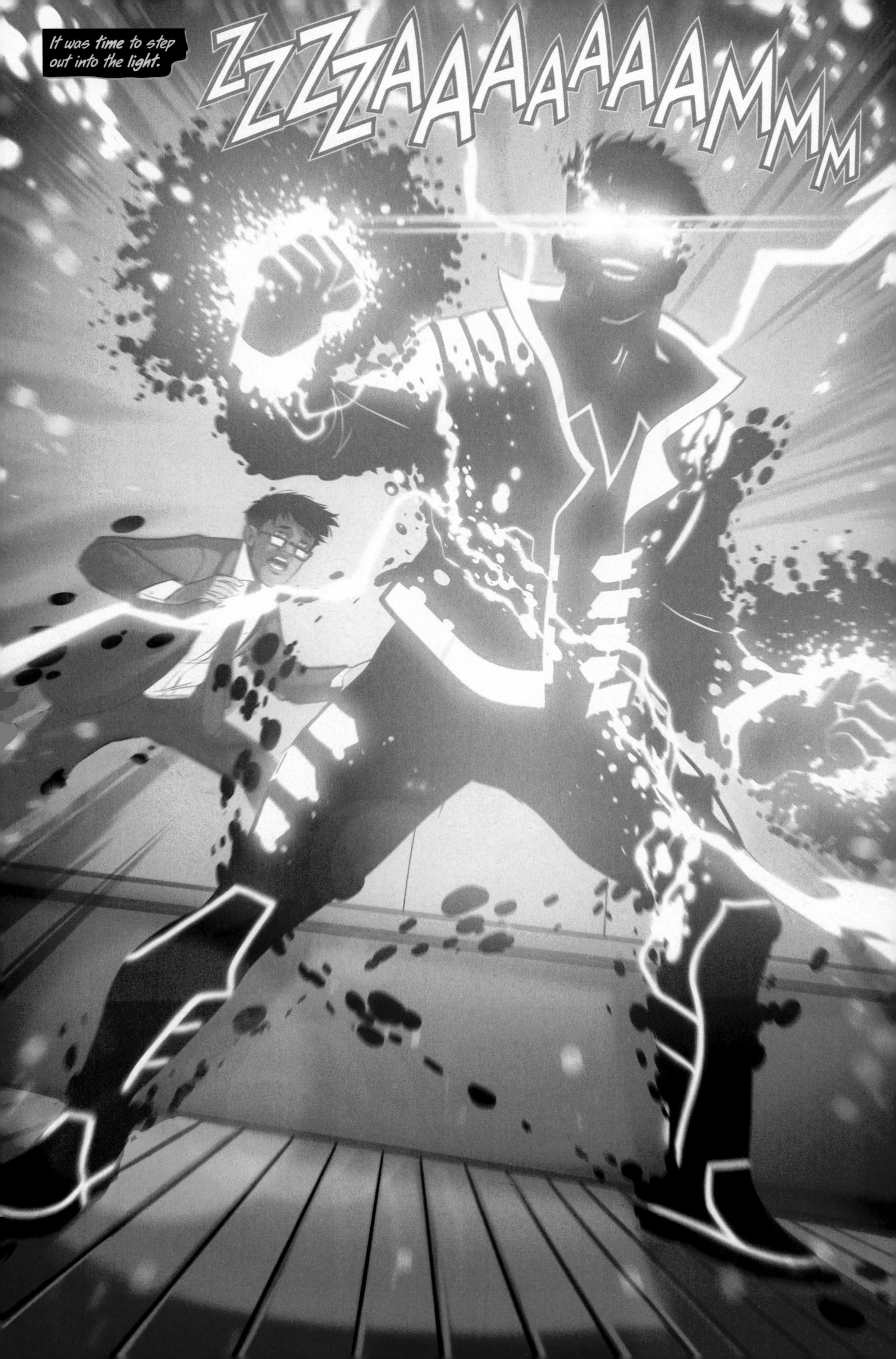
It was time to step out into the light.
ZZZZAAAAAAAAMMMM

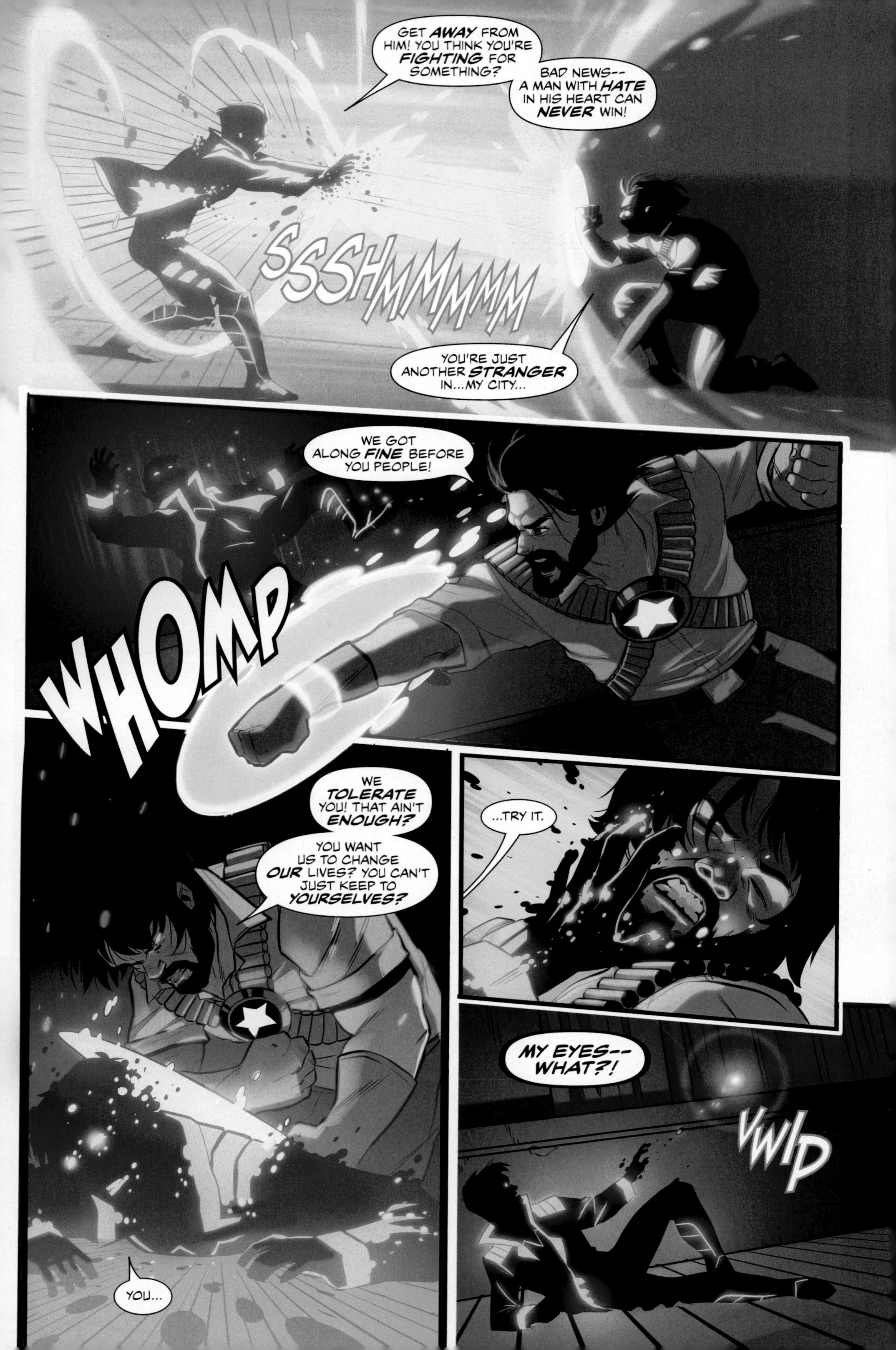
GET AWAY FROM HIM! YOU THINK YOU'RE FIGHTING FOR SOMETHING?
BAD NEWS-- A MAN WITH HATE IN HIS HEART CAN NEVER WIN!
SSSHMMMMMM
YOU'RE JUST ANOTHER STRANGER IN...MY CITY...
WE GOT ALONG FINE BEFORE YOU PEOPLE!
WHOMP
WE TOLERATE YOU! THAT AIN'T ENOUGH?
YOU WANT US TO CHANGE OUR LIVES? YOU CAN'T JUST KEEP TO YOURSELVES?
YOU...
...TRY IT.
MY EYES-- WHAT?!
VWIP

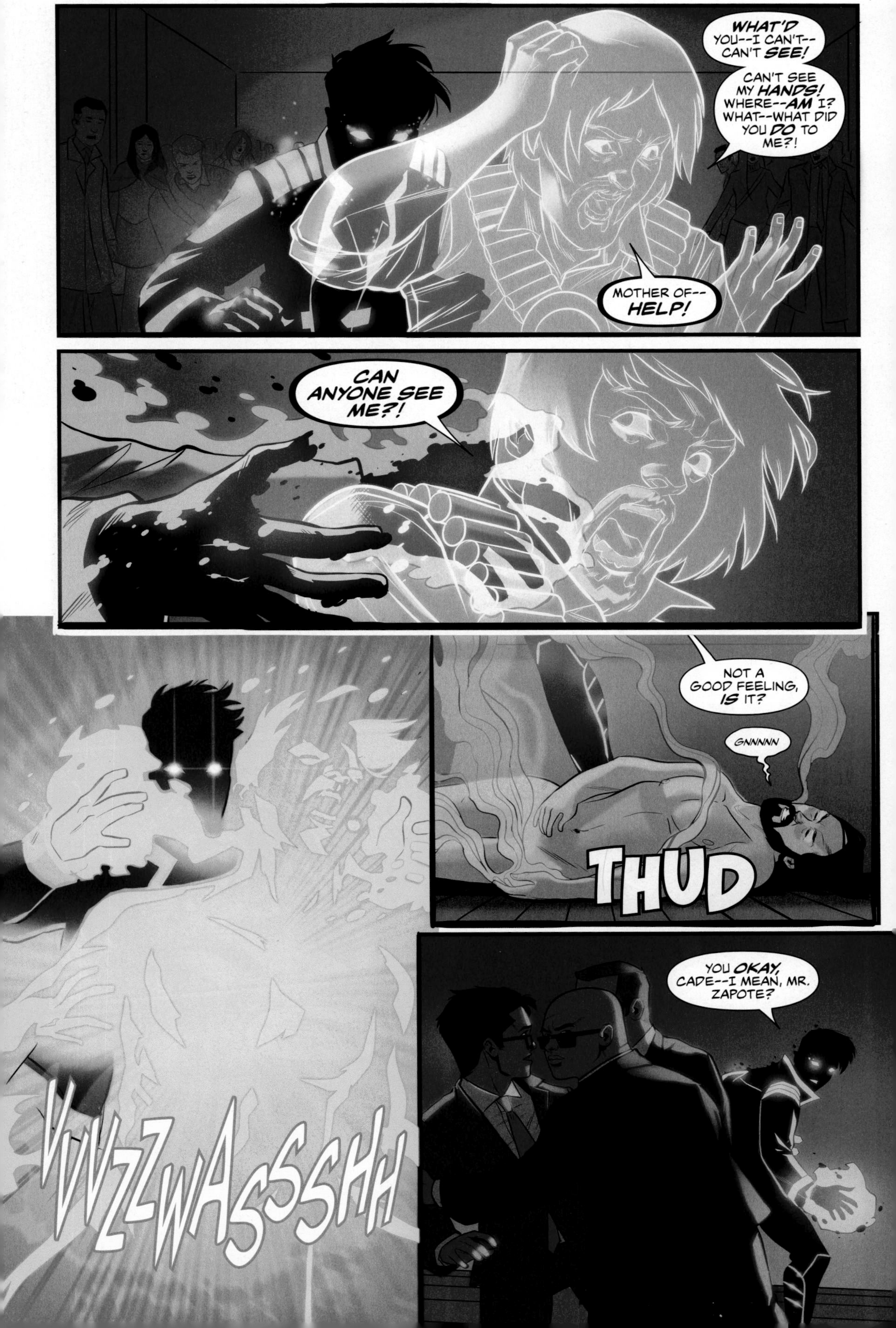
WHAT'D YOU--I CAN'T--CAN'T SEE!
CAN'T SEE MY HANDS! WHERE--AM I? WHAT--WHAT DID YOU DO TO ME?!
MOTHER OF--HELP!
CAN ANYONE SEE ME?!
VVVZZWASSSHH
NOT A GOOD FEELING, IS IT?
GNNNNN
THUD
YOU OKAY, CADE--I MEAN, MR. ZAPOTE?

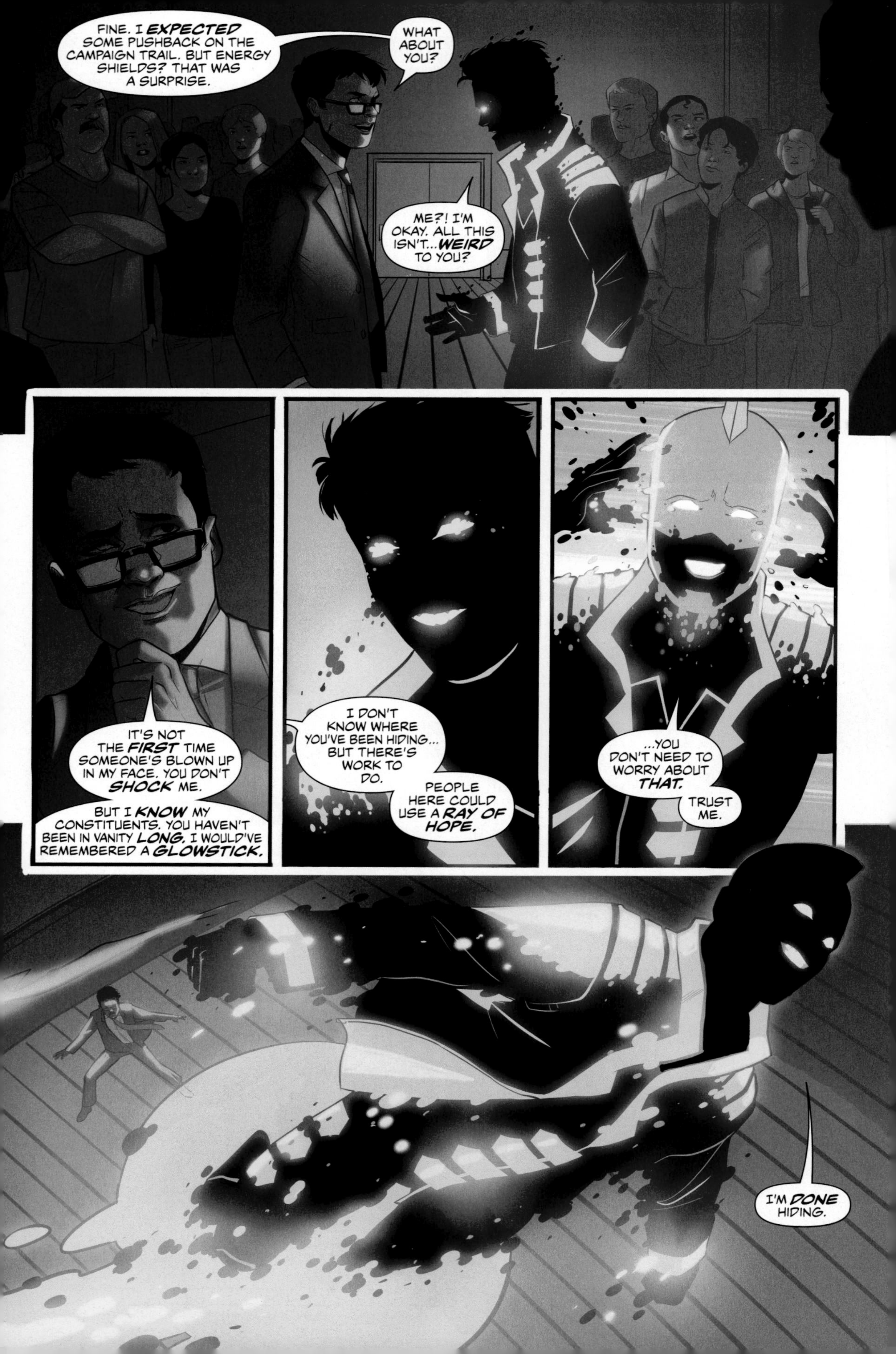
FINE. I EXPECTED SOME PUSHBACK ON THE CAMPAIGN TRAIL. BUT ENERGY SHIELDS? THAT WAS A SURPRISE.
WHAT ABOUT YOU?
ME?! I'M OKAY. ALL THIS ISN'T...WEIRD TO YOU?
IT'S NOT THE FIRST TIME SOMEONE'S BLOWN UP IN MY FACE. YOU DON'T SHOCK ME.
BUT I KNOW MY CONSTITUENTS. YOU HAVEN'T BEEN IN VANITY LONG. I WOULD'VE REMEMBERED A GLOWSTICK.
I DON'T KNOW WHERE YOU'VE BEEN HIDING... BUT THERE'S WORK TO DO.
PEOPLE HERE COULD USE A RAY OF HOPE.
...YOU DON'T NEED TO WORRY ABOUT THAT.
TRUST ME.
I'M DONE HIDING.

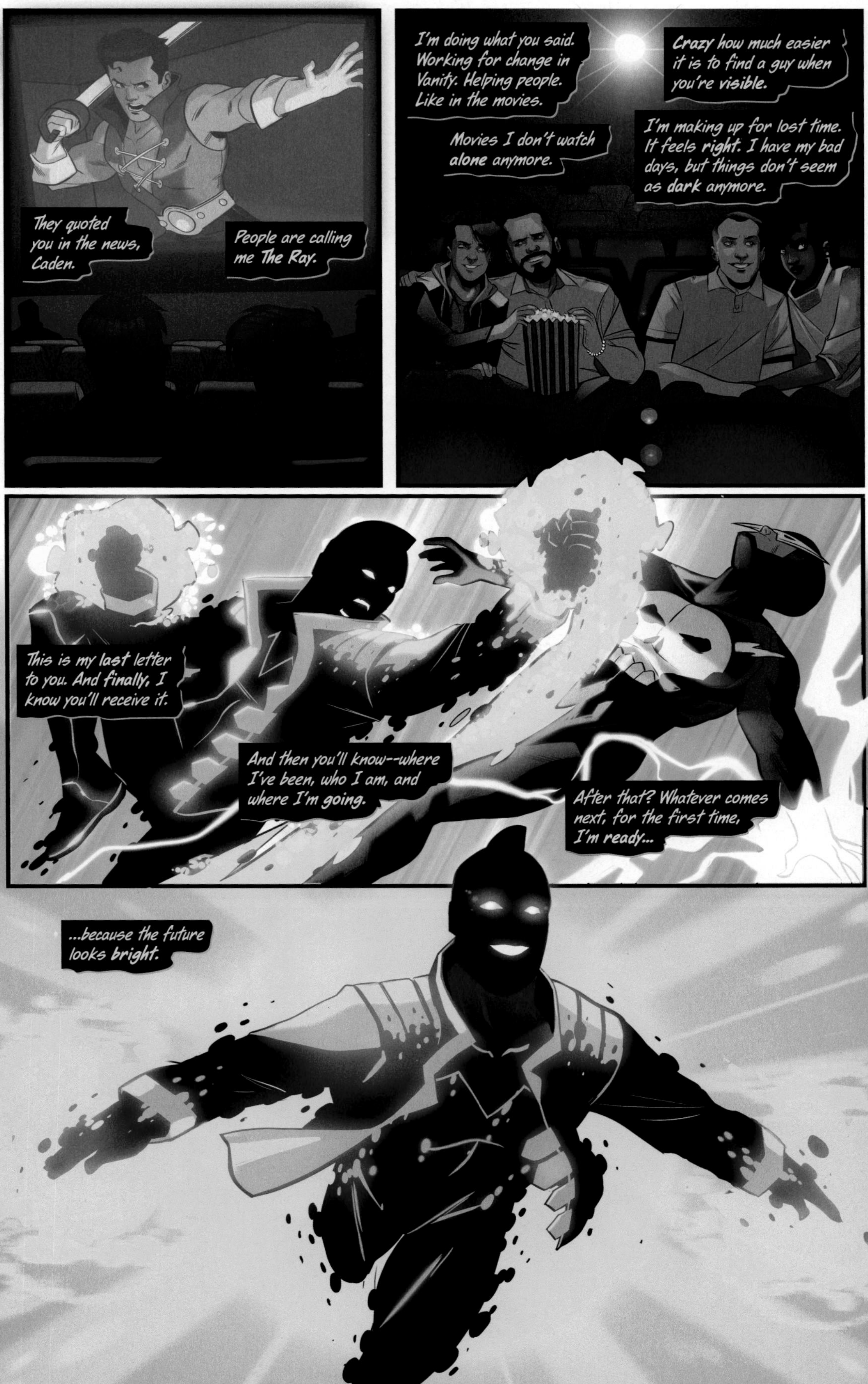
They quoted you in the news, Caden.
People are calling me The Ray.
I'm doing what you said. Working for change in Vanity. Helping people. Like in the movies.
Movies I don't watch alone anymore.
Crazy how much easier it is to find a guy when you're visible.
I'm making up for lost time. It feels right. I have my bad days, but things don't seem as dark anymore.
This is my last letter to you. And finally, I know you'll receive it.
And then you'll know--where I've been, who I am, and where I'm going.
After that? Whatever comes next, for the first time, I'm ready...
...because the future looks bright.

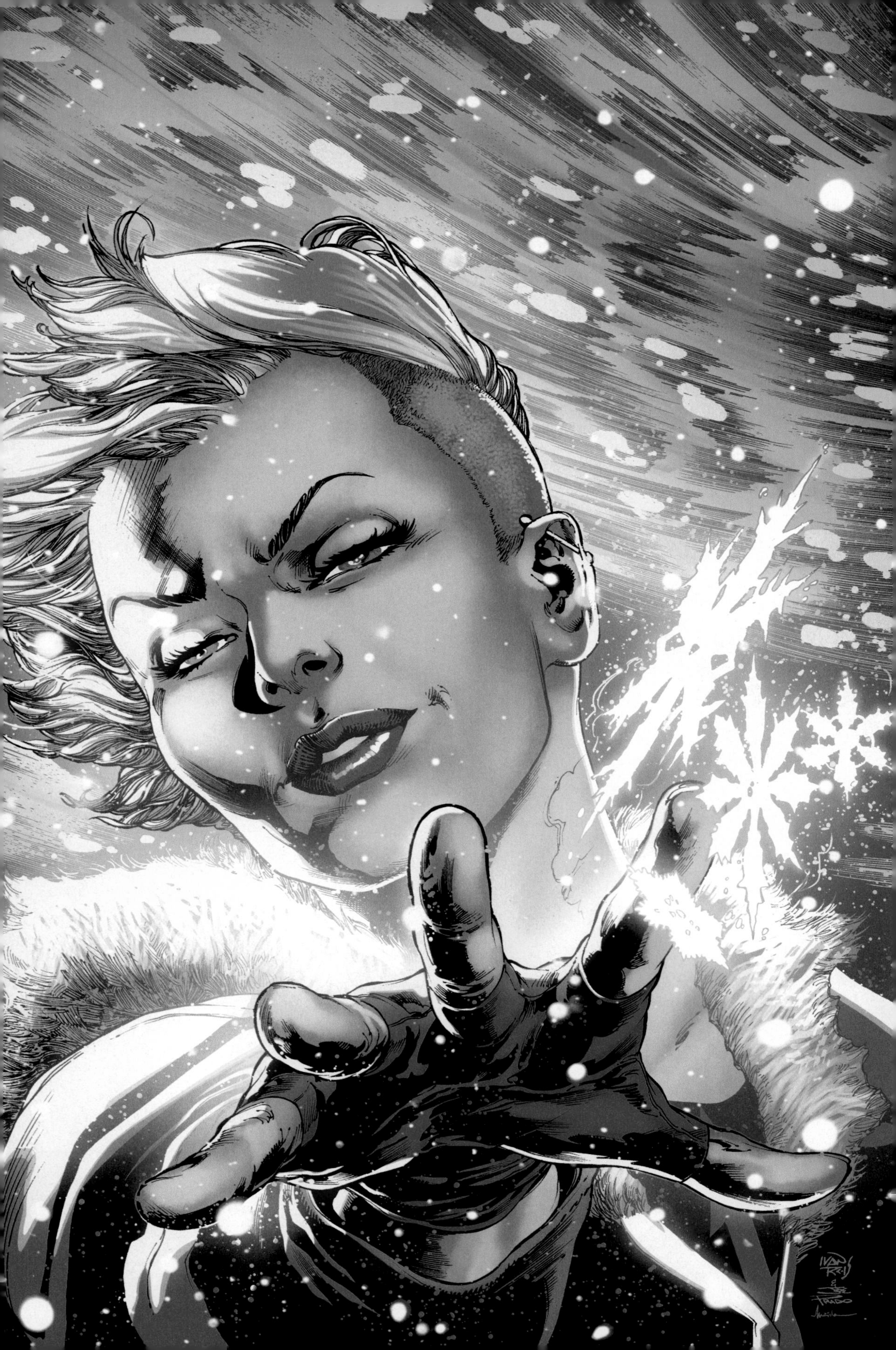

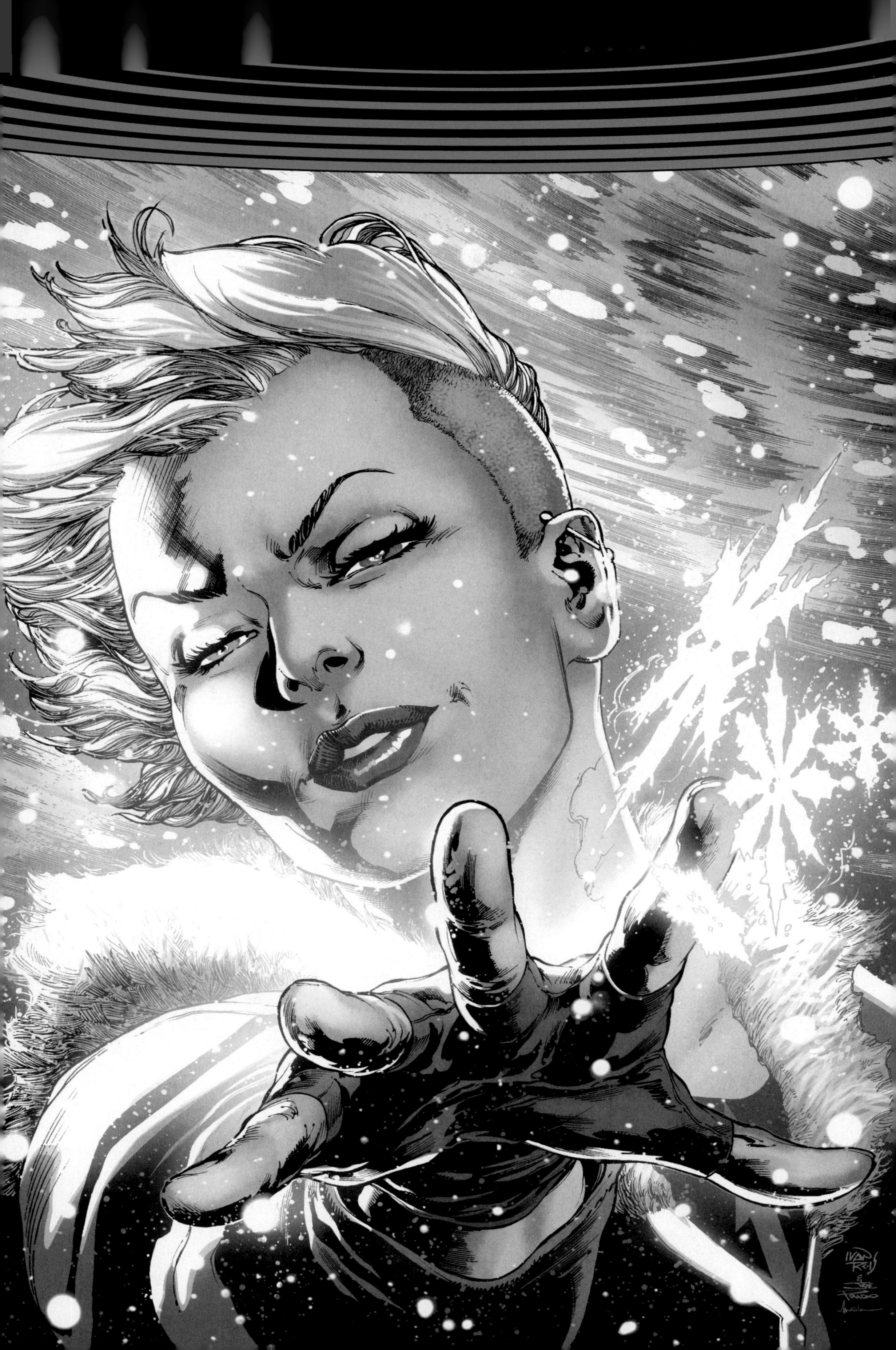

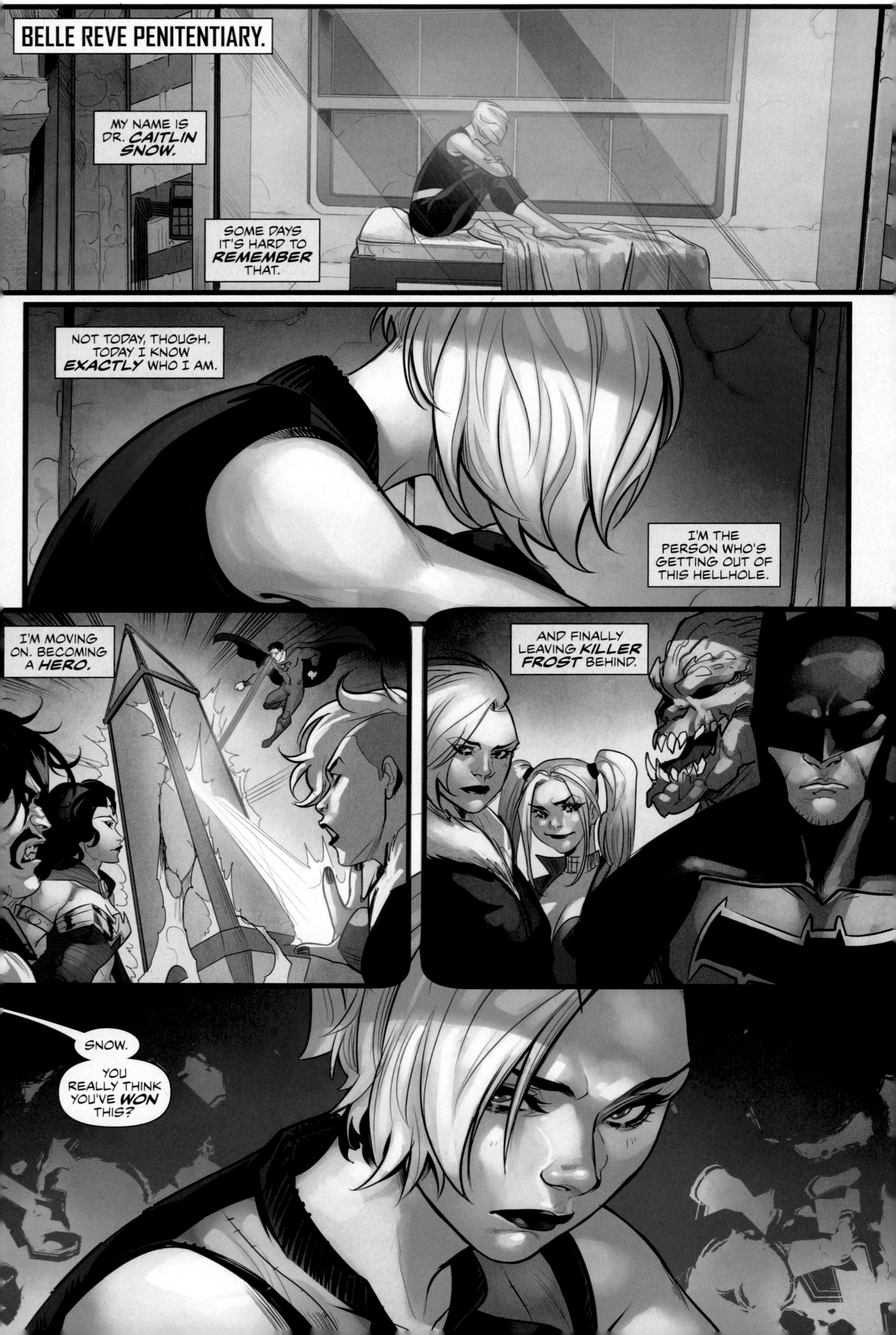
BELLE REVE PENITENTIARY.
MY NAME IS DR. CAITLIN SNOW.
SOME DAYS IT'S HARD TO REMEMBER THAT.
NOT TODAY, THOUGH. TODAY I KNOW EXACTLY WHO I AM.
I'M THE PERSON WHO'S GETTING OUT OF THIS HELLHOLE.
I'M MOVING ON. BECOMING A HERO.
AND FINALLY LEAVING KILLER FROST BEHIND.
SNOW.
YOU REALLY THINK YOU'VE WON THIS?

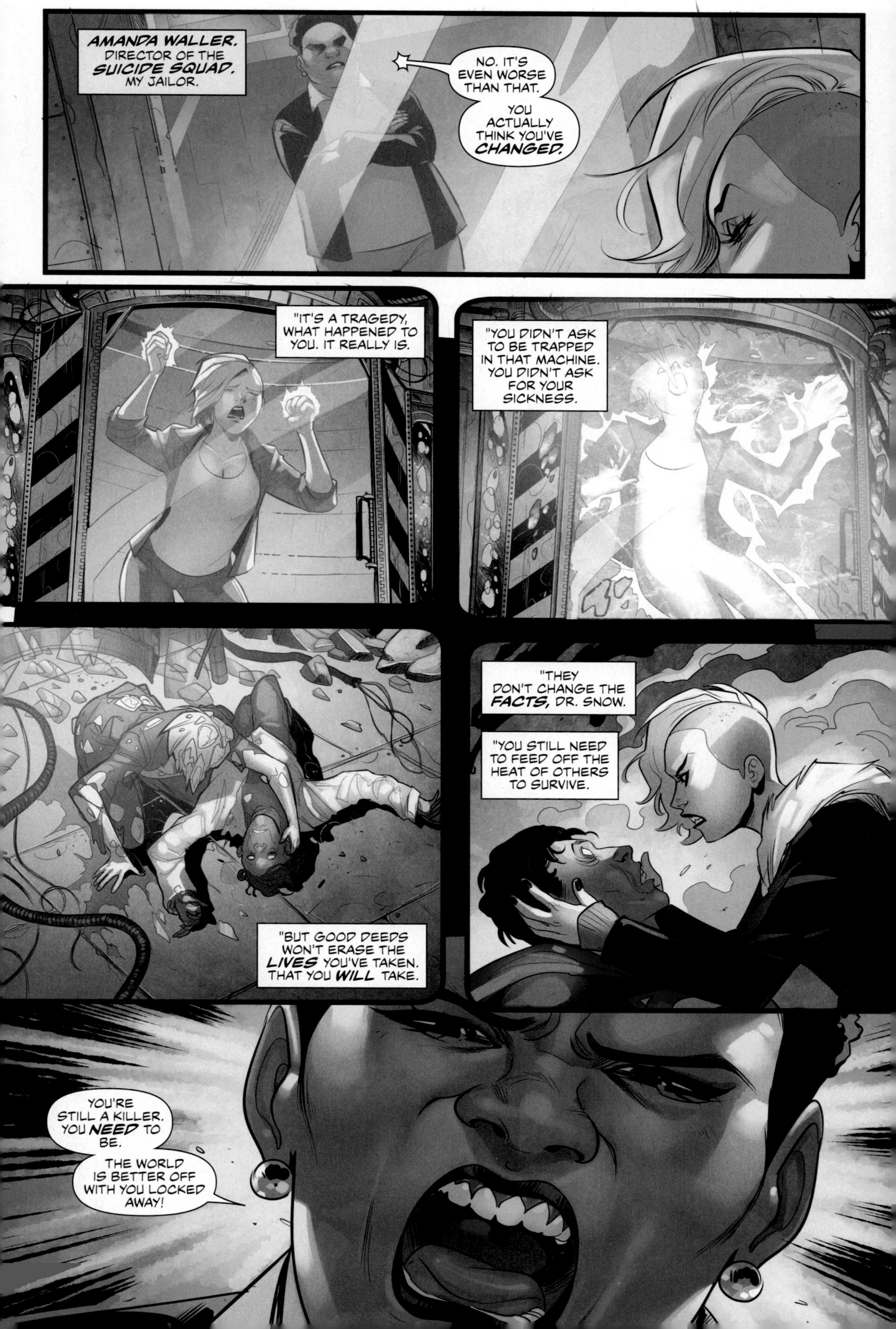
AMANDA WALLER. DIRECTOR OF THE SUICIDE SQUAD. MY JAILOR.
NO. IT'S EVEN WORSE THAN THAT.
YOU ACTUALLY THINK YOU'VE CHANGED.
"IT'S A TRAGEDY, WHAT HAPPENED TO YOU. IT REALLY IS.
"YOU DIDN'T ASK TO BE TRAPPED IN THAT MACHINE. YOU DIDN'T ASK FOR YOUR SICKNESS.
"BUT GOOD DEEDS WON'T ERASE THE LIVES YOU'VE TAKEN. THAT YOU WILL TAKE.
"THEY DON'T CHANGE THE FACTS, DR. SNOW.
"YOU STILL NEED TO FEED OFF THE HEAT OF OTHERS TO SURVIVE.
YOU'RE STILL A KILLER. YOU NEED TO BE.
THE WORLD IS BETTER OFF WITH YOU LOCKED AWAY!

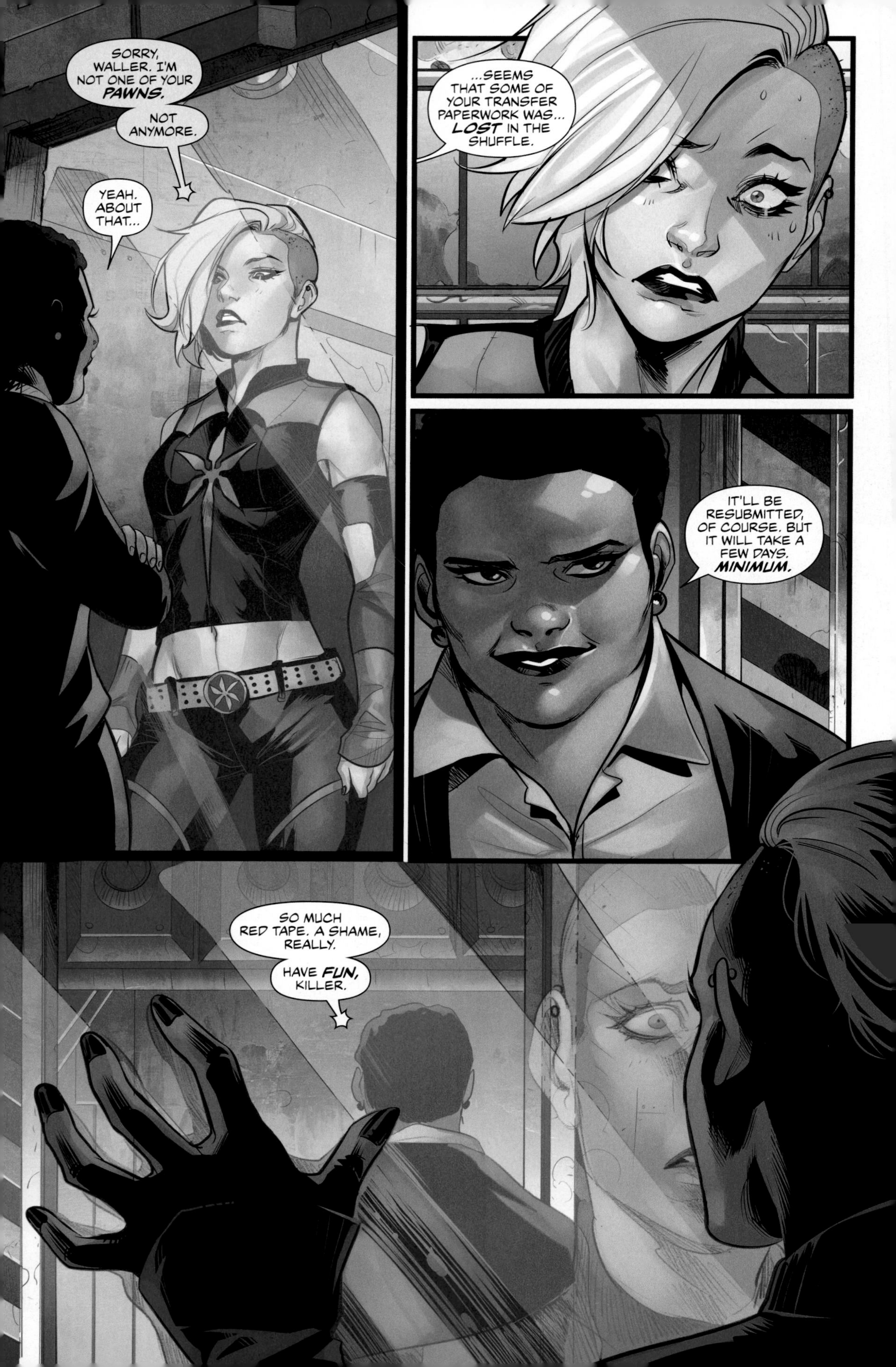
SORRY, WALLER. I'M NOT ONE OF YOUR PAWNS.
NOT ANYMORE.
YEAH. ABOUT THAT...
...SEEMS THAT SOME OF YOUR TRANSFER PAPERWORK WAS... LOST IN THE SHUFFLE.
IT'LL BE RESUBMITTED, OF COURSE. BUT IT WILL TAKE A FEW DAYS. MINIMUM.
SO MUCH RED TAPE. A SHAME, REALLY.
HAVE FUN, KILLER.

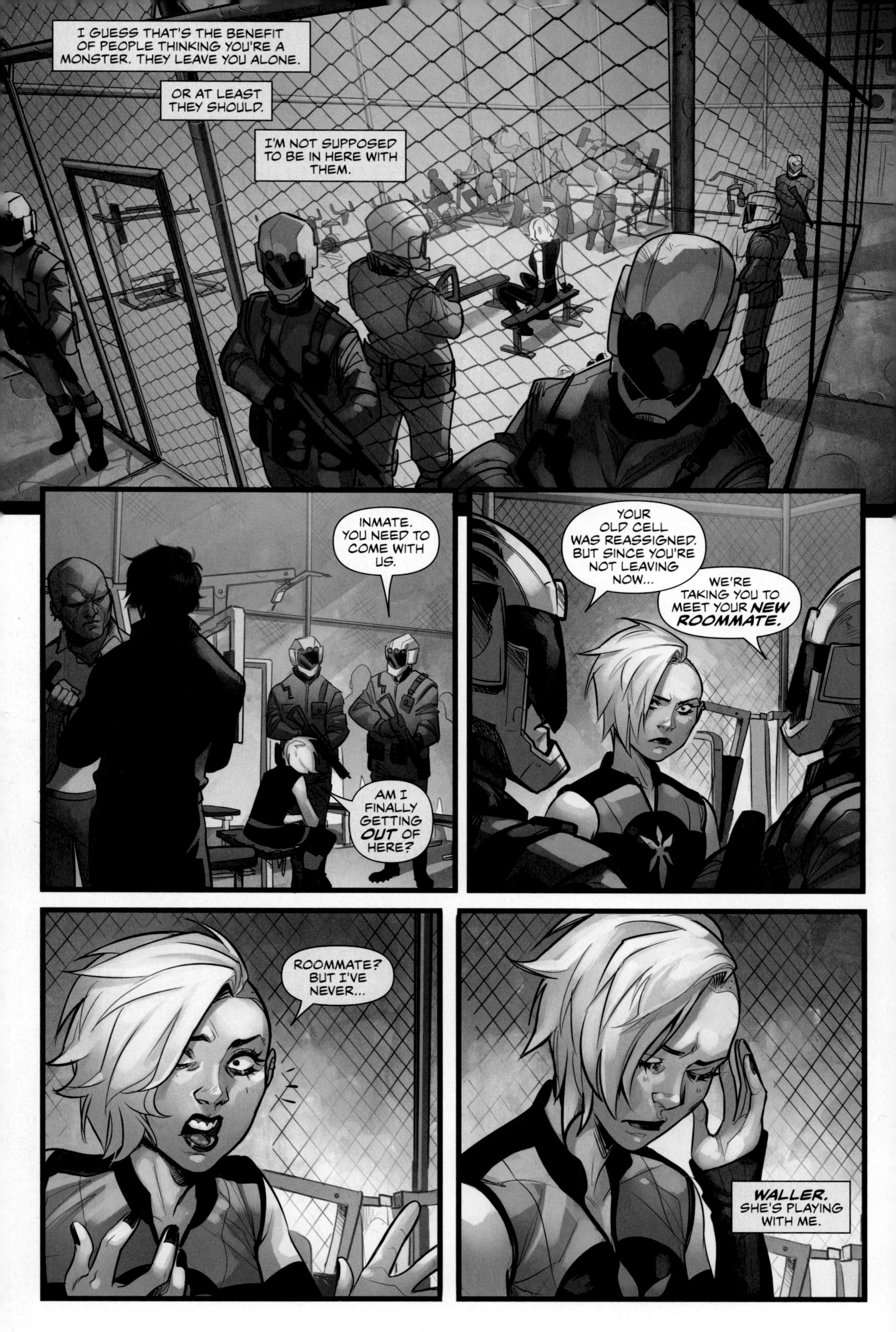
I GUESS THAT'S THE BENEFIT OF PEOPLE THINKING YOU'RE A MONSTER. THEY LEAVE YOU ALONE.
OR AT LEAST THEY SHOULD.
I'M NOT SUPPOSED TO BE IN HERE WITH THEM.
INMATE. YOU NEED TO COME WITH US.
AM I FINALLY GETTING OUT OF HERE?
YOUR OLD CELL WAS REASSIGNED. BUT SINCE YOU'RE NOT LEAVING NOW...
WE'RE TAKING YOU TO MEET YOUR NEW ROOMMATE.
ROOMMATE? BUT I'VE NEVER...
WALLER. SHE'S PLAYING WITH ME.

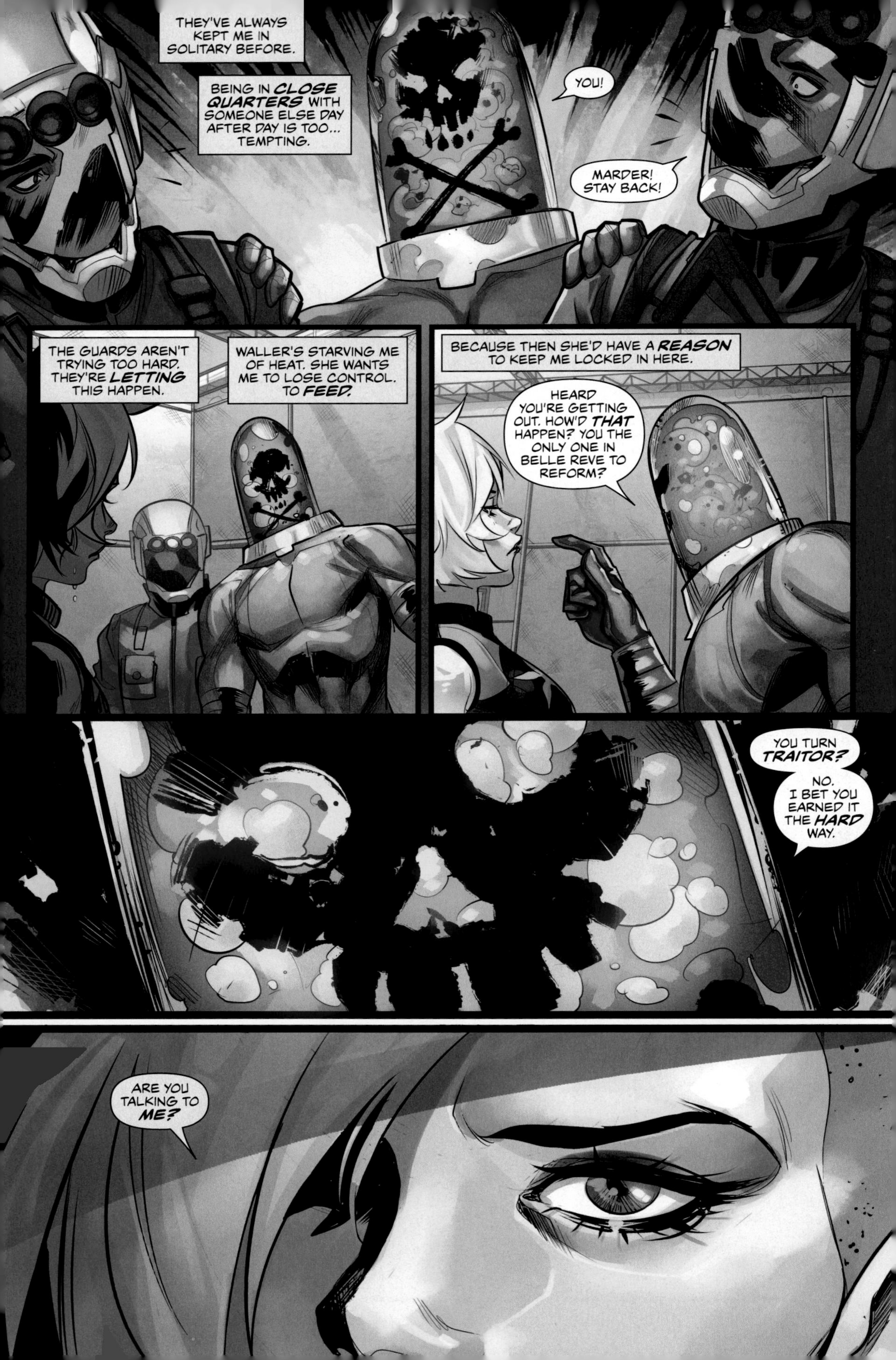
THEY'VE ALWAYS KEPT ME IN SOLITARY BEFORE.
BEING IN CLOSE QUARTERS WITH SOMEONE ELSE DAY AFTER DAY IS TOO... TEMPTING.
YOU!
MARDER! STAY BACK!
THE GUARDS AREN'T TRYING TOO HARD. THEY'RE LETTING THIS HAPPEN.
WALLER'S STARVING ME OF HEAT. SHE WANTS ME TO LOSE CONTROL. TO FEED.
BECAUSE THEN SHE'D HAVE A REASON TO KEEP ME LOCKED IN HERE.
HEARD YOU'RE GETTING OUT. HOW'D THAT HAPPEN? YOU THE ONLY ONE IN BELLE REVE TO REFORM?
YOU TURN TRAITOR?
NO. I BET YOU EARNED IT THE HARD WAY.
ARE YOU TALKING TO ME?

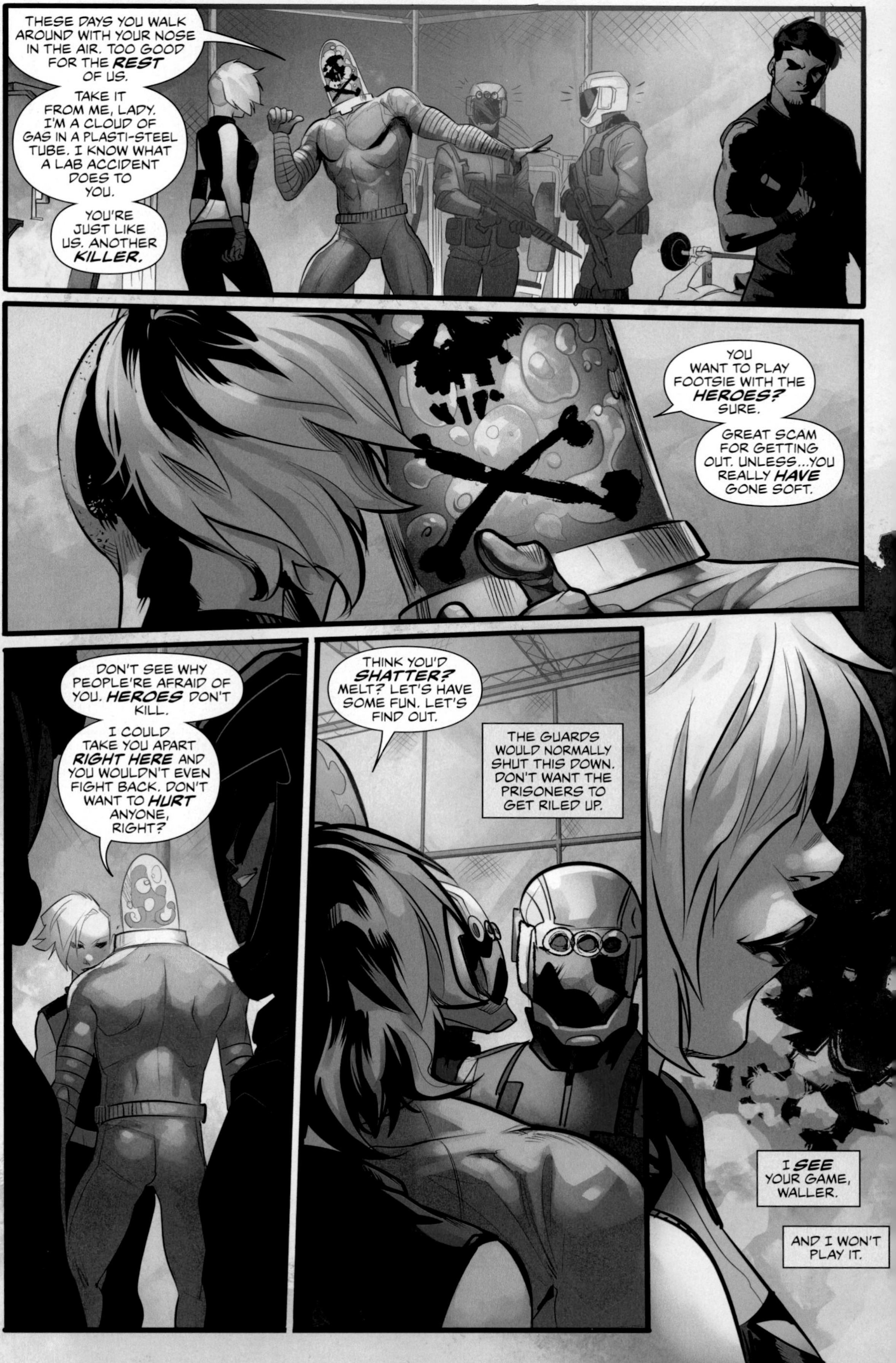
THESE DAYS YOU WALK AROUND WITH YOUR NOSE IN THE AIR. TOO GOOD FOR THE REST OF US.
TAKE IT FROM ME, LADY. I'M A CLOUD OF GAS IN A PLASTI-STEEL TUBE. I KNOW WHAT A LAB ACCIDENT DOES TO YOU.
YOU'RE JUST LIKE US. ANOTHER KILLER.
YOU WANT TO PLAY FOOTSIE WITH THE HEROES? SURE.
GREAT SCAM FOR GETTING OUT. UNLESS...YOU REALLY HAVE GONE SOFT.
DON'T SEE WHY PEOPLE'RE AFRAID OF YOU. HEROES DON'T KILL.
I COULD TAKE YOU APART RIGHT HERE AND YOU WOULDN'T EVEN FIGHT BACK. DON'T WANT TO HURT ANYONE, RIGHT?
THINK YOU'D SHATTER? MELT? LET'S HAVE SOME FUN. LET'S FIND OUT.
THE GUARDS WOULD NORMALLY SHUT THIS DOWN. DON'T WANT THE PRISONERS TO GET RILED UP.
I SEE YOUR GAME, WALLER.
AND I WON'T PLAY IT.

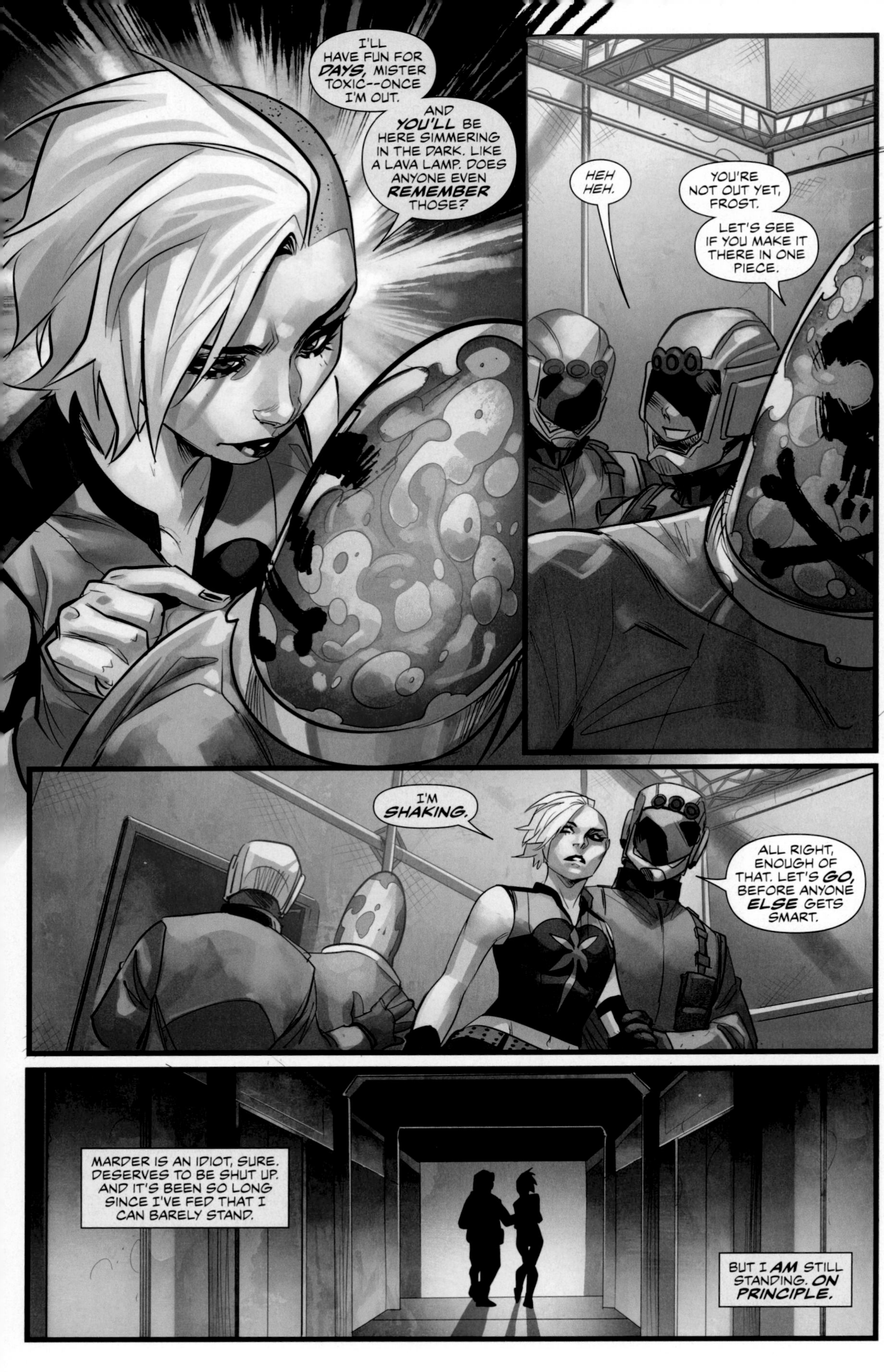
I'LL HAVE FUN FOR DAYS, MISTER TOXIC--ONCE I'M OUT.
AND YOU'LL BE HERE SIMMERING IN THE DARK. LIKE A LAVA LAMP. DOES ANYONE EVEN REMEMBER THOSE?
HEH HEH.
YOU'RE NOT OUT YET, FROST.
LET'S SEE IF YOU MAKE IT THERE IN ONE PIECE.
I'M SHAKING.
ALL RIGHT, ENOUGH OF THAT. LET'S GO, BEFORE ANYONE ELSE GETS SMART.
MARDER IS AN IDIOT, SURE. DESERVES TO BE SHUT UP. AND IT'S BEEN SO LONG SINCE I'VE FED THAT I CAN BARELY STAND.
BUT I AM STILL STANDING. ON PRINCIPLE.

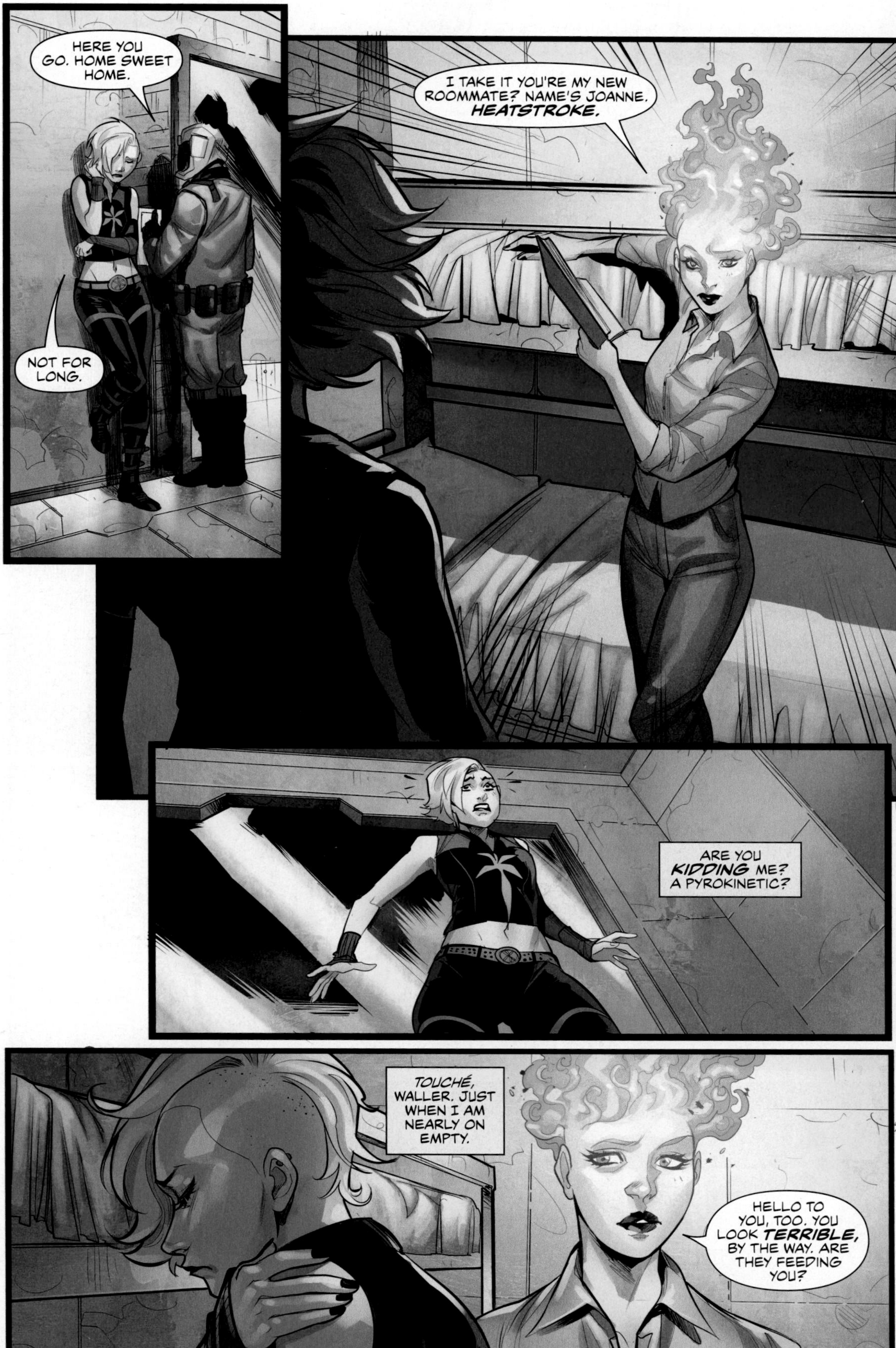
HERE YOU GO. HOME SWEET HOME.
NOT FOR LONG.
I TAKE IT YOU'RE MY NEW ROOMMATE? NAME'S JOANNE. ***HEATSTROKE.***
ARE YOU ***KIDDING*** ME? A PYROKINETIC?
TOUCHÉ, WALLER. JUST WHEN I AM NEARLY ON EMPTY.
HELLO TO YOU, TOO. YOU LOOK ***TERRIBLE,*** BY THE WAY. ARE THEY FEEDING YOU?

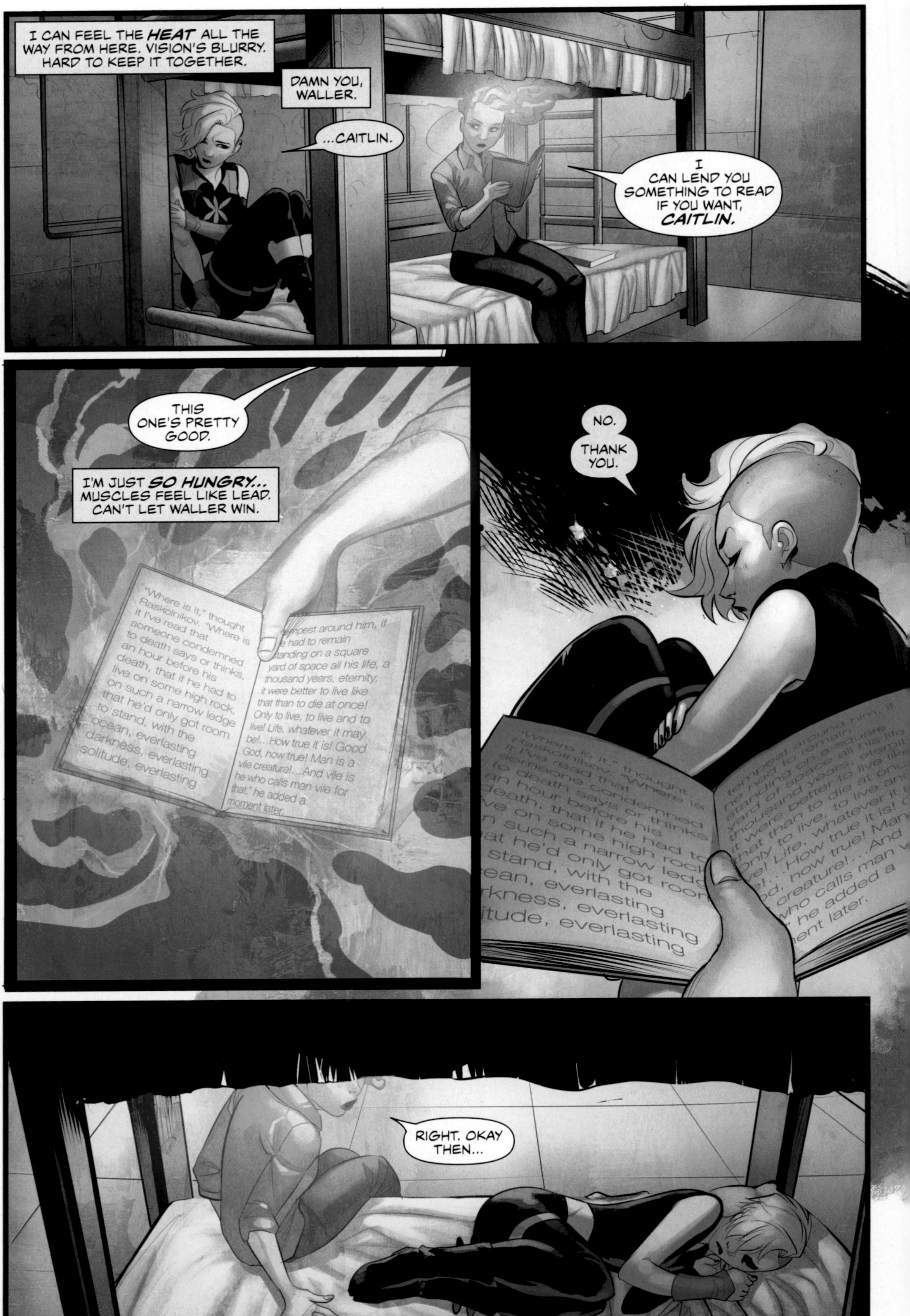
I CAN FEEL THE ***HEAT*** ALL THE WAY FROM HERE. VISION'S BLURRY. HARD TO KEEP IT TOGETHER.
DAMN YOU, WALLER.
...CAITLIN.
I CAN LEND YOU SOMETHING TO READ IF YOU WANT, ***CAITLIN.***
THIS ONE'S PRETTY GOOD.
I'M JUST ***SO HUNGRY...*** MUSCLES FEEL LIKE LEAD. CAN'T LET WALLER WIN.
"Where is it," thought Raskolnikov. "Where is it I've read that someone condemned to death says or thinks, an hour before his death, that if he had to live on some high rock, on such a narrow ledge that he'd only got room to stand, with the ocean, everlasting darkness, everlasting solitude, everlasting
tempest around him, if he had to remain standing on a square yard of space all his life, a thousand years, eternity, it were better to live like that than to die at once! Only to live, to live and to live! Life, whatever it may be!...How true it is! Good God, how true! Man is a vile creature!...And vile is he who calls man vile for that," he added a moment later.
NO.
THANK YOU.
RIGHT. OKAY THEN...

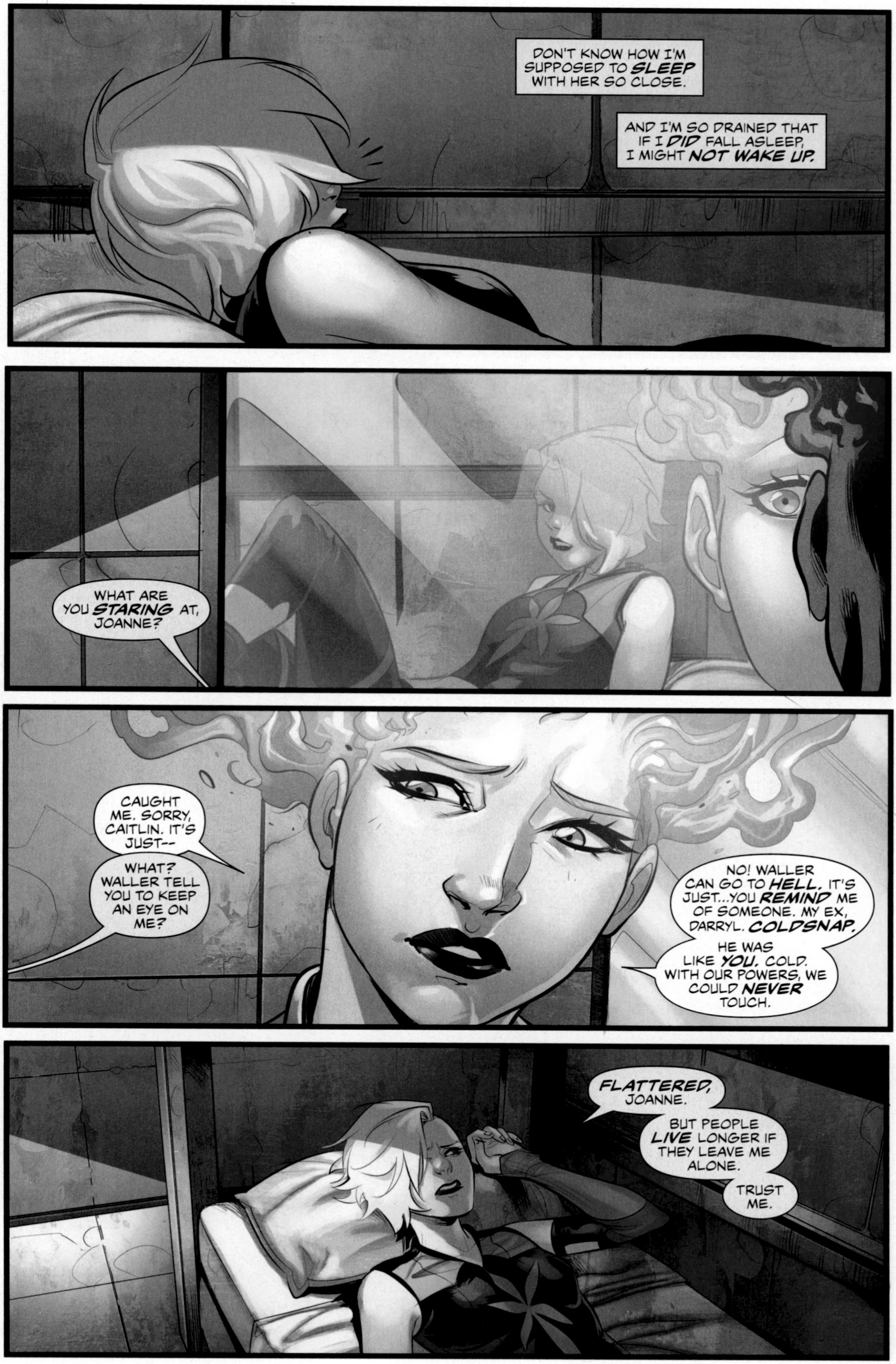

DON'T KNOW HOW I'M SUPPOSED TO SLEEP WITH HER SO CLOSE.
AND I'M SO DRAINED THAT IF I DID FALL ASLEEP, I MIGHT NOT WAKE UP.
WHAT ARE YOU STARING AT, JOANNE?
CAUGHT ME. SORRY, CAITLIN. IT'S JUST--
WHAT? WALLER TELL YOU TO KEEP AN EYE ON ME?
NO! WALLER CAN GO TO HELL. IT'S JUST...YOU REMIND ME OF SOMEONE. MY EX, DARRYL. COLDSNAP.
HE WAS LIKE YOU. COLD. WITH OUR POWERS, WE COULD NEVER TOUCH.
FLATTERED, JOANNE.
BUT PEOPLE LIVE LONGER IF THEY LEAVE ME ALONE.
TRUST ME.

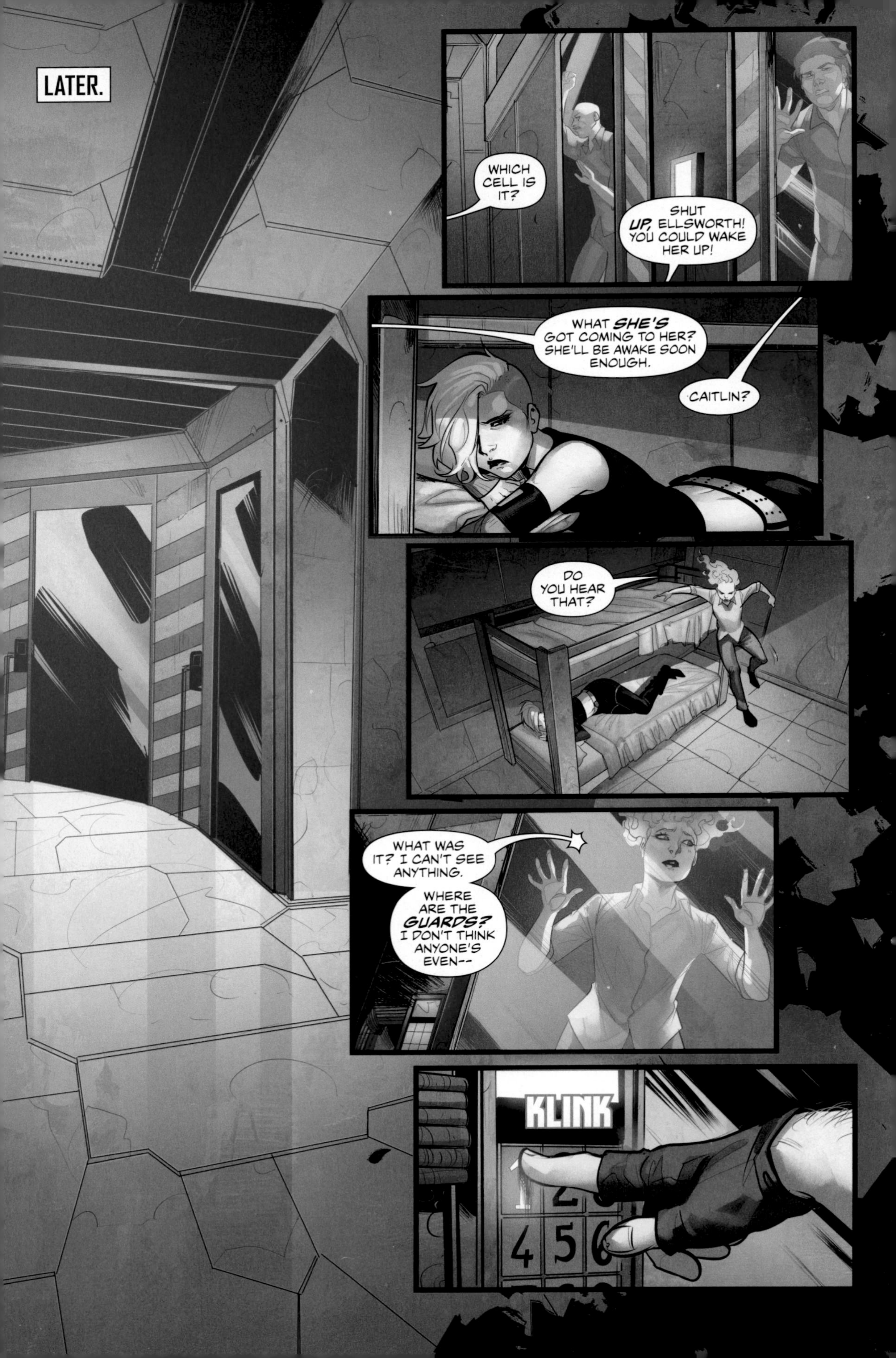
LATER.
WHICH CELL IS IT?
SHUT UP, ELLSWORTH! YOU COULD WAKE HER UP!
WHAT SHE'S GOT COMING TO HER? SHE'LL BE AWAKE SOON ENOUGH.
CAITLIN?
DO YOU HEAR THAT?
WHAT WAS IT? I CAN'T SEE ANYTHING.
WHERE ARE THE GUARDS? I DON'T THINK ANYONE'S EVEN--
KLINK
456

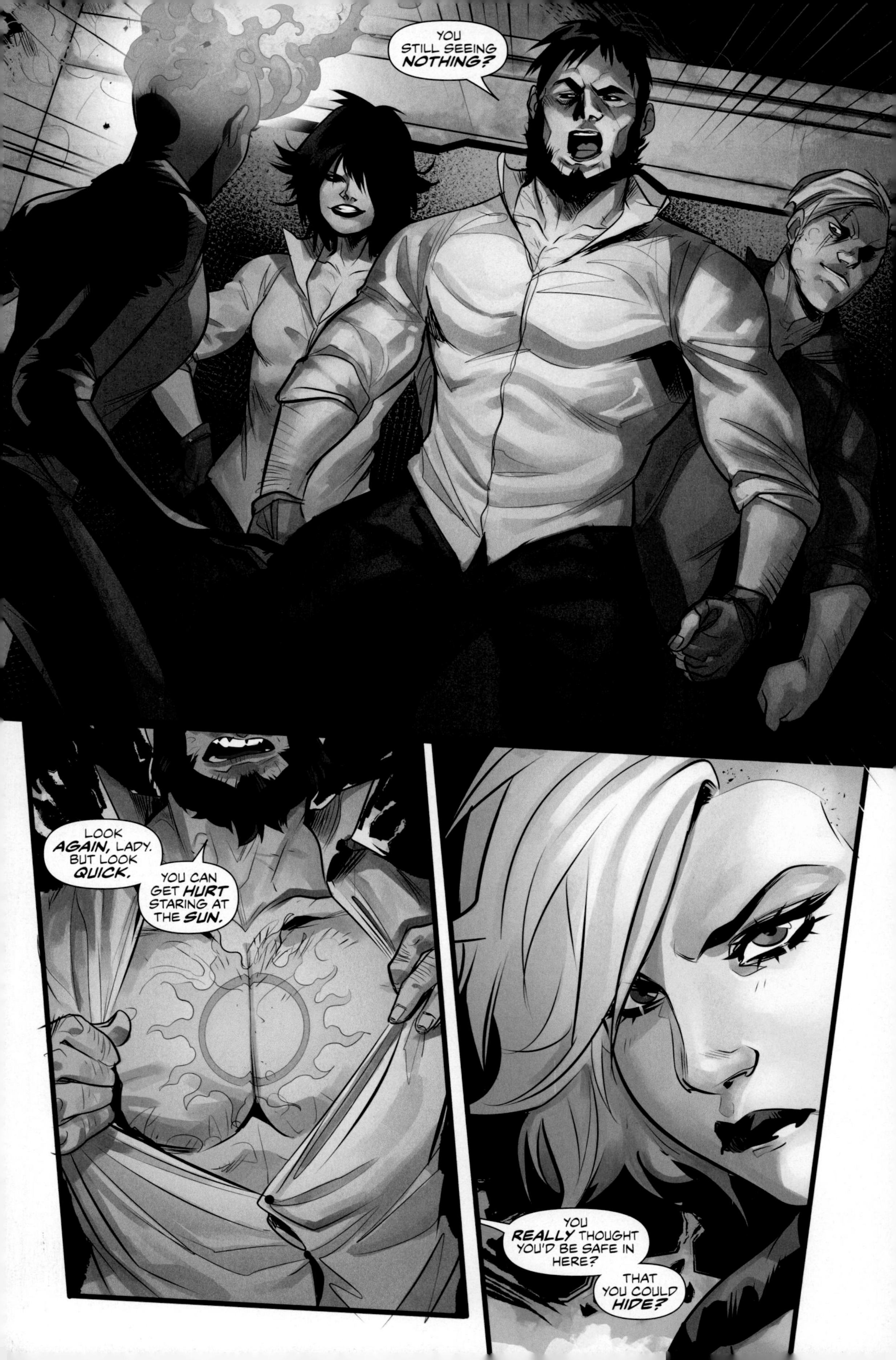

YOU STILL SEEING NOTHING?
LOOK AGAIN, LADY. BUT LOOK QUICK.
YOU CAN GET HURT STARING AT THE SUN.
YOU REALLY THOUGHT YOU'D BE SAFE IN HERE?
THAT YOU COULD HIDE?

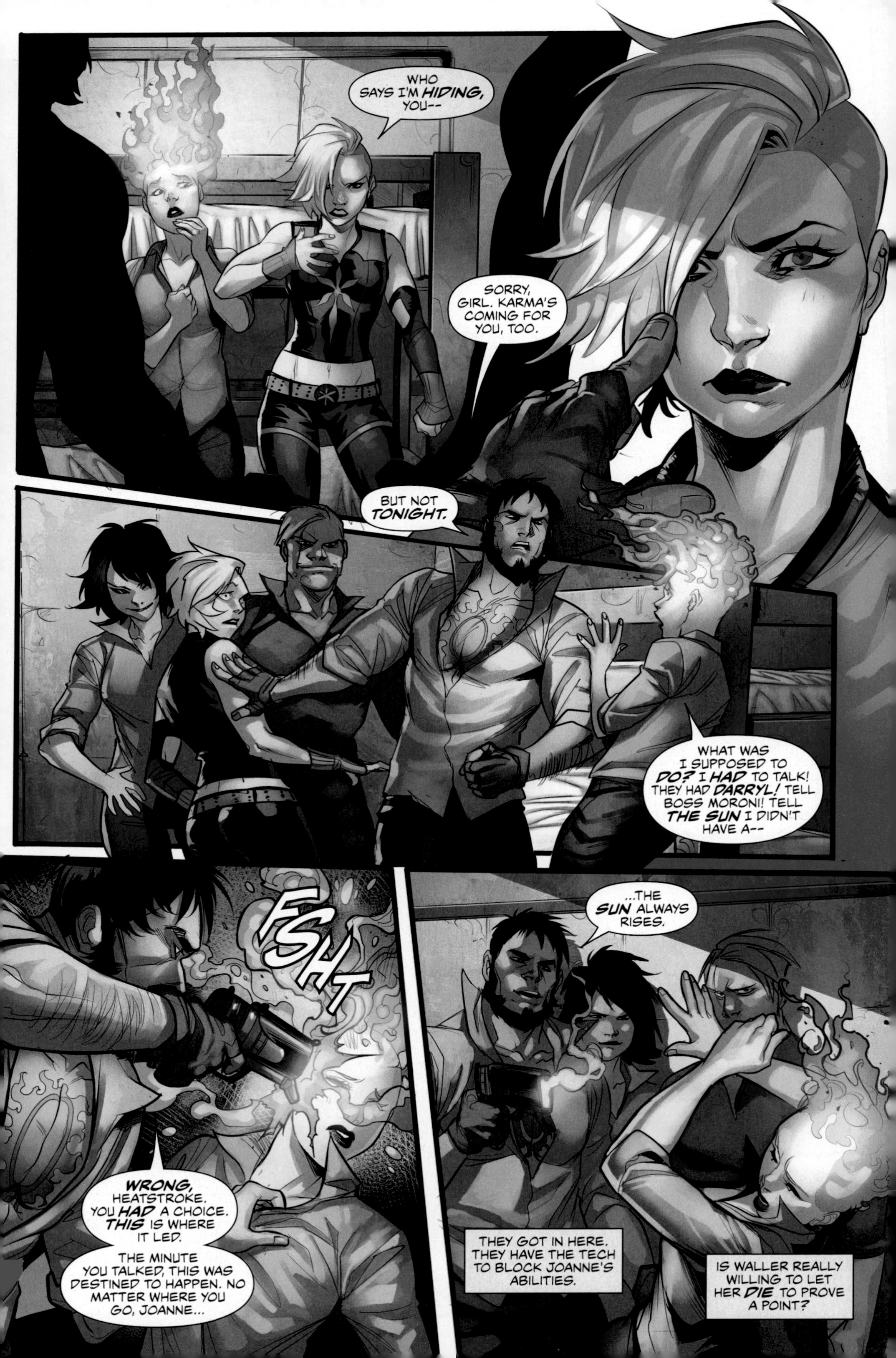
WHO SAYS I'M HIDING, YOU--
SORRY, GIRL. KARMA'S COMING FOR YOU, TOO.
BUT NOT TONIGHT.
WHAT WAS I SUPPOSED TO DO? I HAD TO TALK! THEY HAD DARRYL! TELL BOSS MORONI! TELL THE SUN I DIDN'T HAVE A--
FSHT
WRONG, HEATSTROKE. YOU HAD A CHOICE. THIS IS WHERE IT LED.
THE MINUTE YOU TALKED, THIS WAS DESTINED TO HAPPEN. NO MATTER WHERE YOU GO, JOANNE...
...THE SUN ALWAYS RISES.
THEY GOT IN HERE. THEY HAVE THE TECH TO BLOCK JOANNE'S ABILITIES.
IS WALLER REALLY WILLING TO LET HER DIE TO PROVE A POINT?

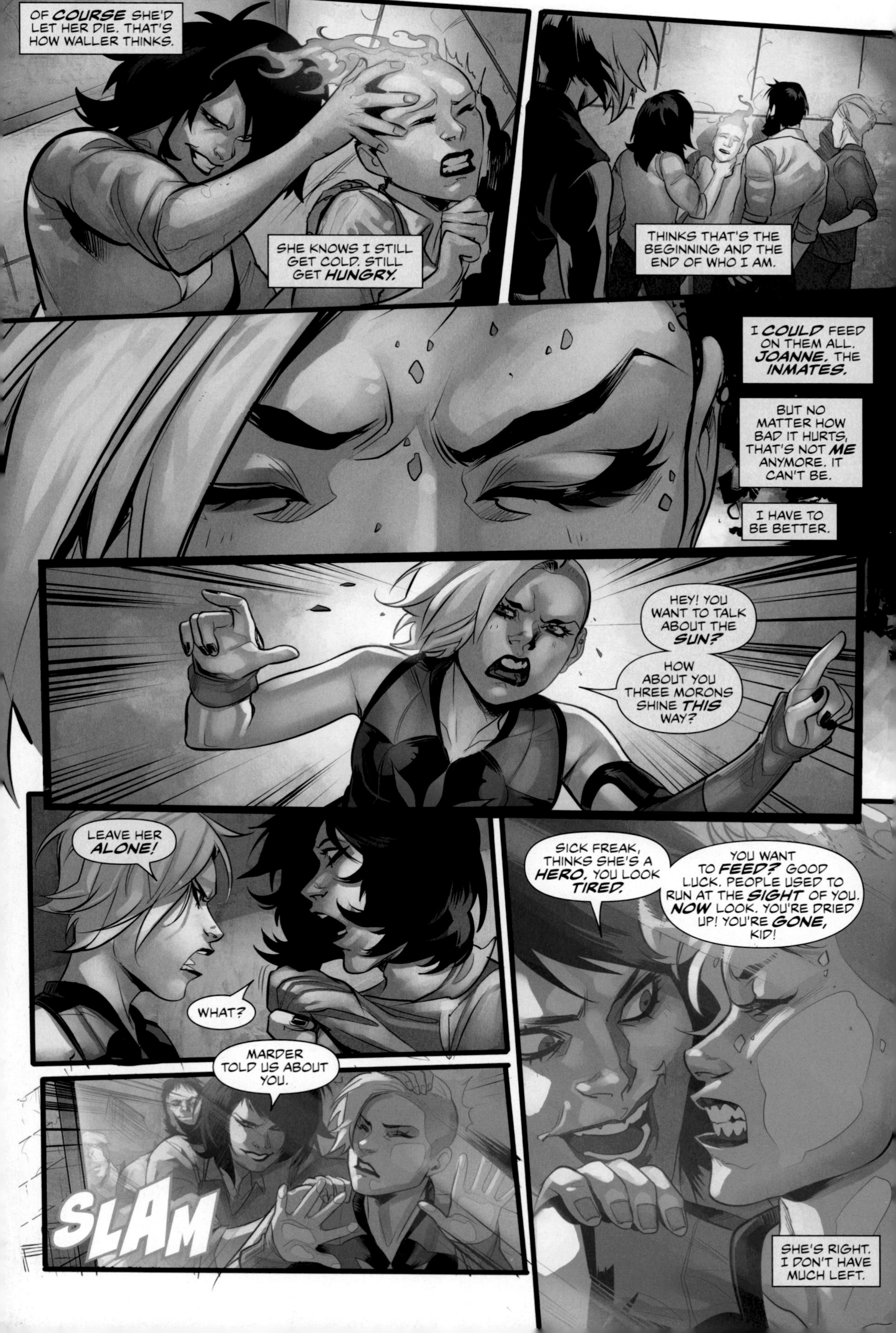

OF COURSE SHE'D LET HER DIE. THAT'S HOW WALLER THINKS.
SHE KNOWS I STILL GET COLD. STILL GET HUNGRY.
THINKS THAT'S THE BEGINNING AND THE END OF WHO I AM.
I COULD FEED ON THEM ALL. JOANNE. THE INMATES.
BUT NO MATTER HOW BAD IT HURTS, THAT'S NOT ME ANYMORE. IT CAN'T BE.
I HAVE TO BE BETTER.
HEY! YOU WANT TO TALK ABOUT THE SUN?
HOW ABOUT YOU THREE MORONS SHINE THIS WAY?
LEAVE HER ALONE!
WHAT?
MARDER TOLD US ABOUT YOU.
SLAM
SICK FREAK, THINKS SHE'S A HERO. YOU LOOK TIRED.
YOU WANT TO FEED? GOOD LUCK. PEOPLE USED TO RUN AT THE SIGHT OF YOU. NOW LOOK. YOU'RE DRIED UP! YOU'RE GONE, KID!
SHE'S RIGHT. I DON'T HAVE MUCH LEFT.

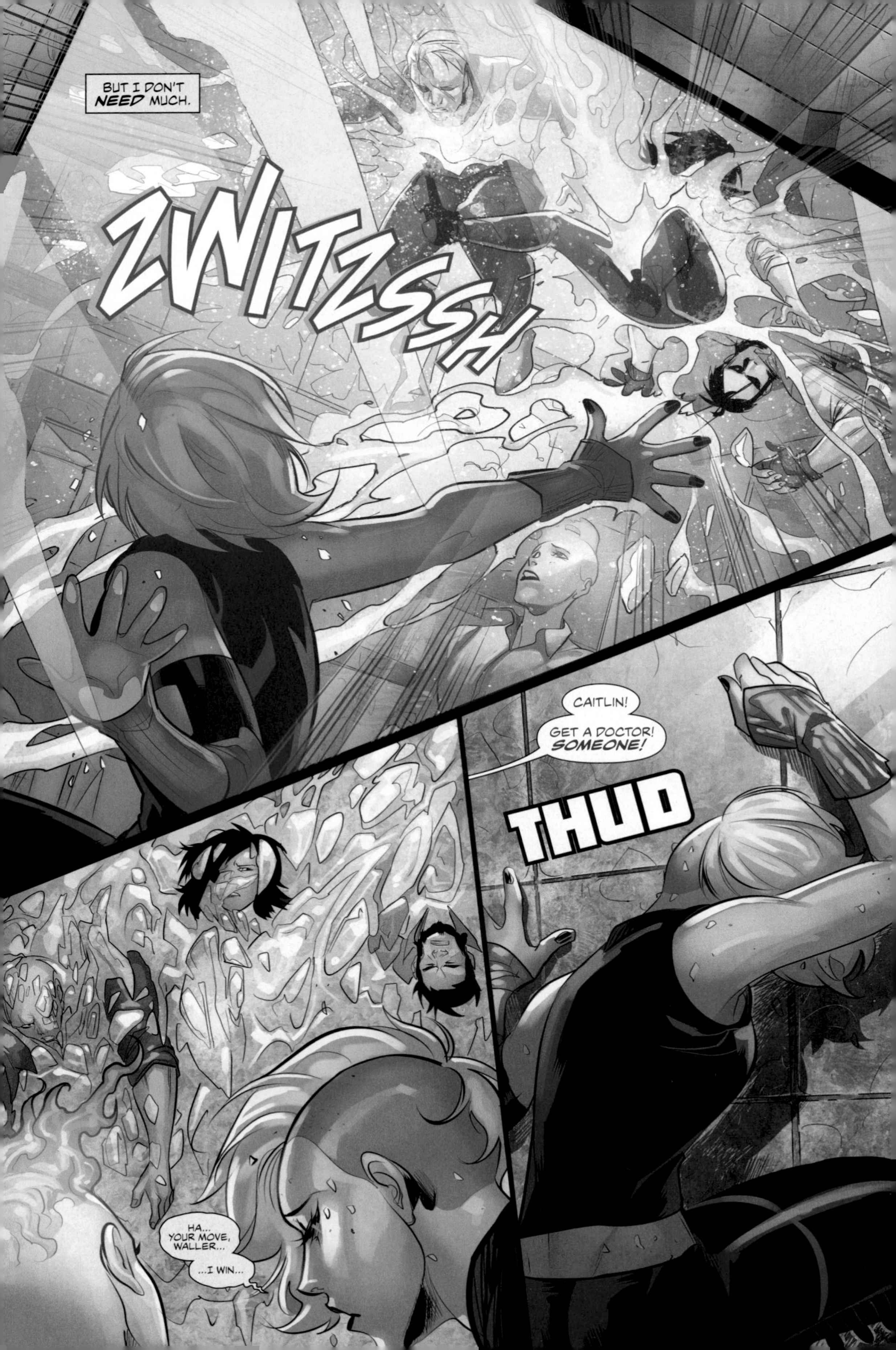
BUT I DON'T NEED MUCH.
ZWITZSSH
CAITLIN!
GET A DOCTOR! SOMEONE!
THUD
HA... YOUR MOVE, WALLER...
...I WIN...

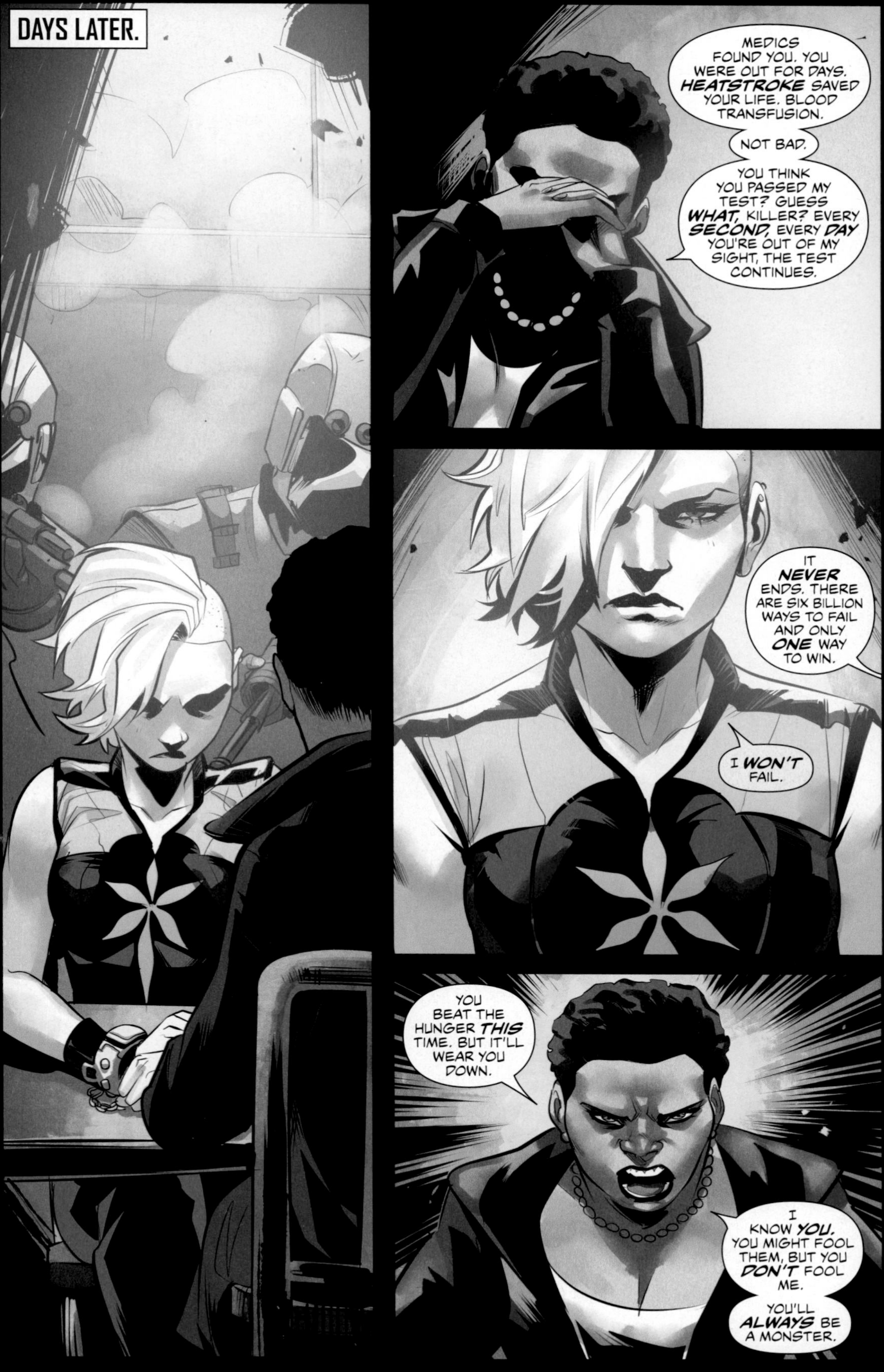
DAYS LATER.
MEDICS FOUND YOU. YOU WERE OUT FOR DAYS. HEATSTROKE SAVED YOUR LIFE. BLOOD TRANSFUSION.
NOT BAD.
YOU THINK YOU PASSED MY TEST? GUESS WHAT, KILLER? EVERY SECOND, EVERY DAY YOU'RE OUT OF MY SIGHT, THE TEST CONTINUES.
IT NEVER ENDS. THERE ARE SIX BILLION WAYS TO FAIL AND ONLY ONE WAY TO WIN.
I WON'T FAIL.
YOU BEAT THE HUNGER THIS TIME. BUT IT'LL WEAR YOU DOWN.
I KNOW YOU. YOU MIGHT FOOL THEM, BUT YOU DON'T FOOL ME.
YOU'LL ALWAYS BE A MONSTER.

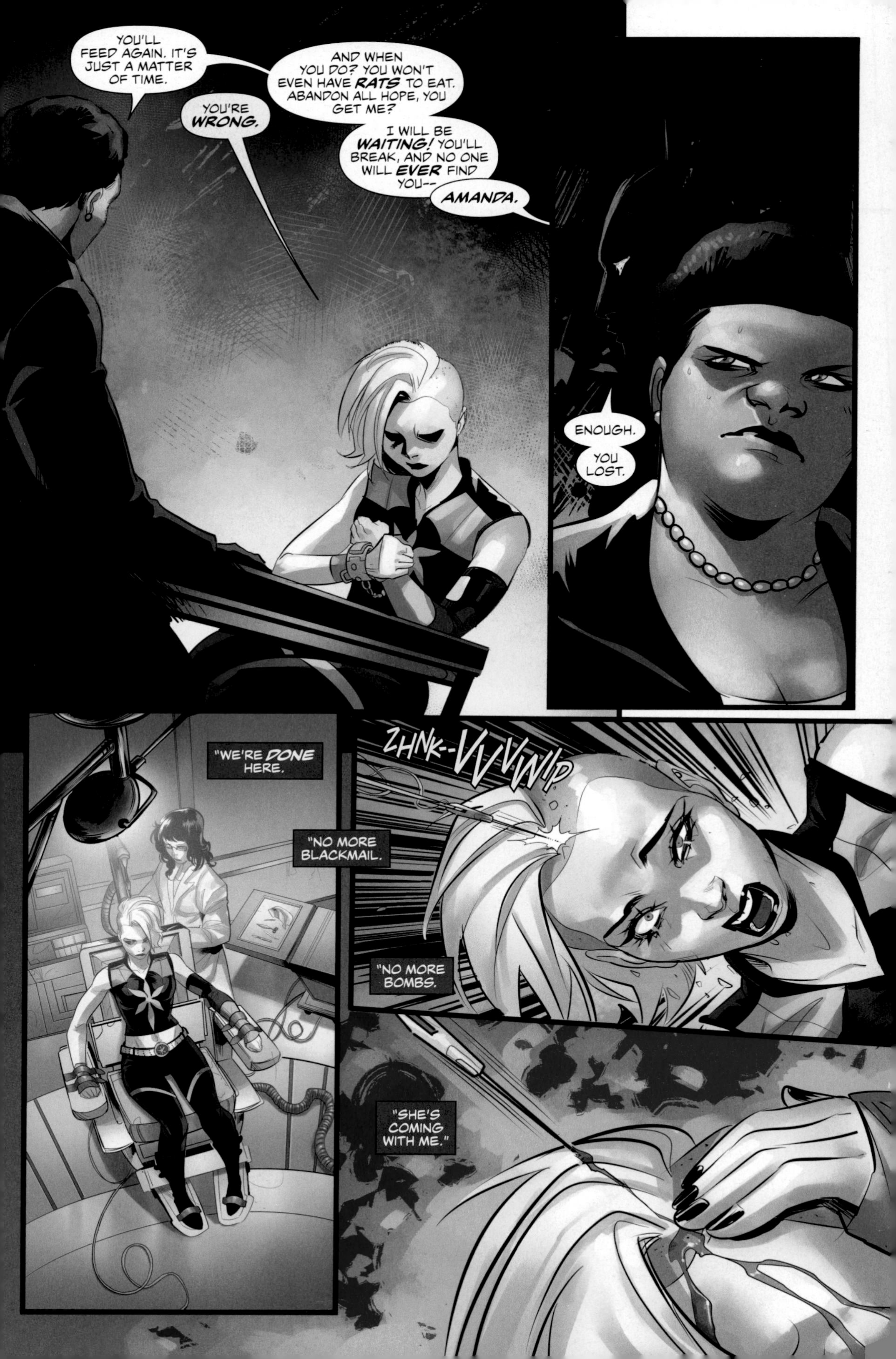
YOU'LL FEED AGAIN. IT'S JUST A MATTER OF TIME.
YOU'RE WRONG.
AND WHEN YOU DO? YOU WON'T EVEN HAVE RATS TO EAT. ABANDON ALL HOPE, YOU GET ME?
I WILL BE WAITING! YOU'LL BREAK, AND NO ONE WILL EVER FIND YOU--
AMANDA.
ENOUGH.
YOU LOST.
"WE'RE DONE HERE.
ZHNK--VVVVWIP
"NO MORE BLACKMAIL.
"NO MORE BOMBS.
"SHE'S COMING WITH ME."

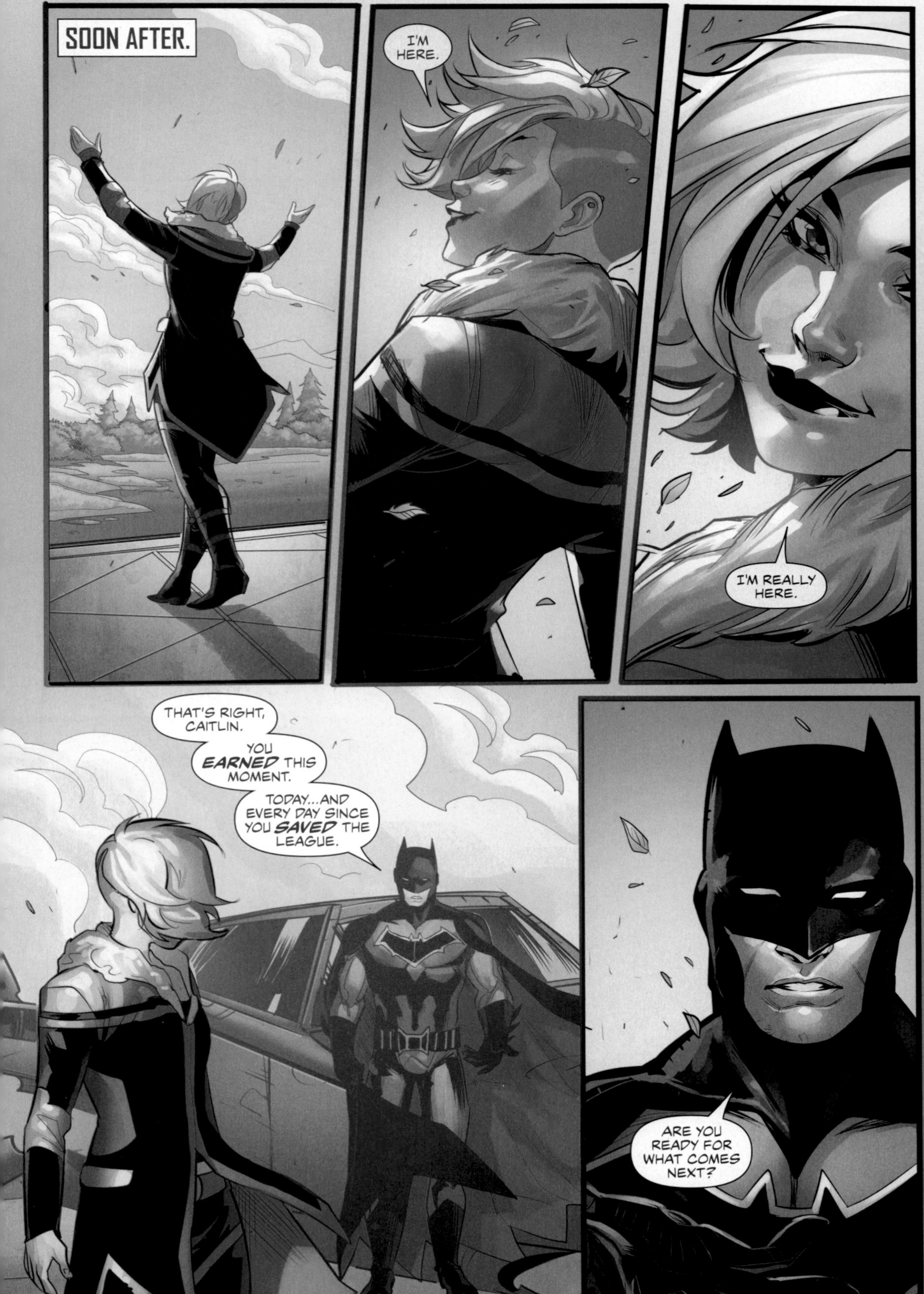
SOON AFTER.
I'M HERE.
I'M REALLY HERE.
THAT'S RIGHT, CAITLIN.
YOU EARNED THIS MOMENT.
TODAY...AND EVERY DAY SINCE YOU SAVED THE LEAGUE.
ARE YOU READY FOR WHAT COMES NEXT?

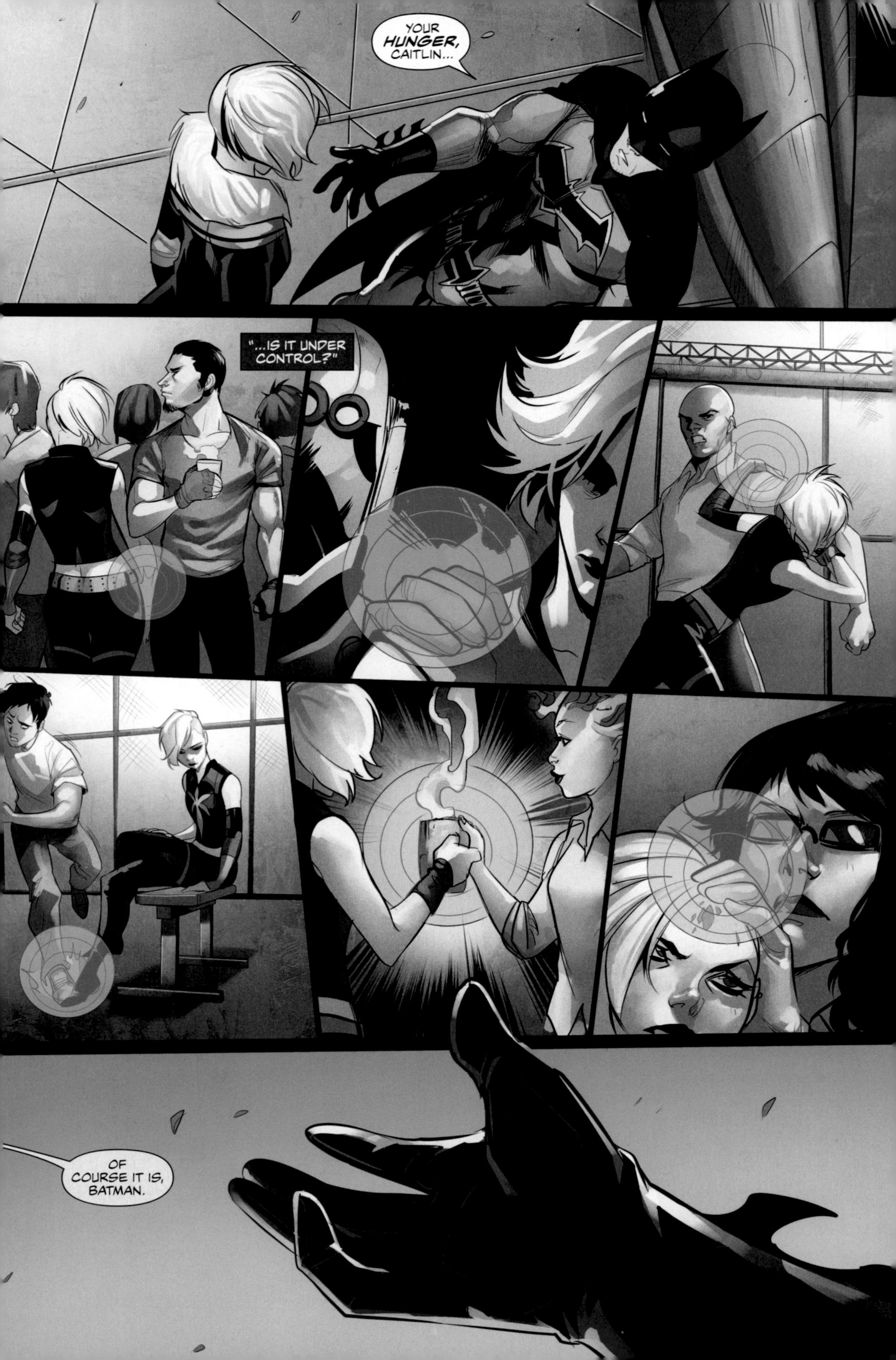
YOUR HUNGER, CAITLIN...
"...IS IT UNDER CONTROL?"
OF COURSE IT IS, BATMAN.

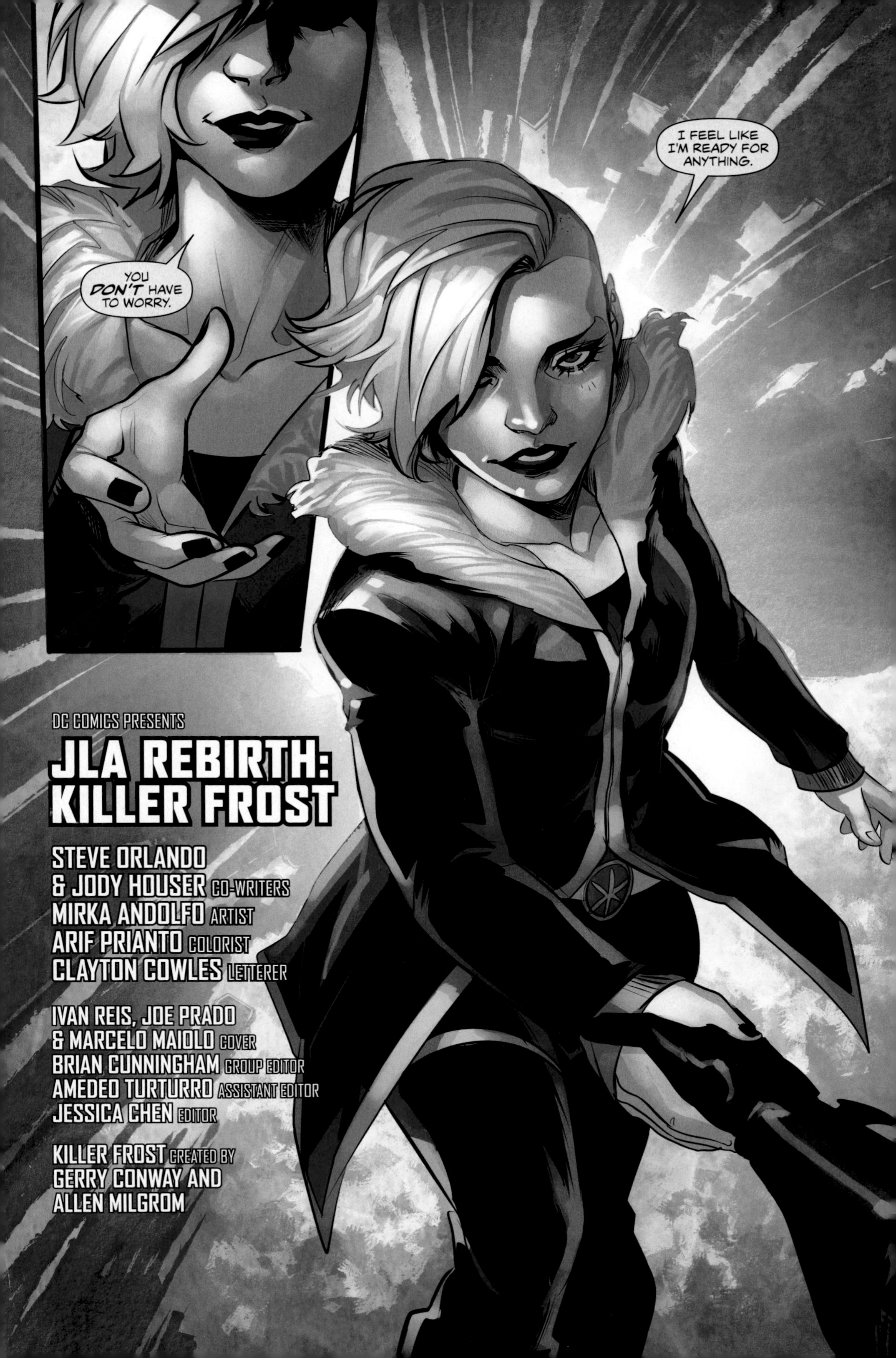
YOU *DON'T* HAVE TO WORRY.
I FEEL LIKE I'M READY FOR ANYTHING.

DC COMICS PRESENTS

JLA REBIRTH: KILLER FROST

STEVE ORLANDO
& JODY HOUSER CO-WRITERS
MIRKA ANDOLFO ARTIST
ARIF PRIANTO COLORIST
CLAYTON COWLES LETTERER

IVAN REIS, JOE PRADO
& MARCELO MAIOLO COVER
BRIAN CUNNINGHAM GROUP EDITOR
AMEDED TURTURRO ASSISTANT EDITOR
JESSICA CHEN EDITOR

KILLER FROST CREATED BY
GERRY CONWAY AND
ALLEN MILGROM

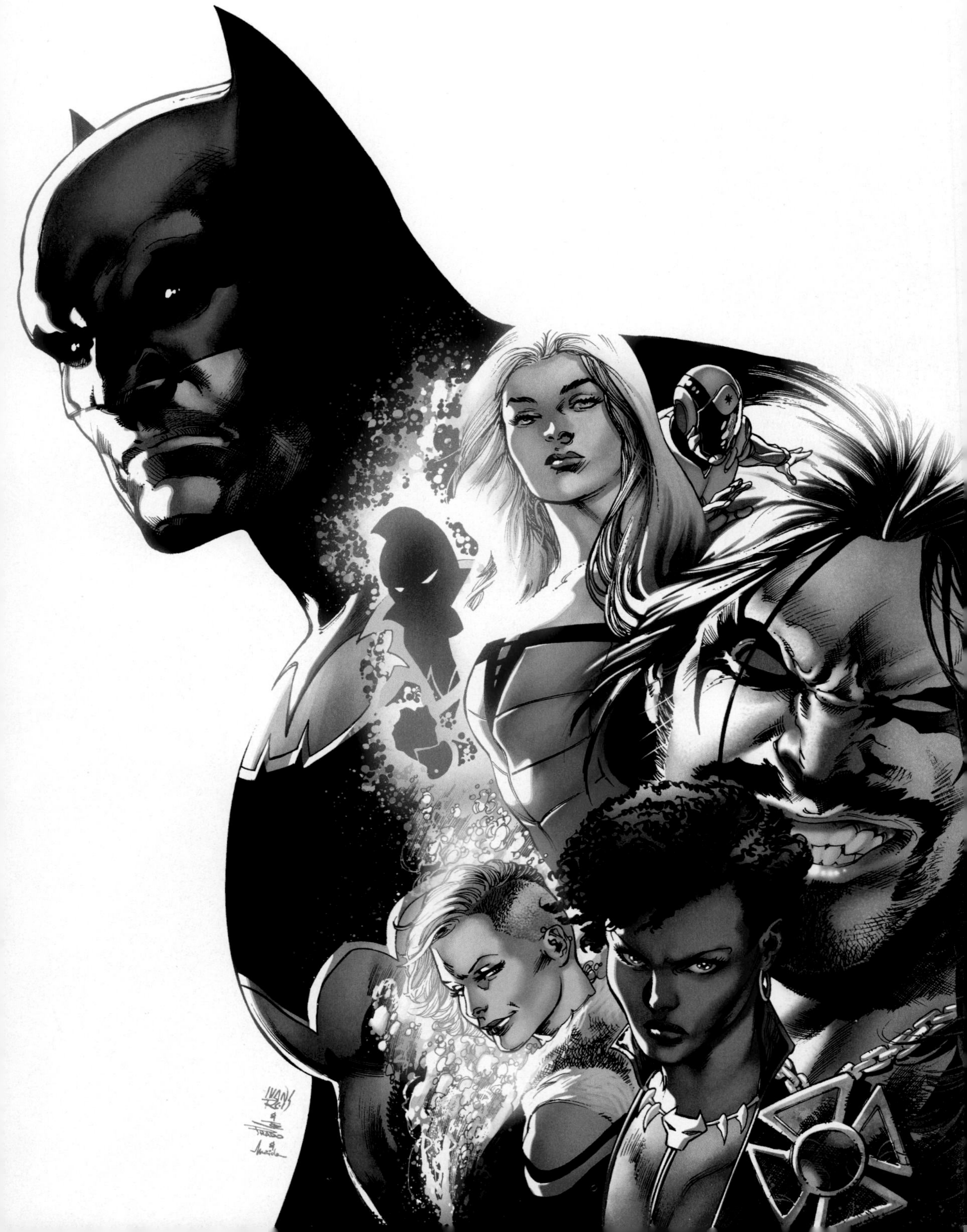

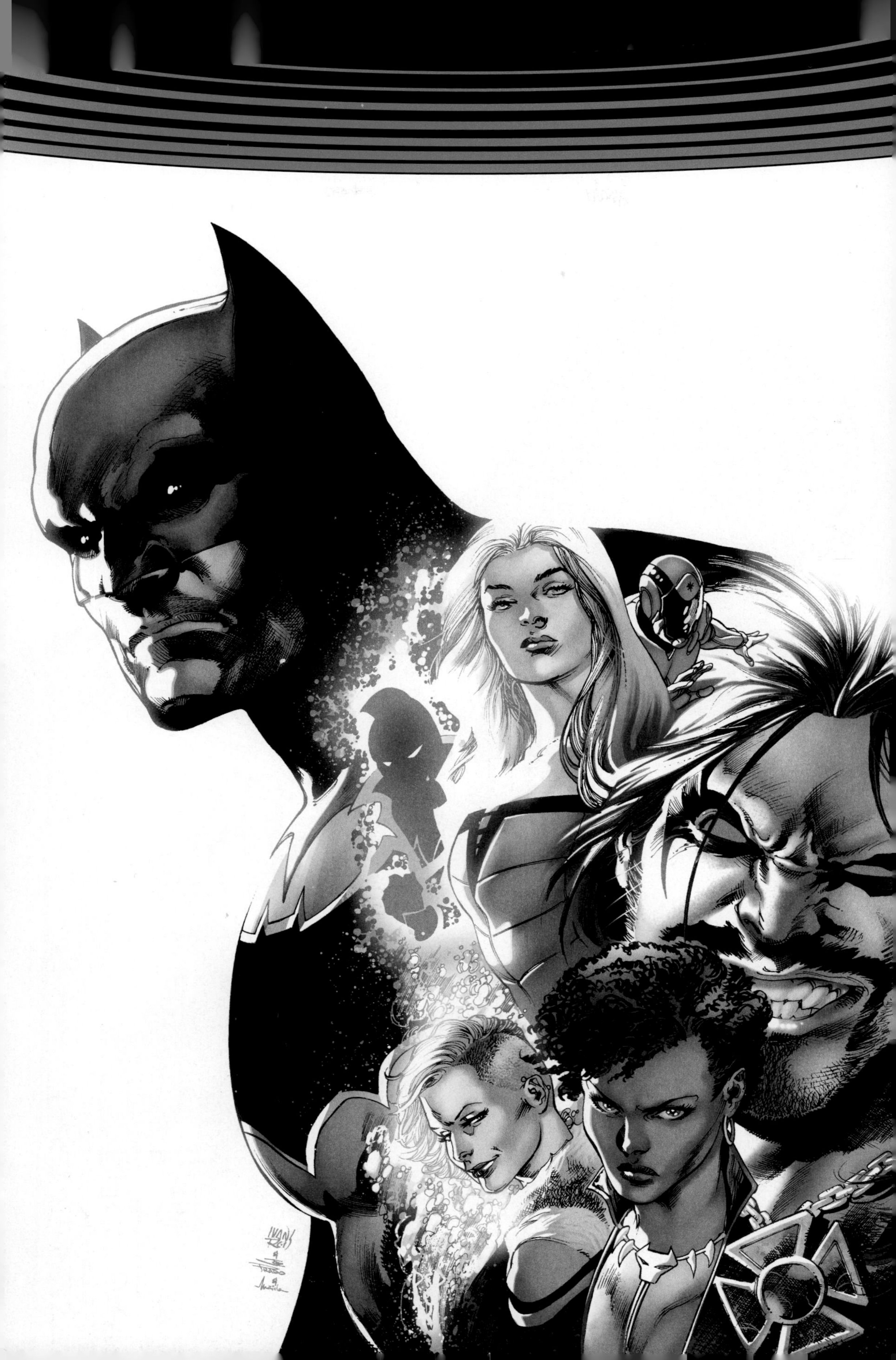

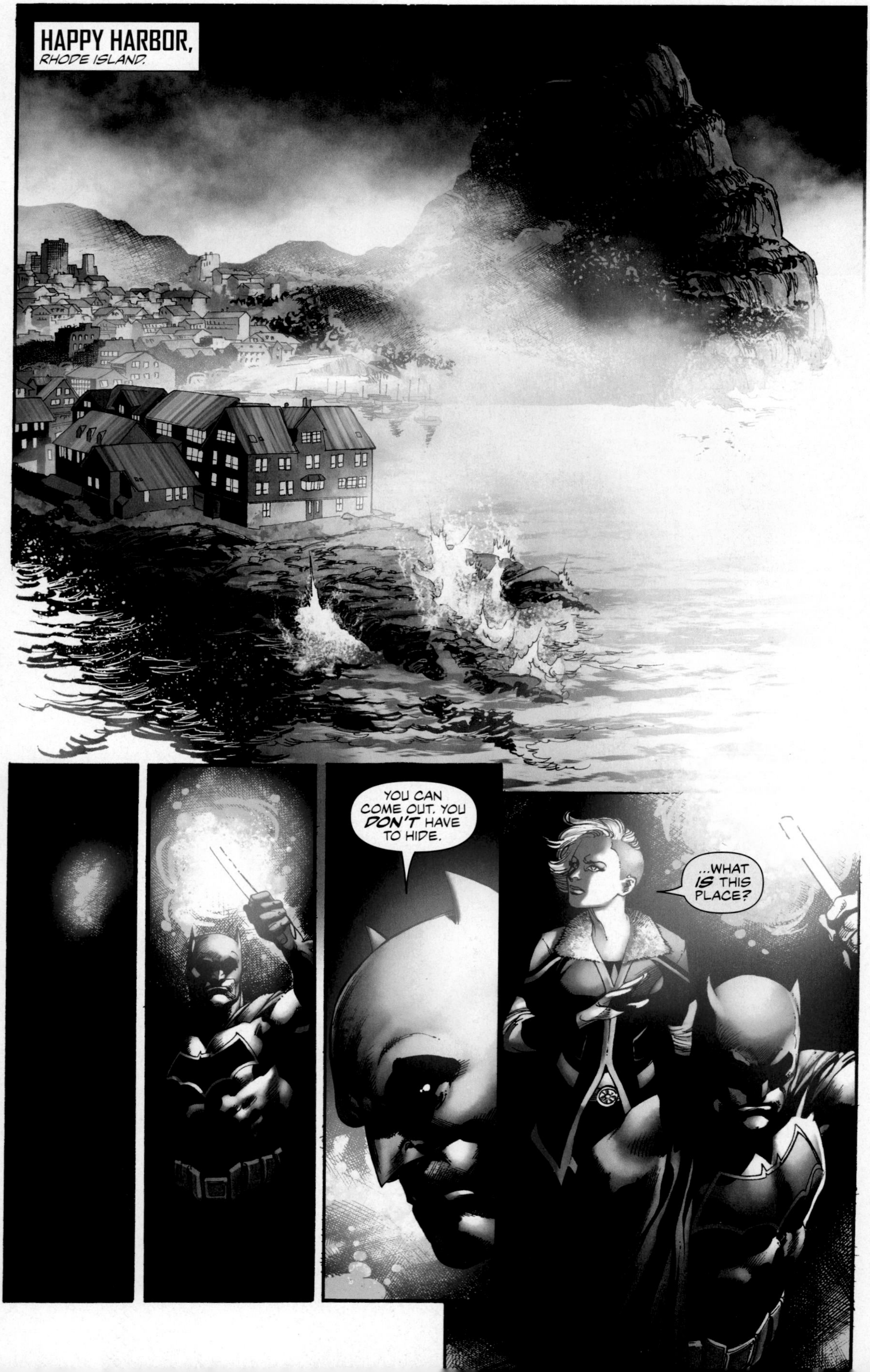
HAPPY HARBOR,
RHODE ISLAND.
YOU CAN COME OUT. YOU DON'T HAVE TO HIDE.
...WHAT IS THIS PLACE?

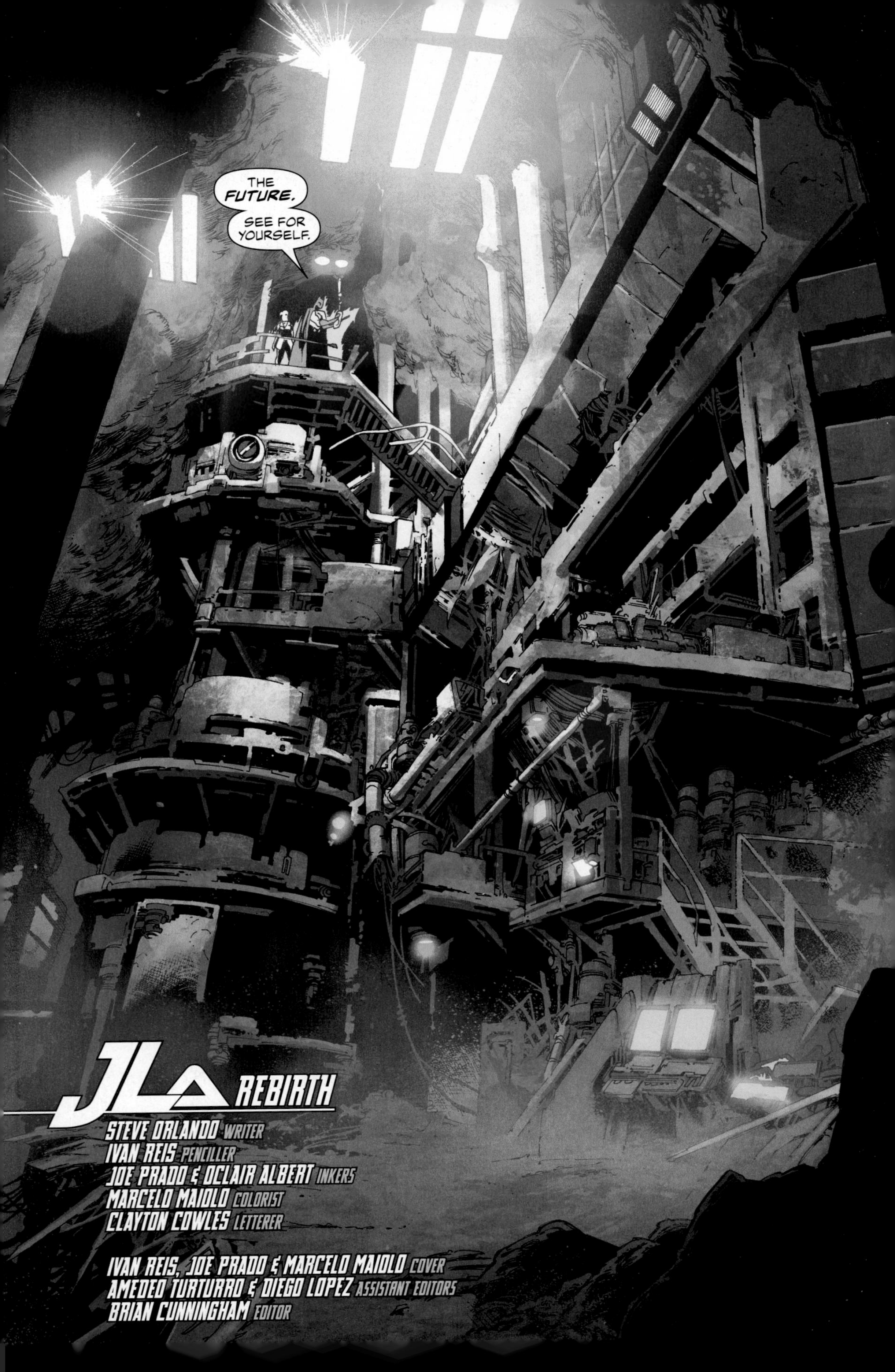
THE FUTURE. SEE FOR YOURSELF.
JLA REBIRTH
STEVE ORLANDO WRITER
IVAN REIS PENCILLER
JOE PRADO & OCLAIR ALBERT INKERS
MARCELO MAIOLO COLORIST
CLAYTON COWLES LETTERER
IVAN REIS, JOE PRADO & MARCELO MAIOLO COVER
AMEDEO TURTURRO & DIEGO LOPEZ ASSISTANT EDITORS
BRIAN CUNNINGHAM EDITOR

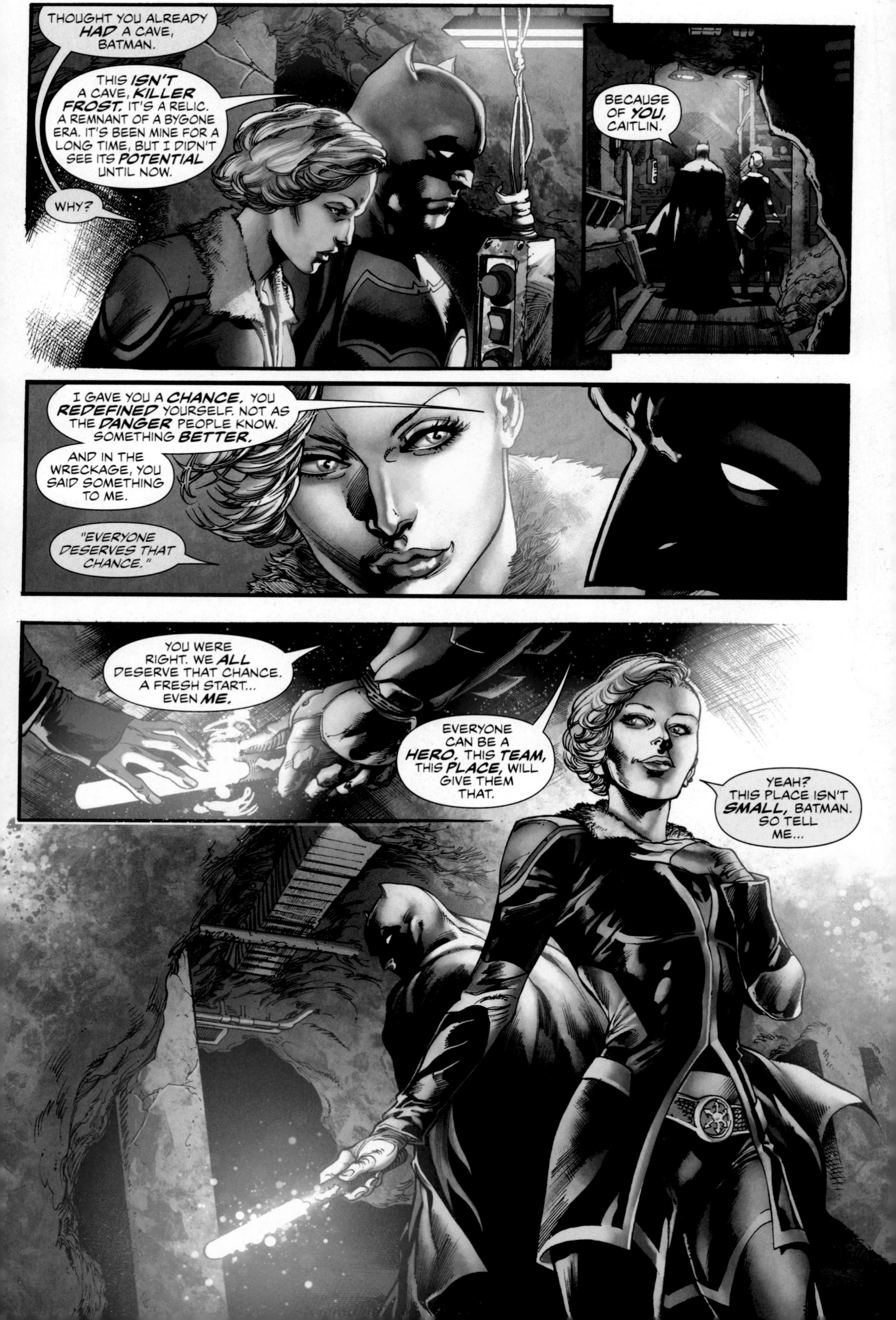
THOUGHT YOU ALREADY HAD A CAVE, BATMAN.
THIS ISN'T A CAVE, KILLER FROST. IT'S A RELIC. A REMNANT OF A BYGONE ERA. IT'S BEEN MINE FOR A LONG TIME, BUT I DIDN'T SEE ITS POTENTIAL UNTIL NOW.
WHY?
BECAUSE OF YOU, CAITLIN.
I GAVE YOU A CHANCE. YOU REDEFINED YOURSELF. NOT AS THE DANGER PEOPLE KNOW. SOMETHING BETTER.
AND IN THE WRECKAGE, YOU SAID SOMETHING TO ME.
"EVERYONE DESERVES THAT CHANCE."
YOU WERE RIGHT. WE ALL DESERVE THAT CHANCE. A FRESH START... EVEN ME.
EVERYONE CAN BE A HERO. THIS TEAM, THIS PLACE, WILL GIVE THEM THAT.
YEAH? THIS PLACE ISN'T SMALL, BATMAN. SO TELL ME...

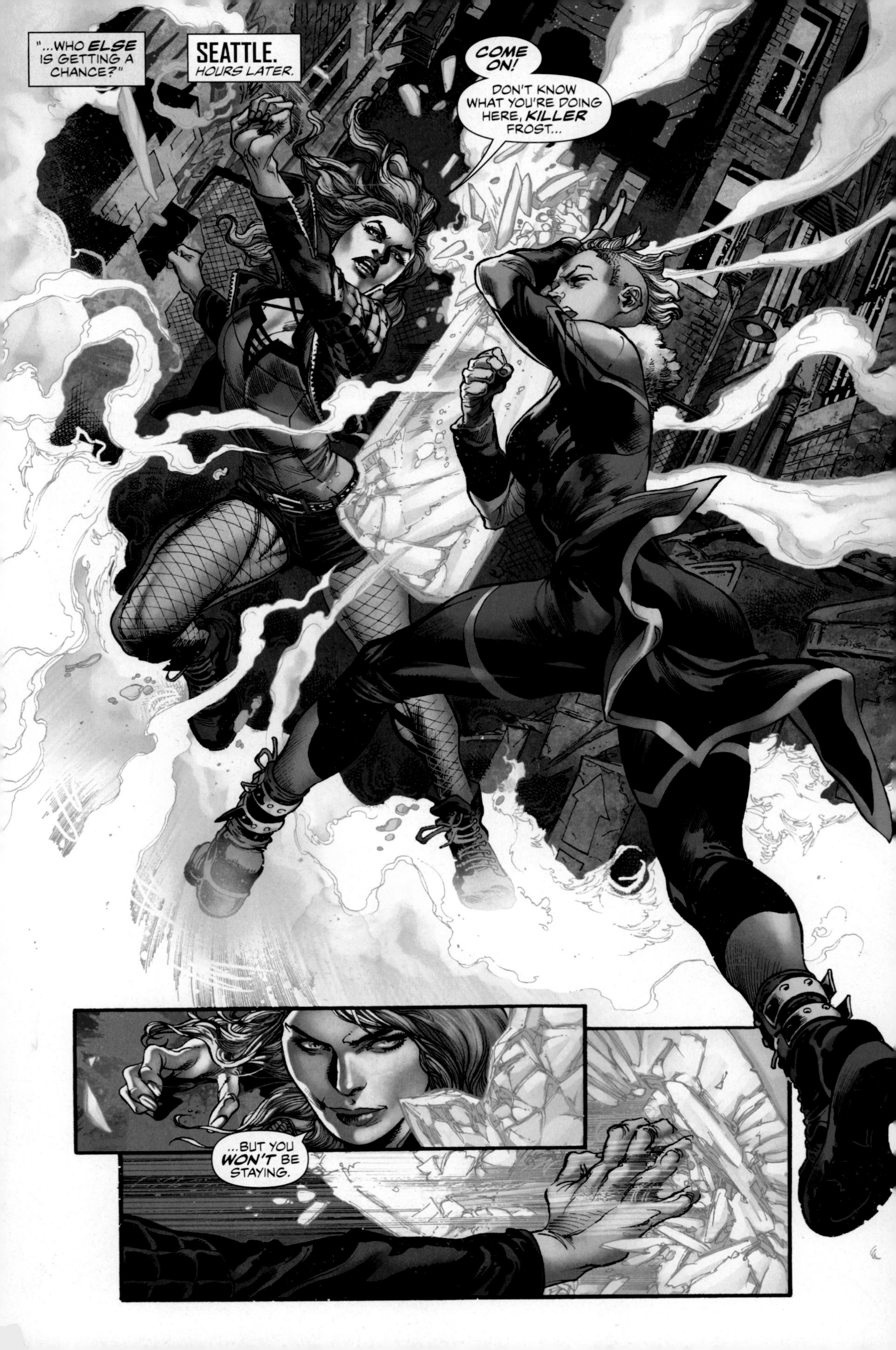
"...WHO ELSE IS GETTING A CHANCE?"
SEATTLE. HOURS LATER.
COME ON!
DON'T KNOW WHAT YOU'RE DOING HERE, KILLER FROST...
...BUT YOU WON'T BE STAYING.

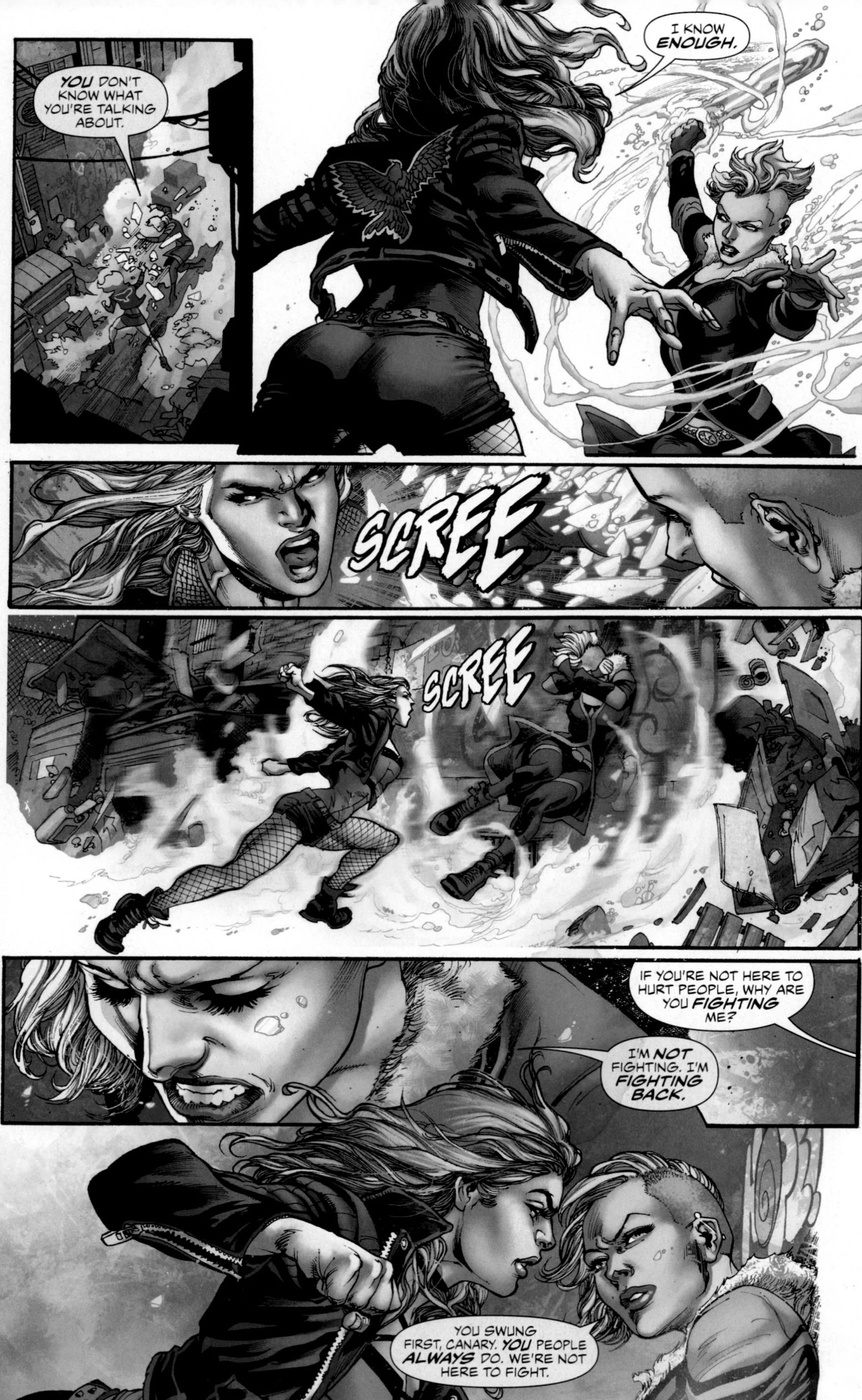
YOU DON'T KNOW WHAT YOU'RE TALKING ABOUT.
I KNOW ENOUGH.
SCREE
SCREE
IF YOU'RE NOT HERE TO HURT PEOPLE, WHY ARE YOU FIGHTING ME?
I'M NOT FIGHTING. I'M FIGHTING BACK.
YOU SWUNG FIRST, CANARY. YOU PEOPLE ALWAYS DO. WE'RE NOT HERE TO FIGHT.

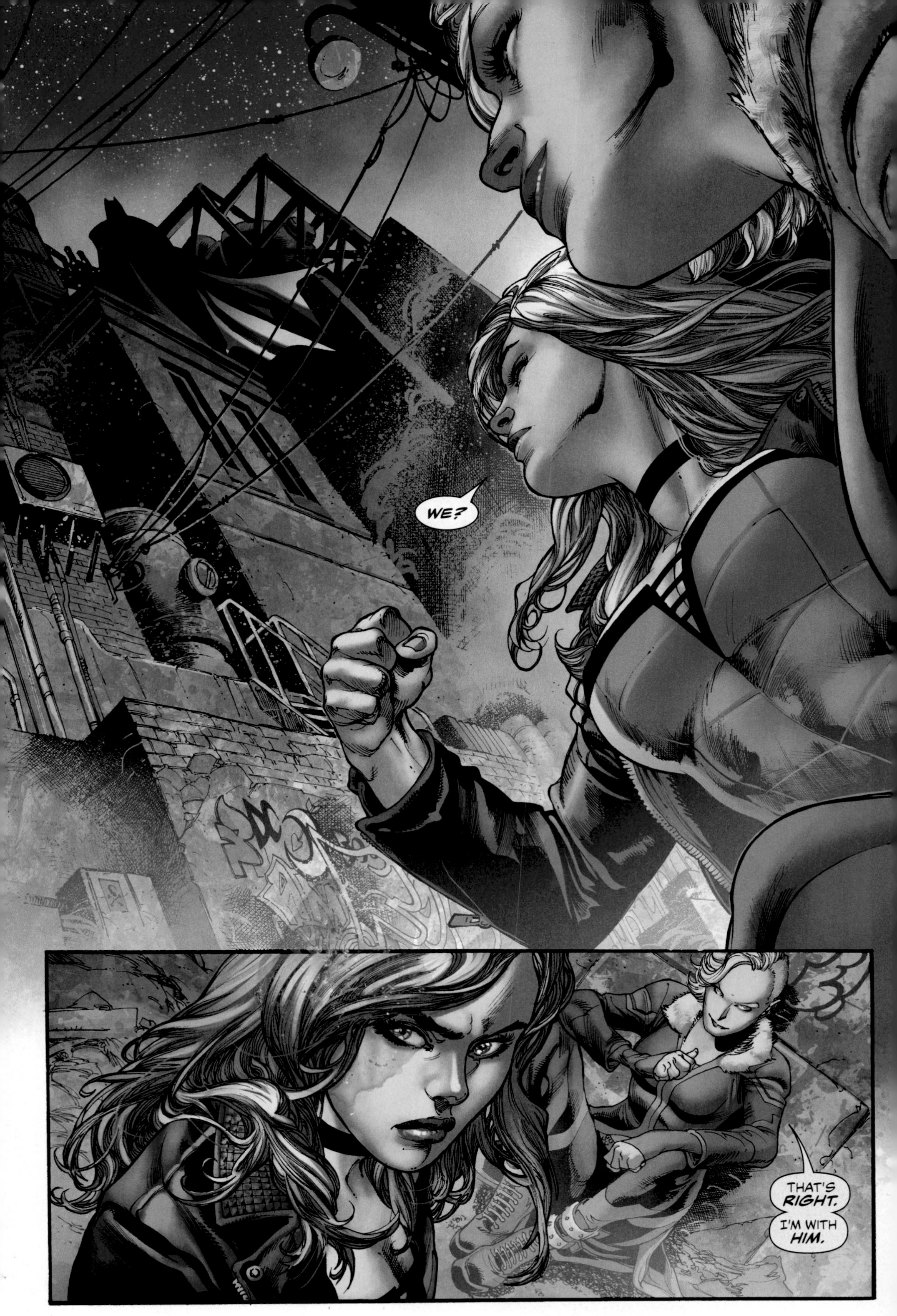
WE?
THAT'S RIGHT.
I'M WITH HIM.

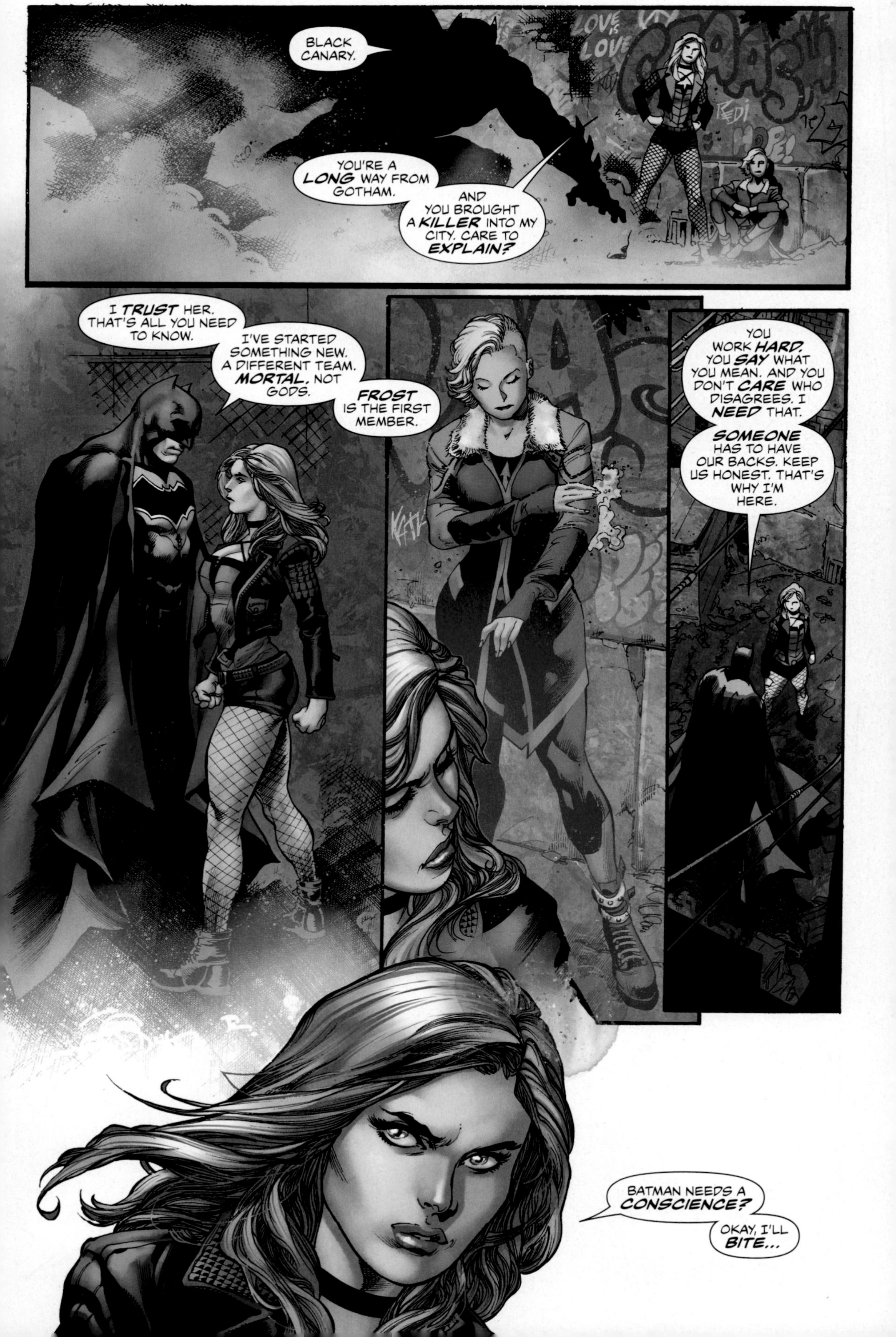
LOVE IS LOVE
HOPE!
BLACK CANARY.
YOU'RE A LONG WAY FROM GOTHAM.
AND YOU BROUGHT A KILLER INTO MY CITY. CARE TO EXPLAIN?
I TRUST HER. THAT'S ALL YOU NEED TO KNOW.
I'VE STARTED SOMETHING NEW. A DIFFERENT TEAM. MORTAL, NOT GODS.
FROST IS THE FIRST MEMBER.
YOU WORK HARD. YOU SAY WHAT YOU MEAN. AND YOU DON'T CARE WHO DISAGREES. I NEED THAT.
SOMEONE HAS TO HAVE OUR BACKS. KEEP US HONEST. THAT'S WHY I'M HERE.
BATMAN NEEDS A CONSCIENCE?
OKAY, I'LL BITE...

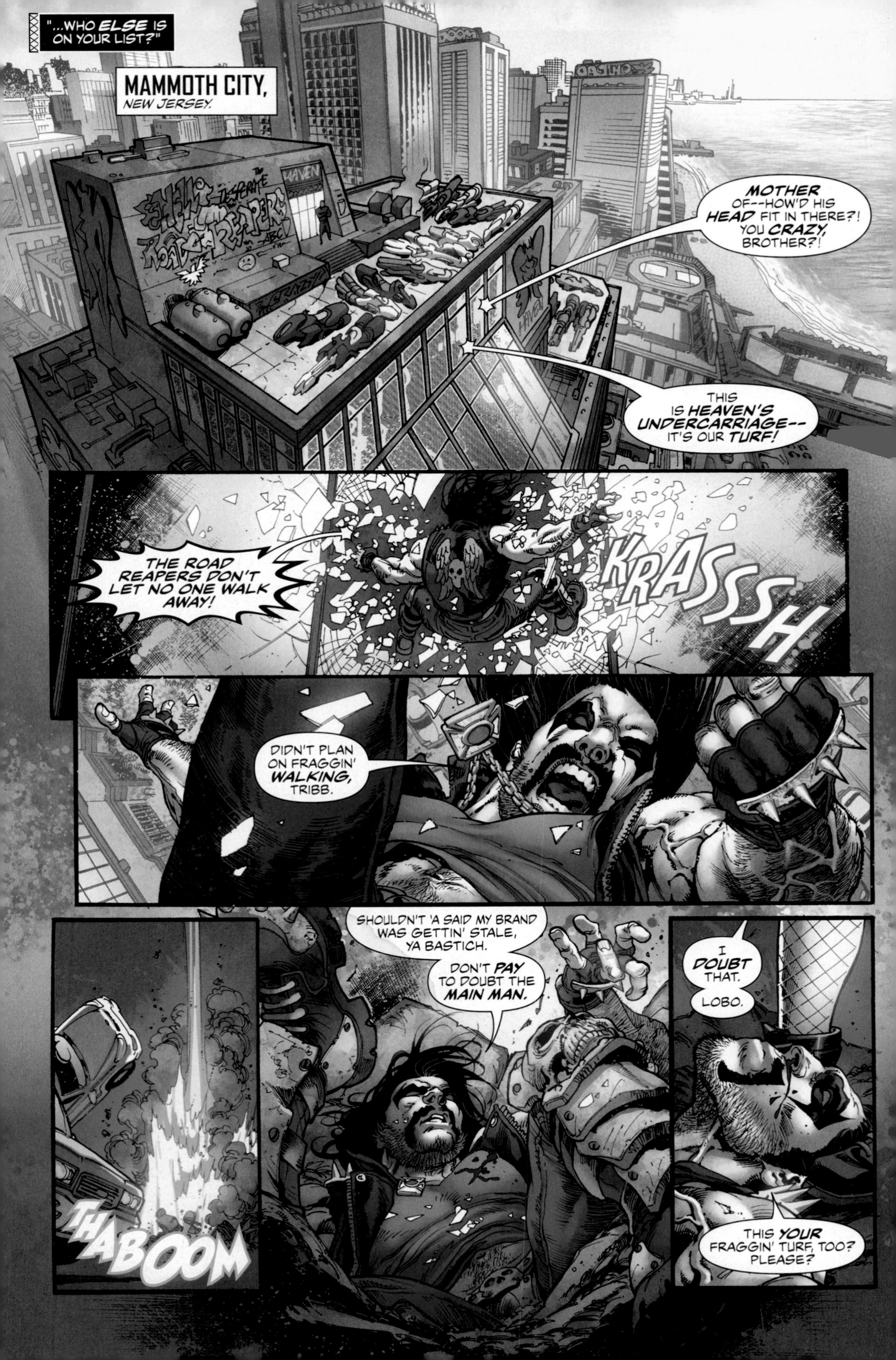
"...WHO ELSE IS ON YOUR LIST?"
MAMMOTH CITY, NEW JERSEY.
MOTHER OF--HOW'D HIS HEAD FIT IN THERE?! YOU CRAZY, BROTHER?!
THIS IS HEAVEN'S UNDERCARRIAGE-- IT'S OUR TURF!
THE ROAD REAPERS DON'T LET NO ONE WALK AWAY!
KRASSSH
DIDN'T PLAN ON FRAGGIN' WALKING, TRIBB.
THABOOM
SHOULDN'T 'A SAID MY BRAND WAS GETTIN' STALE, YA BASTICH.
DON'T PAY TO DOUBT THE MAIN MAN.
I DOUBT THAT.
LOBO.
THIS YOUR FRAGGIN' TURF, TOO? PLEASE?

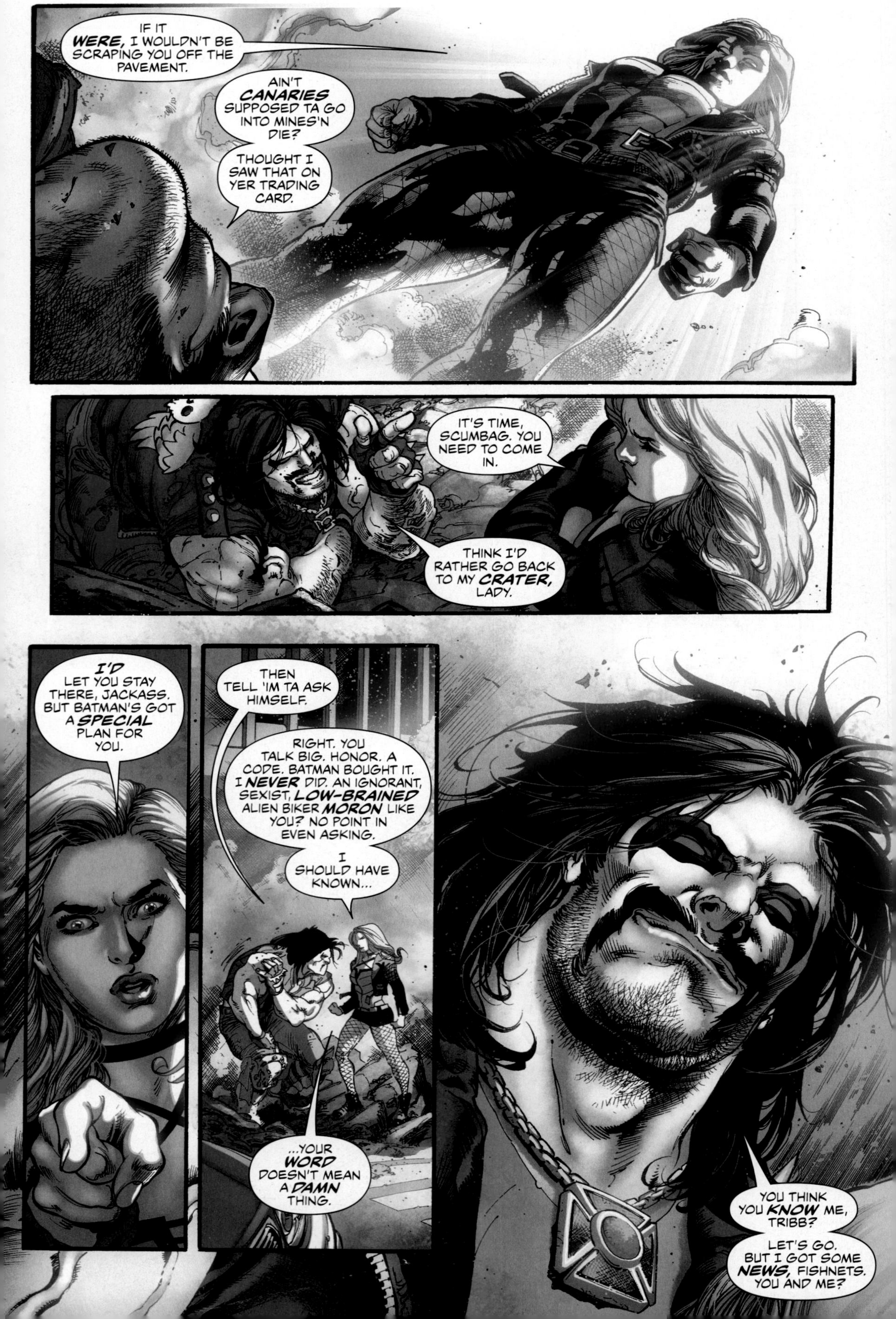
IF IT WERE, I WOULDN'T BE SCRAPING YOU OFF THE PAVEMENT.
AIN'T CANARIES SUPPOSED TA GO INTO MINES'N DIE?
THOUGHT I SAW THAT ON YER TRADING CARD.
IT'S TIME, SCUMBAG. YOU NEED TO COME IN.
THINK I'D RATHER GO BACK TO MY CRATER, LADY.
I'D LET YOU STAY THERE, JACKASS. BUT BATMAN'S GOT A SPECIAL PLAN FOR YOU.
THEN TELL 'IM TA ASK HIMSELF.
RIGHT. YOU TALK BIG. HONOR. A CODE. BATMAN BOUGHT IT. I NEVER DID. AN IGNORANT, SEXIST, LOW-BRAINED ALIEN BIKER MORON LIKE YOU? NO POINT IN EVEN ASKING.
I SHOULD HAVE KNOWN...
...YOUR WORD DOESN'T MEAN A DAMN THING.
YOU THINK YOU KNOW ME, TRIBB?
LET'S GO. BUT I GOT SOME NEWS, FISHNETS. YOU AND ME?

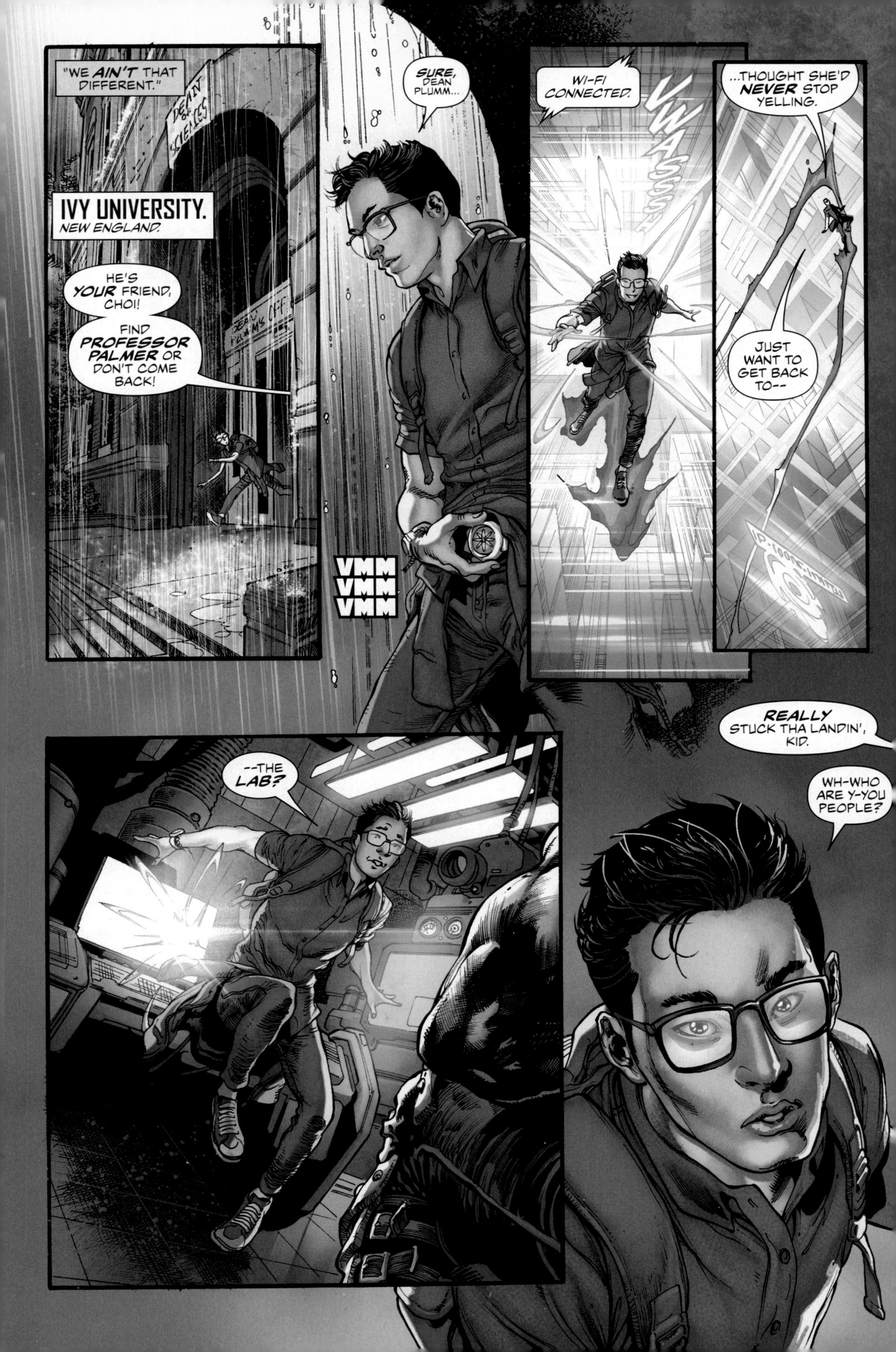
"WE AIN'T THAT DIFFERENT."
IVY UNIVERSITY. NEW ENGLAND.
HE'S YOUR FRIEND, CHOI!
FIND PROFESSOR PALMER OR DON'T COME BACK!
SURE, DEAN PLUMM...
VMM VMM VMM
WI-FI CONNECTED.
VWASSS!
...THOUGHT SHE'D NEVER STOP YELLING.
JUST WANT TO GET BACK TO--
--THE LAB?
REALLY STUCK THA LANDIN', KID.
WH-WHO ARE Y-YOU PEOPLE?

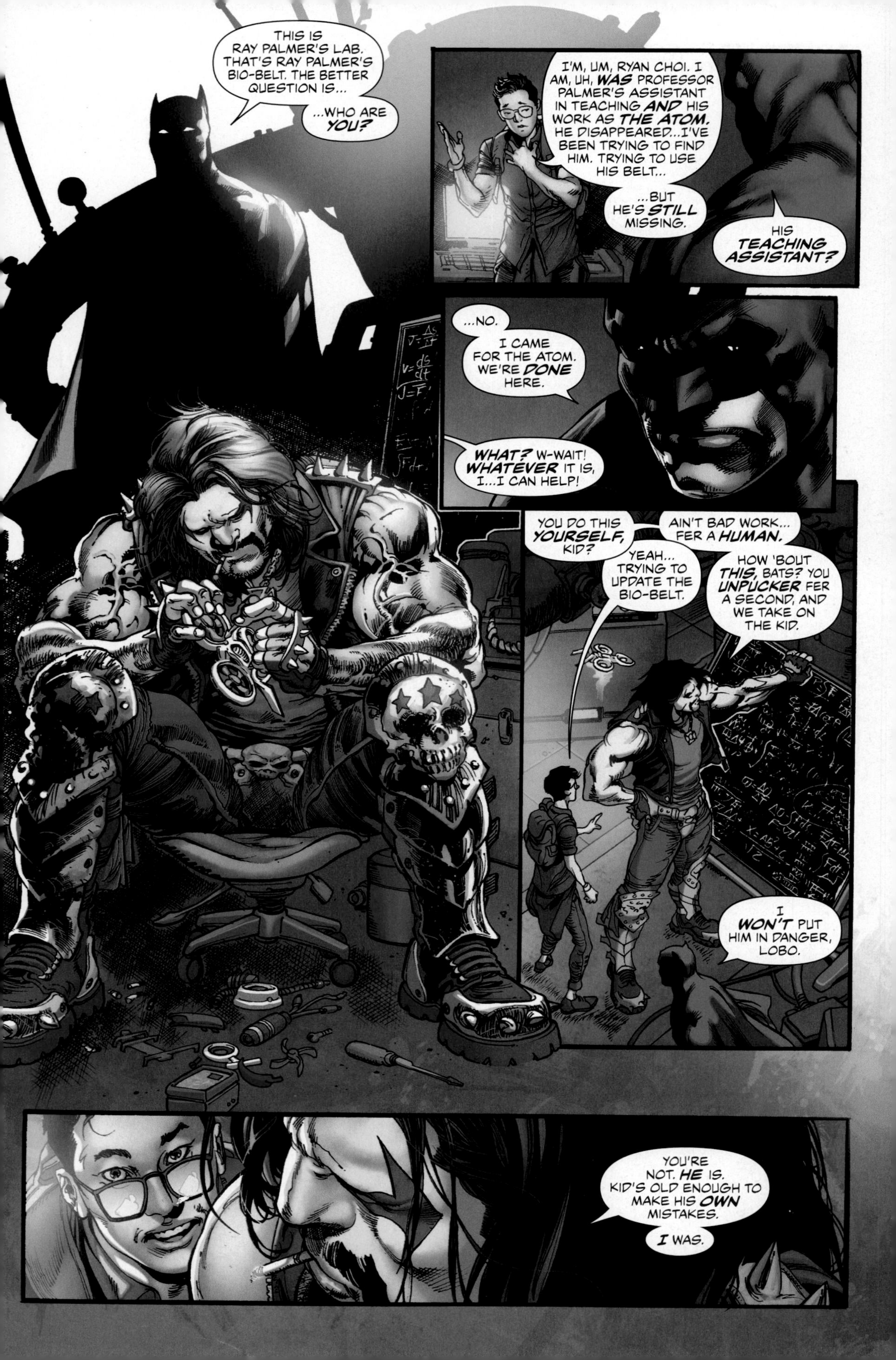

THIS IS RAY PALMER'S LAB. THAT'S RAY PALMER'S BIO-BELT. THE BETTER QUESTION IS...
...WHO ARE YOU?
I'M, UM, RYAN CHOI. I AM, UH, WAS PROFESSOR PALMER'S ASSISTANT IN TEACHING AND HIS WORK AS THE ATOM. HE DISAPPEARED...I'VE BEEN TRYING TO FIND HIM. TRYING TO USE HIS BELT...
...BUT HE'S STILL MISSING.
HIS TEACHING ASSISTANT?
...NO.
I CAME FOR THE ATOM. WE'RE DONE HERE.
WHAT? W-WAIT! WHATEVER IT IS, I...I CAN HELP!
YOU DO THIS YOURSELF, KID?
AIN'T BAD WORK... FER A HUMAN.
YEAH... TRYING TO UPDATE THE BIO-BELT.
HOW 'BOUT THIS, BATS? YOU UNPUCKER FER A SECOND, AND WE TAKE ON THE KID.
I WON'T PUT HIM IN DANGER, LOBO.
YOU'RE NOT. HE IS. KID'S OLD ENOUGH TO MAKE HIS OWN MISTAKES.
I WAS.

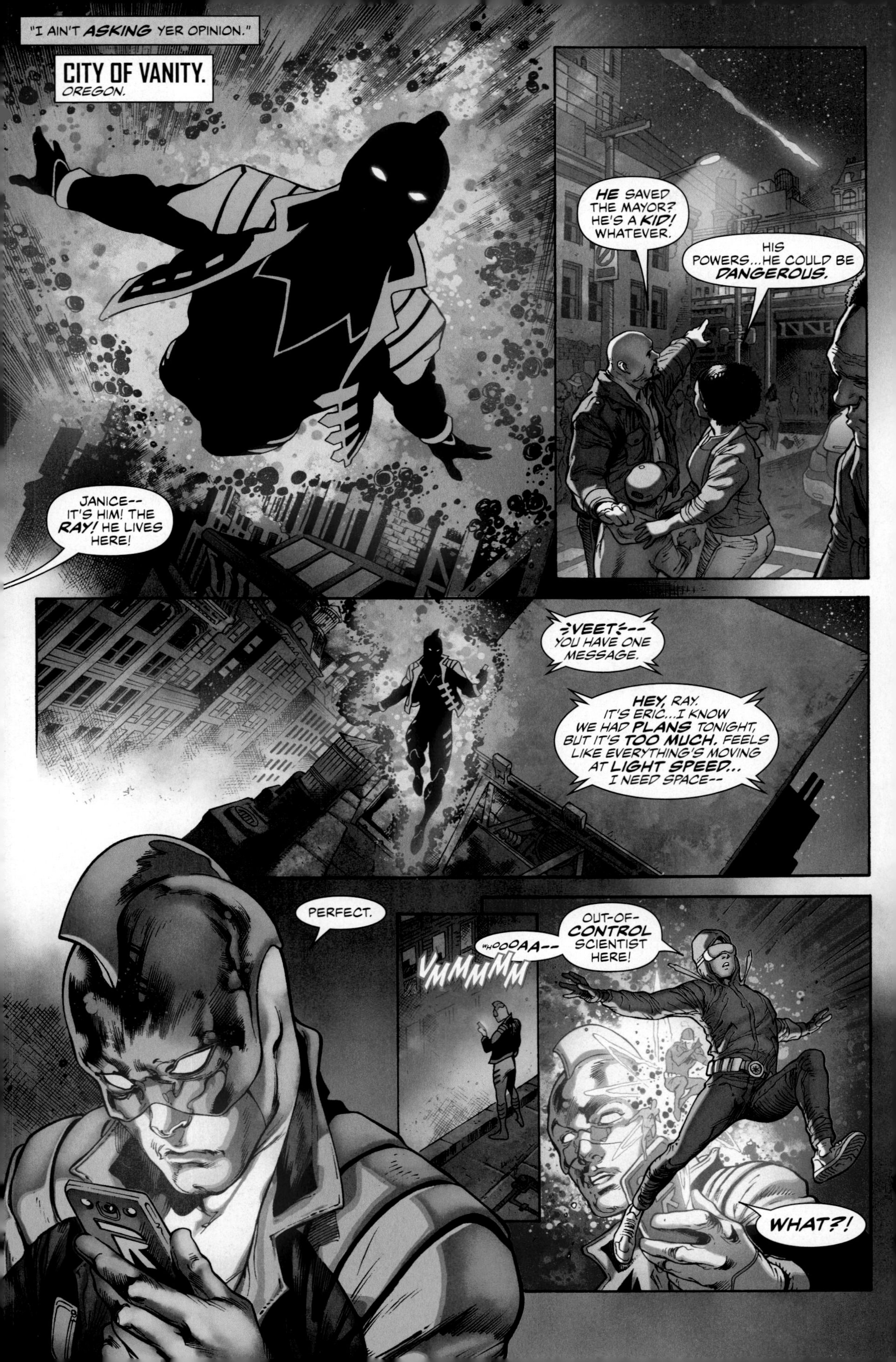
"I AIN'T ASKING YER OPINION."
CITY OF VANITY. OREGON.
JANICE-- IT'S HIM! THE RAY! HE LIVES HERE!
HE SAVED THE MAYOR? HE'S A KID! WHATEVER.
HIS POWERS...HE COULD BE DANGEROUS.
=VEET=-- YOU HAVE ONE MESSAGE.
HEY, RAY. IT'S ERIC...I KNOW WE HAD PLANS TONIGHT, BUT IT'S TOO MUCH. FEELS LIKE EVERYTHING'S MOVING AT LIGHT SPEED... I NEED SPACE--
PERFECT.
VMMMMM
WHOOOAA--
OUT-OF-CONTROL SCIENTIST HERE!
WHAT?!

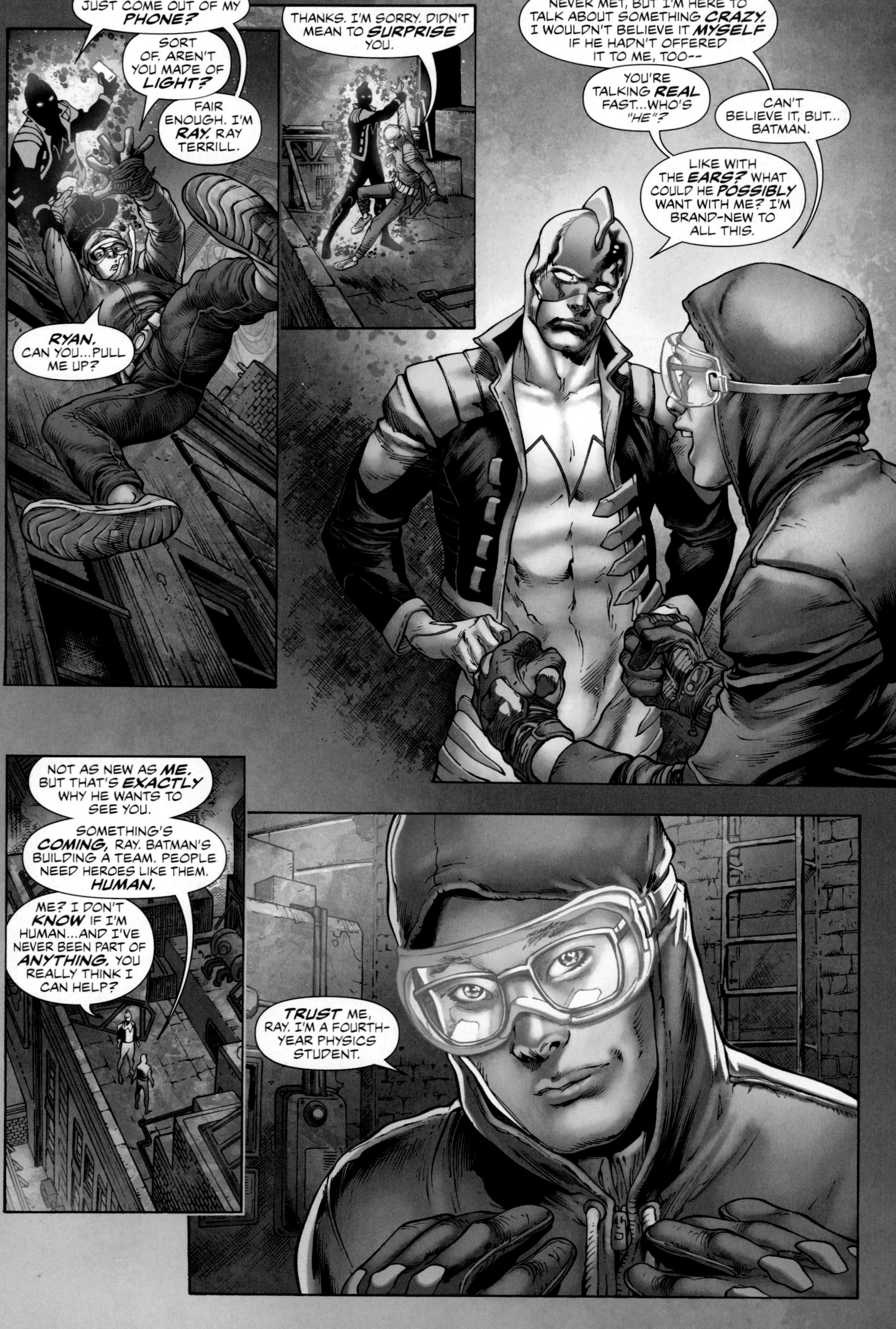
DID YOU JUST COME OUT OF MY PHONE?
SORT OF. AREN'T YOU MADE OF LIGHT?
FAIR ENOUGH. I'M RAY. RAY TERRILL.
RYAN. CAN YOU...PULL ME UP?
THANKS. I'M SORRY. DIDN'T MEAN TO SURPRISE YOU.
I KNOW WE'VE NEVER MET, BUT I'M HERE TO TALK ABOUT SOMETHING CRAZY. I WOULDN'T BELIEVE IT MYSELF IF HE HADN'T OFFERED IT TO ME, TOO--
YOU'RE TALKING REAL FAST...WHO'S "HE"?
CAN'T BELIEVE IT, BUT... BATMAN.
LIKE WITH THE EARS? WHAT COULD HE POSSIBLY WANT WITH ME? I'M BRAND-NEW TO ALL THIS.
NOT AS NEW AS ME. BUT THAT'S EXACTLY WHY HE WANTS TO SEE YOU.
SOMETHING'S COMING, RAY. BATMAN'S BUILDING A TEAM. PEOPLE NEED HEROES LIKE THEM. HUMAN.
ME? I DON'T KNOW IF I'M HUMAN...AND I'VE NEVER BEEN PART OF ANYTHING. YOU REALLY THINK I CAN HELP?
TRUST ME, RAY. I'M A FOURTH-YEAR PHYSICS STUDENT.

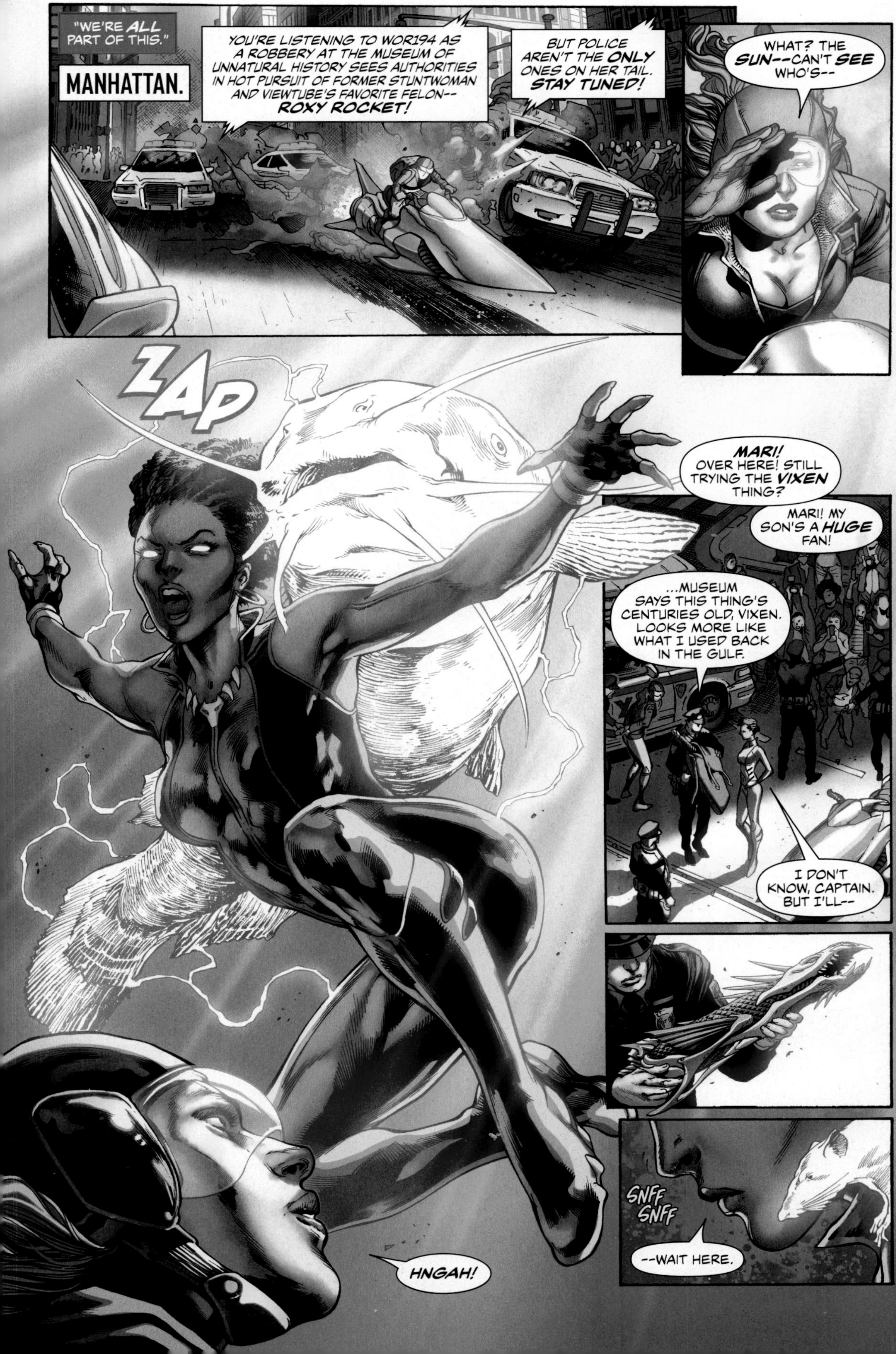
"WE'RE ALL PART OF THIS."
MANHATTAN.
YOU'RE LISTENING TO WOR194 AS A ROBBERY AT THE MUSEUM OF UNNATURAL HISTORY SEES AUTHORITIES IN HOT PURSUIT OF FORMER STUNTWOMAN AND VIEWTUBE'S FAVORITE FELON-- ROXY ROCKET!
BUT POLICE AREN'T THE ONLY ONES ON HER TAIL. STAY TUNED!
WHAT? THE SUN--CAN'T SEE WHO'S--
ZAP
HNGAH!
MARI! OVER HERE! STILL TRYING THE VIXEN THING?
MARI! MY SON'S A HUGE FAN!
...MUSEUM SAYS THIS THING'S CENTURIES OLD, VIXEN. LOOKS MORE LIKE WHAT I USED BACK IN THE GULF.
I DON'T KNOW, CAPTAIN. BUT I'LL--
SNFF SNFF
--WAIT HERE.

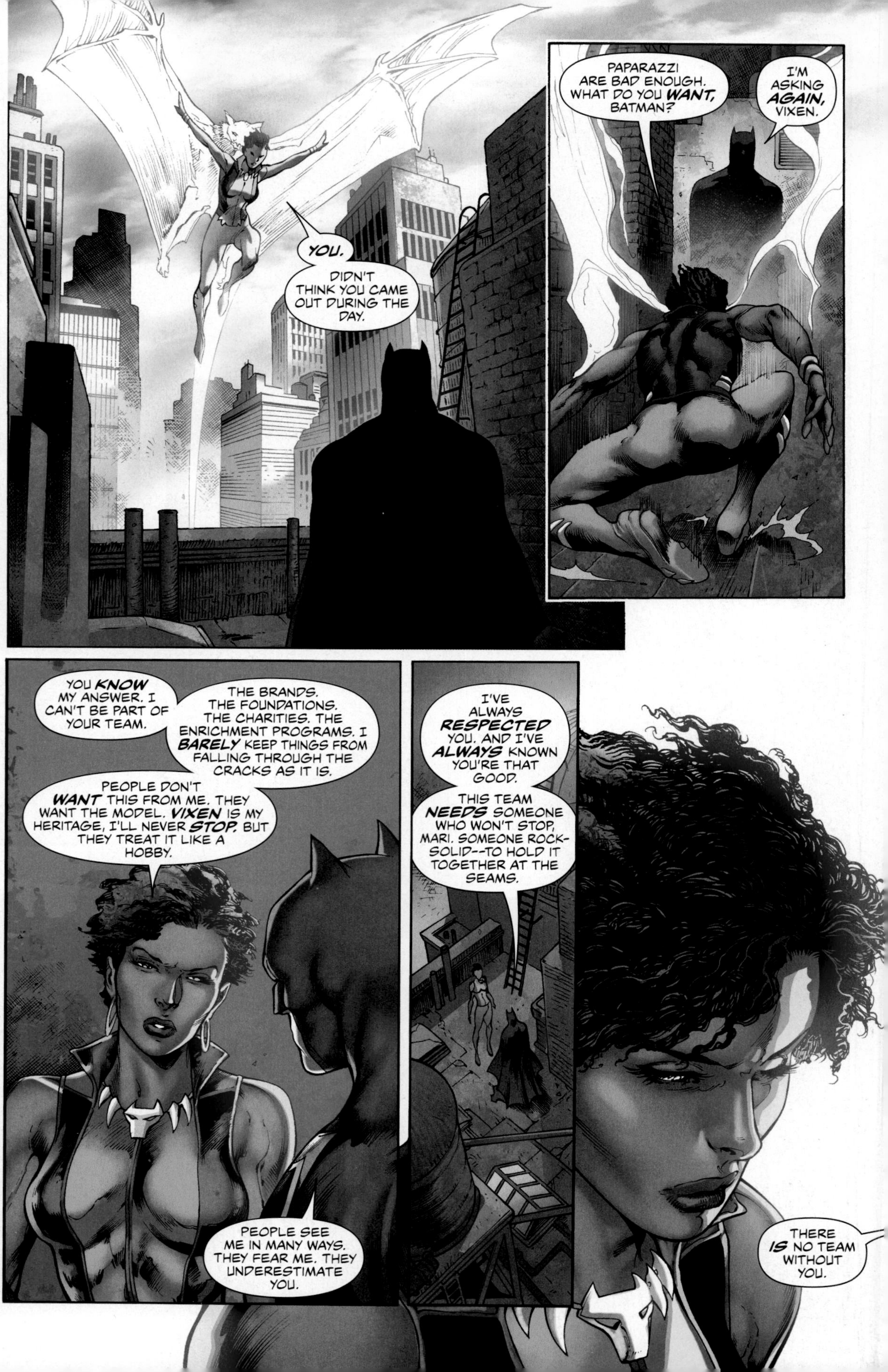
YOU.
DIDN'T THINK YOU CAME OUT DURING THE DAY.
PAPARAZZI ARE BAD ENOUGH. WHAT DO YOU WANT, BATMAN?
I'M ASKING AGAIN, VIXEN.
YOU KNOW MY ANSWER. I CAN'T BE PART OF YOUR TEAM.
THE BRANDS. THE FOUNDATIONS. THE CHARITIES. THE ENRICHMENT PROGRAMS. I BARELY KEEP THINGS FROM FALLING THROUGH THE CRACKS AS IT IS.
PEOPLE DON'T WANT THIS FROM ME. THEY WANT THE MODEL. VIXEN IS MY HERITAGE, I'LL NEVER STOP. BUT THEY TREAT IT LIKE A HOBBY.
PEOPLE SEE ME IN MANY WAYS. THEY FEAR ME. THEY UNDERESTIMATE YOU.
I'VE ALWAYS RESPECTED YOU. AND I'VE ALWAYS KNOWN YOU'RE THAT GOOD.
THIS TEAM NEEDS SOMEONE WHO WON'T STOP, MARI. SOMEONE ROCK-SOLID--TO HOLD IT TOGETHER AT THE SEAMS.
THERE IS NO TEAM WITHOUT YOU.

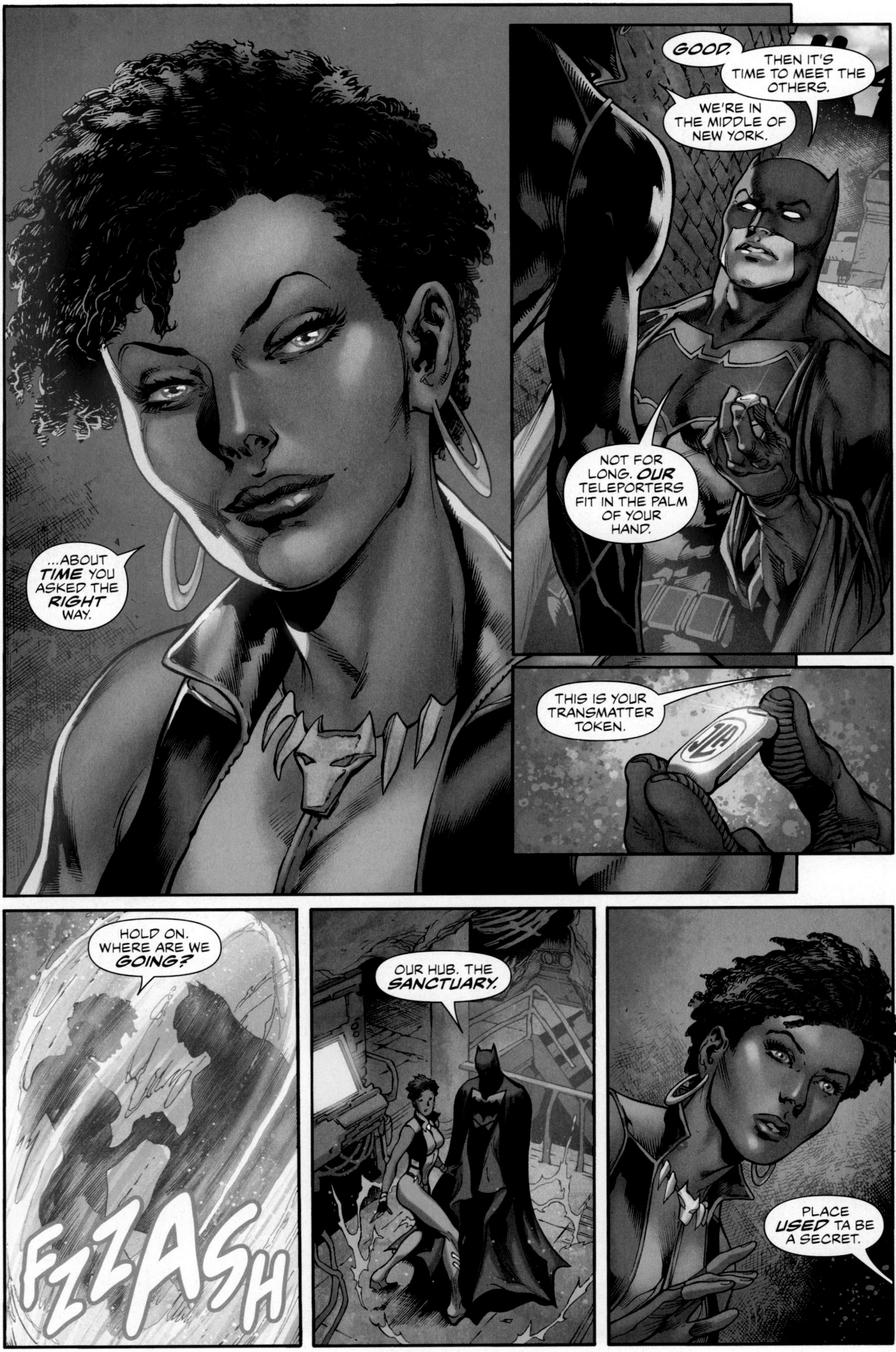
...ABOUT TIME YOU ASKED THE RIGHT WAY.
GOOD.
THEN IT'S TIME TO MEET THE OTHERS.
WE'RE IN THE MIDDLE OF NEW YORK.
NOT FOR LONG. OUR TELEPORTERS FIT IN THE PALM OF YOUR HAND.
THIS IS YOUR TRANSMATTER TOKEN.
JLA
HOLD ON. WHERE ARE WE GOING?
FZZASH
OUR HUB. THE SANCTUARY.
PLACE USED TA BE A SECRET.

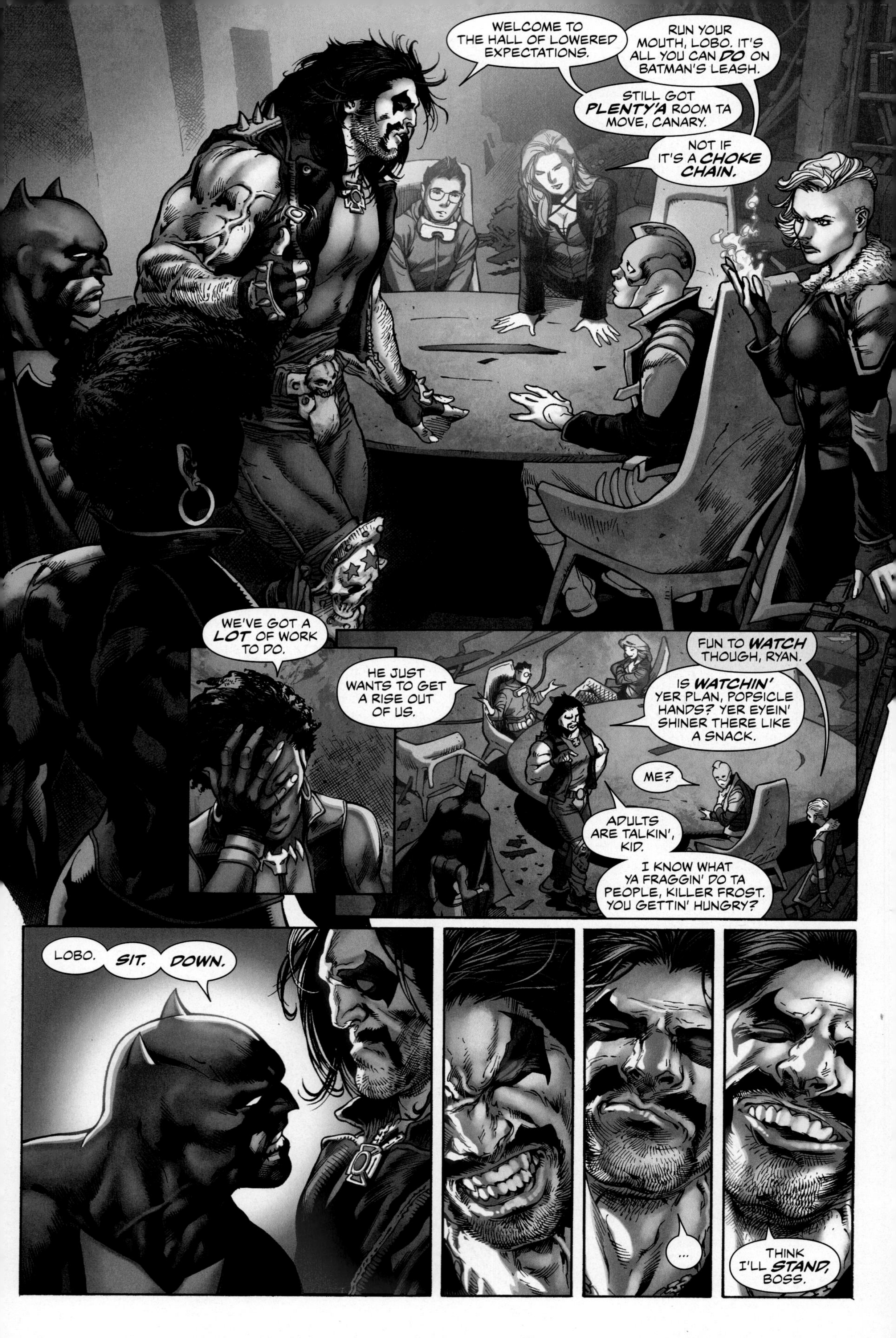
WELCOME TO THE HALL OF LOWERED EXPECTATIONS.
RUN YOUR MOUTH, LOBO. IT'S ALL YOU CAN *DO* ON BATMAN'S LEASH.
STILL GOT *PLENTY'A* ROOM TA MOVE, CANARY.
NOT IF IT'S A *CHOKE CHAIN.*
WE'VE GOT A *LOT* OF WORK TO DO.
HE JUST WANTS TO GET A RISE OUT OF US.
FUN TO *WATCH* THOUGH, RYAN.
IS *WATCHIN'* YER PLAN, POPSICLE HANDS? YER EYEIN' SHINER THERE LIKE A SNACK.
ME?
ADULTS ARE TALKIN', KID.
I KNOW WHAT YA FRAGGIN' DO TA PEOPLE, KILLER FROST. YOU GETTIN' HUNGRY?
LOBO.
SIT.
DOWN.
...
THINK I'LL *STAND,* BOSS.

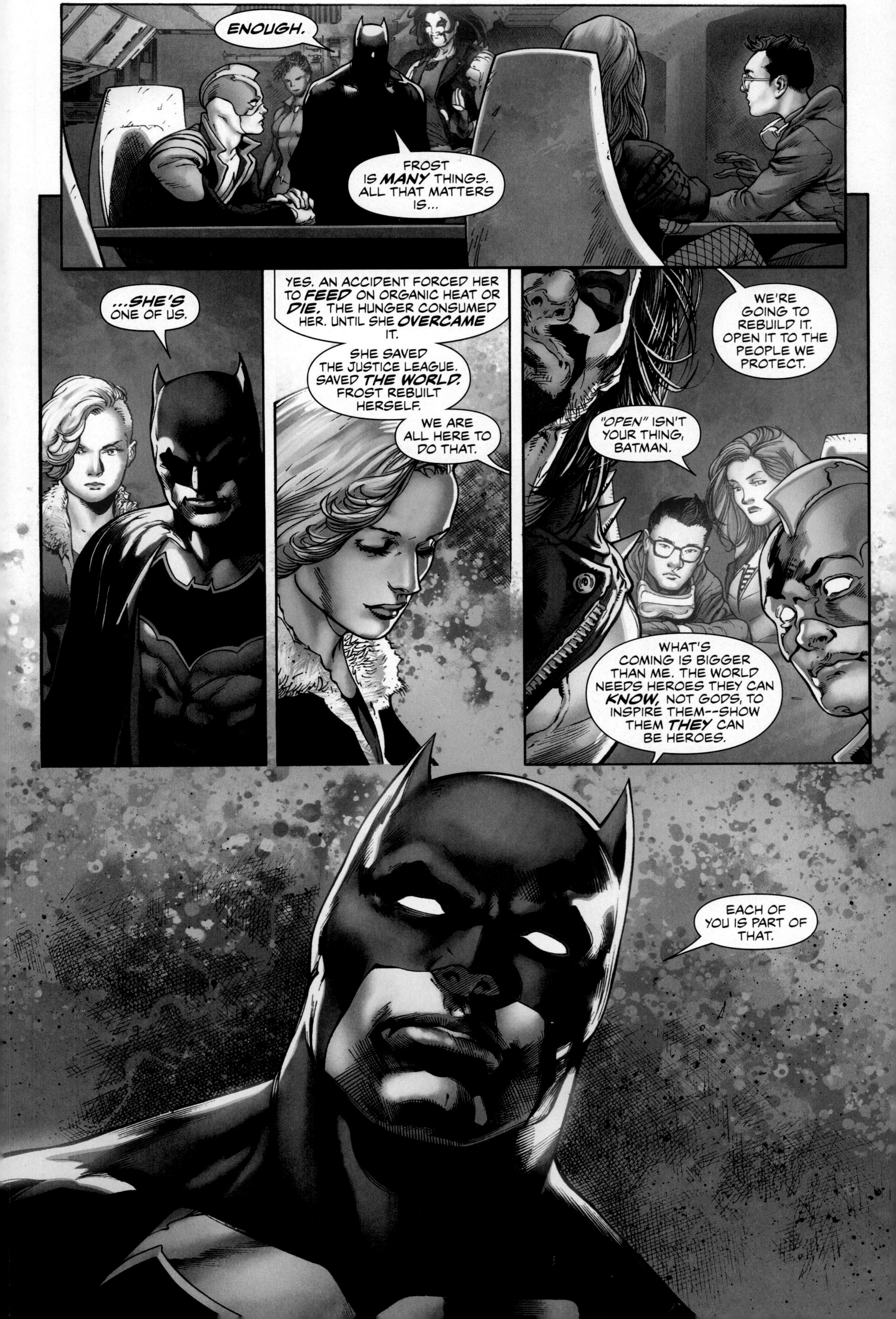
ENOUGH.
FROST IS MANY THINGS. ALL THAT MATTERS IS...
...SHE'S ONE OF US.
YES. AN ACCIDENT FORCED HER TO FEED ON ORGANIC HEAT OR DIE. THE HUNGER CONSUMED HER. UNTIL SHE OVERCAME IT.
SHE SAVED THE JUSTICE LEAGUE. SAVED THE WORLD. FROST REBUILT HERSELF.
WE ARE ALL HERE TO DO THAT.
WE'RE GOING TO REBUILD IT. OPEN IT TO THE PEOPLE WE PROTECT.
"OPEN" ISN'T YOUR THING, BATMAN.
WHAT'S COMING IS BIGGER THAN ME. THE WORLD NEEDS HEROES THEY CAN KNOW, NOT GODS, TO INSPIRE THEM--SHOW THEM THEY CAN BE HEROES.
EACH OF YOU IS PART OF THAT.

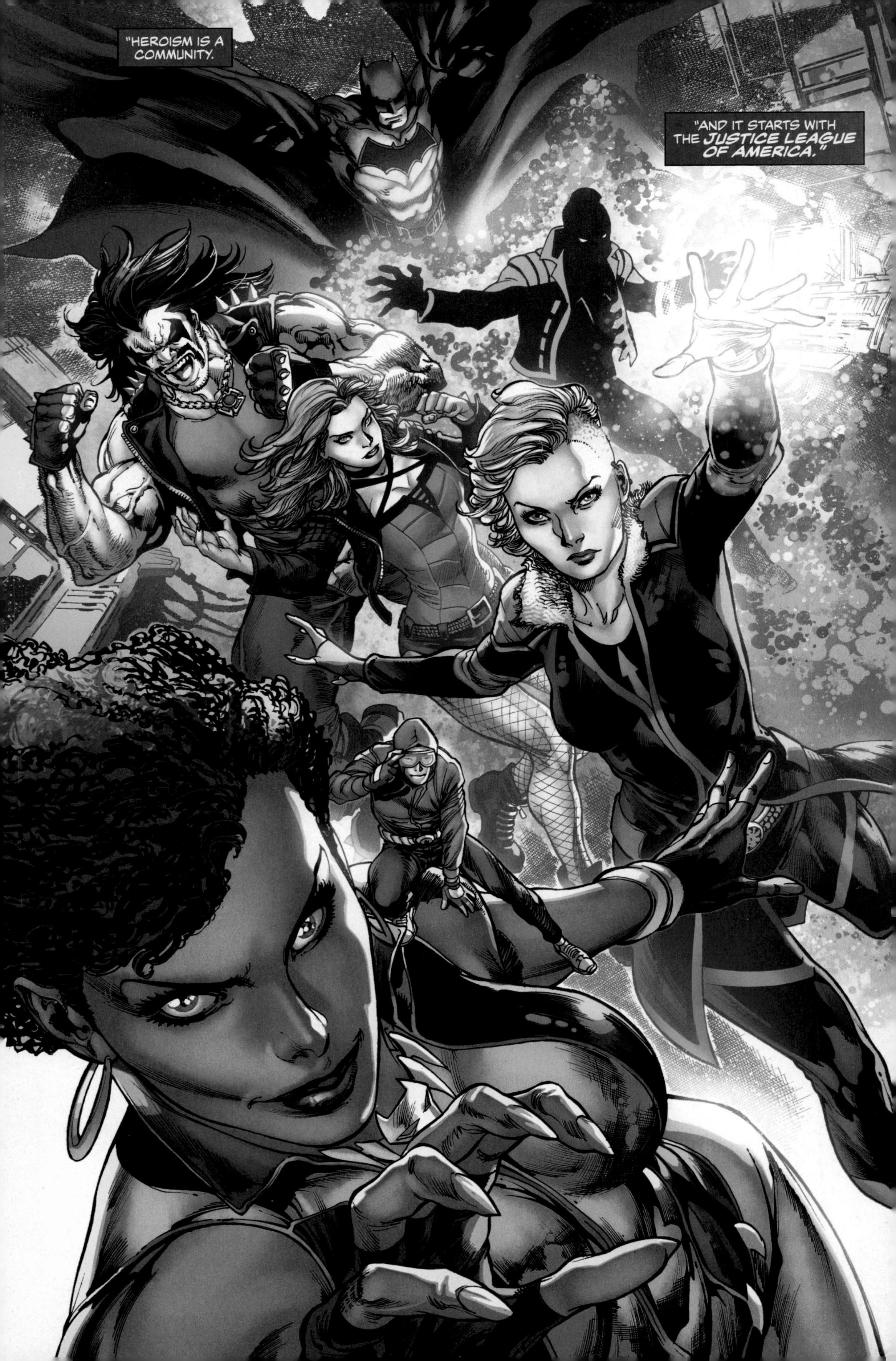
"HEROISM IS A COMMUNITY.
"AND IT STARTS WITH THE *JUSTICE LEAGUE OF AMERICA.*"

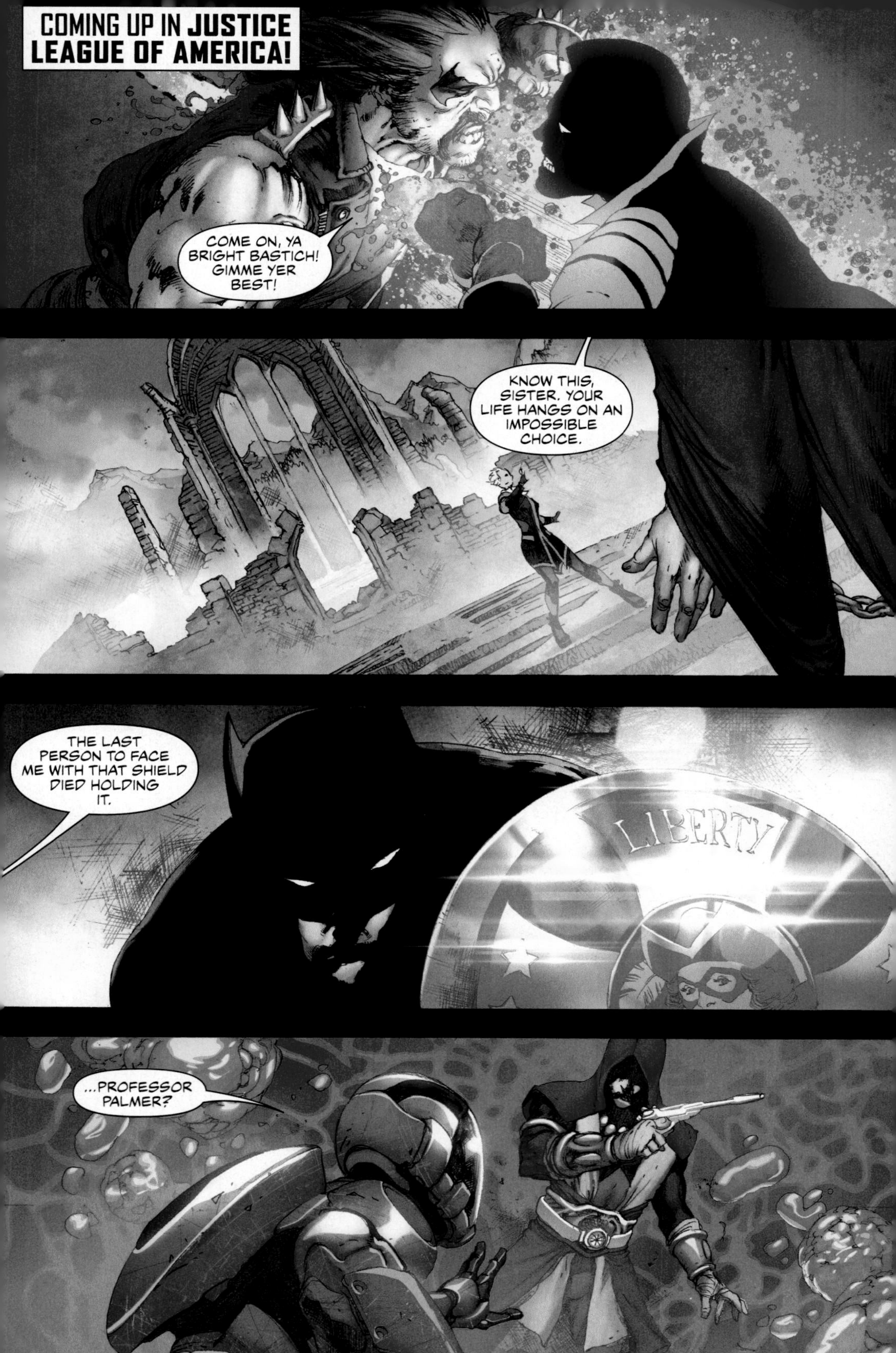
COMING UP IN JUSTICE LEAGUE OF AMERICA!
COME ON, YA BRIGHT BASTICH! GIMME YER BEST!
KNOW THIS, SISTER. YOUR LIFE HANGS ON AN IMPOSSIBLE CHOICE.
THE LAST PERSON TO FACE ME WITH THAT SHIELD DIED HOLDING IT.
LIBERTY
...PROFESSOR PALMER?

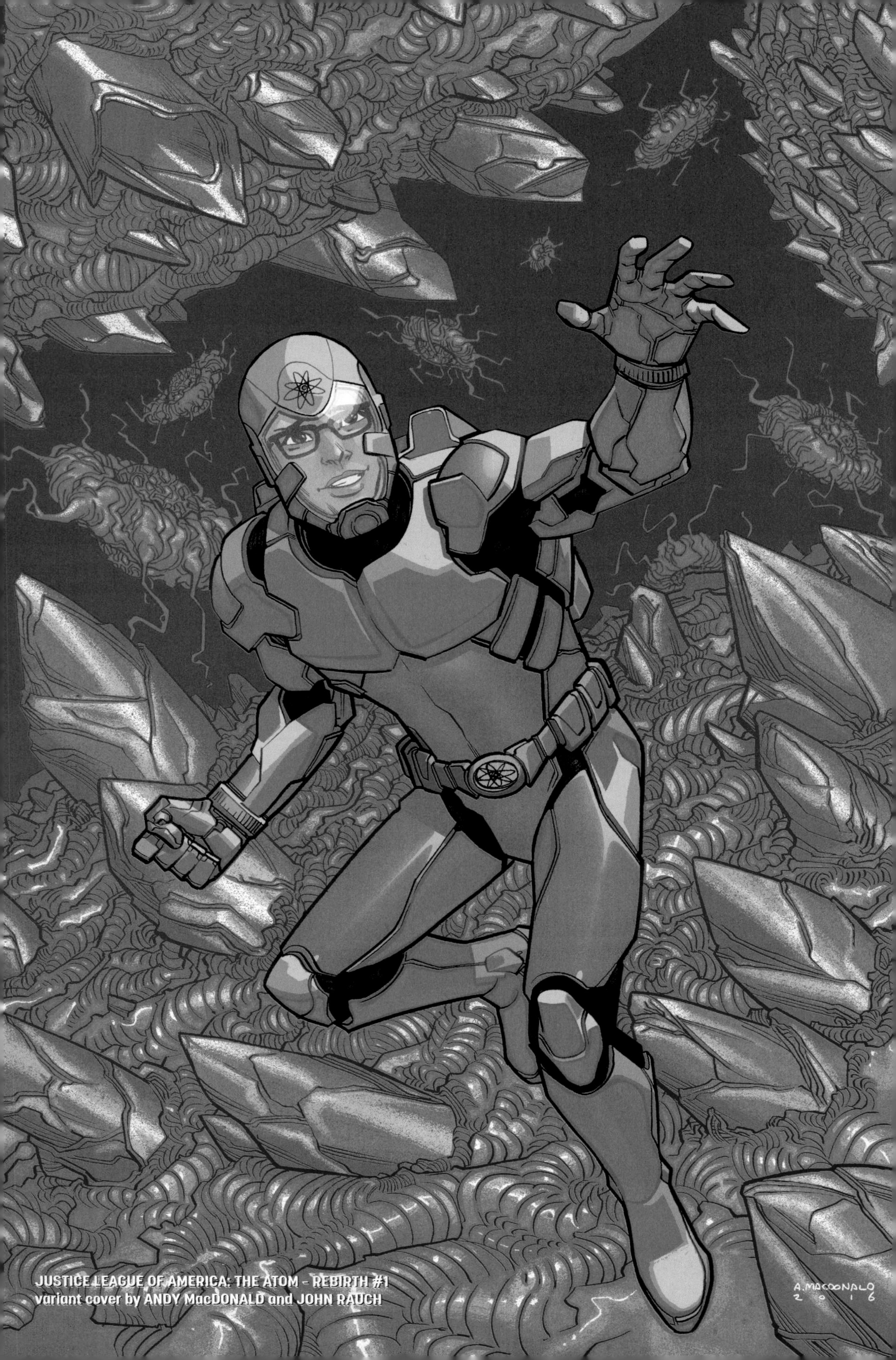
A. MACDONALD
2 0 1 6

JUSTICE LEAGUE OF AMERICA: THE ATOM – REBIRTH #1
variant cover by ANDY MacDONALD and JOHN RAUCH

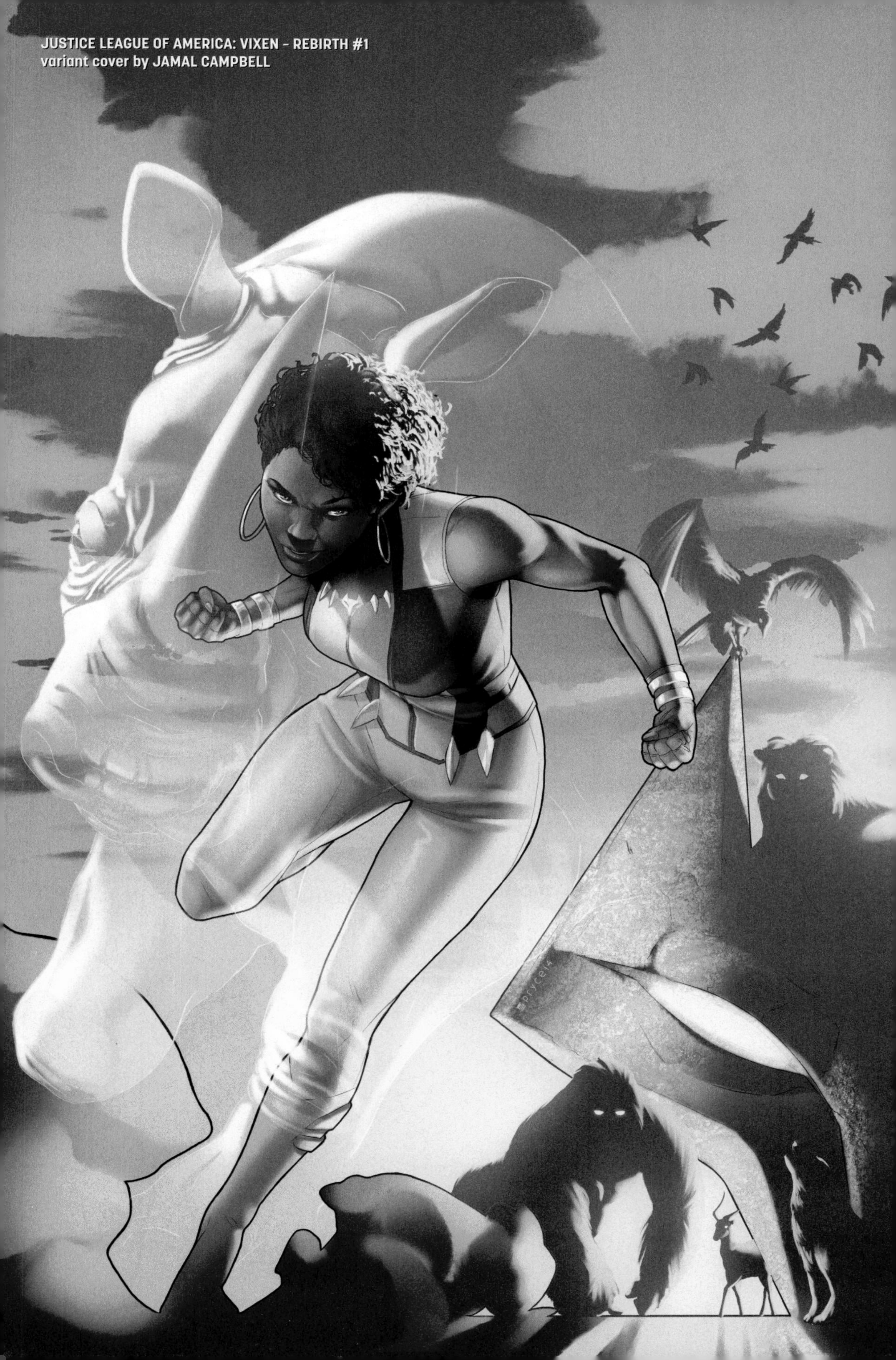
JUSTICE LEAGUE OF AMERICA: VIXEN - REBIRTH #1
variant cover by JAMAL CAMPBELL

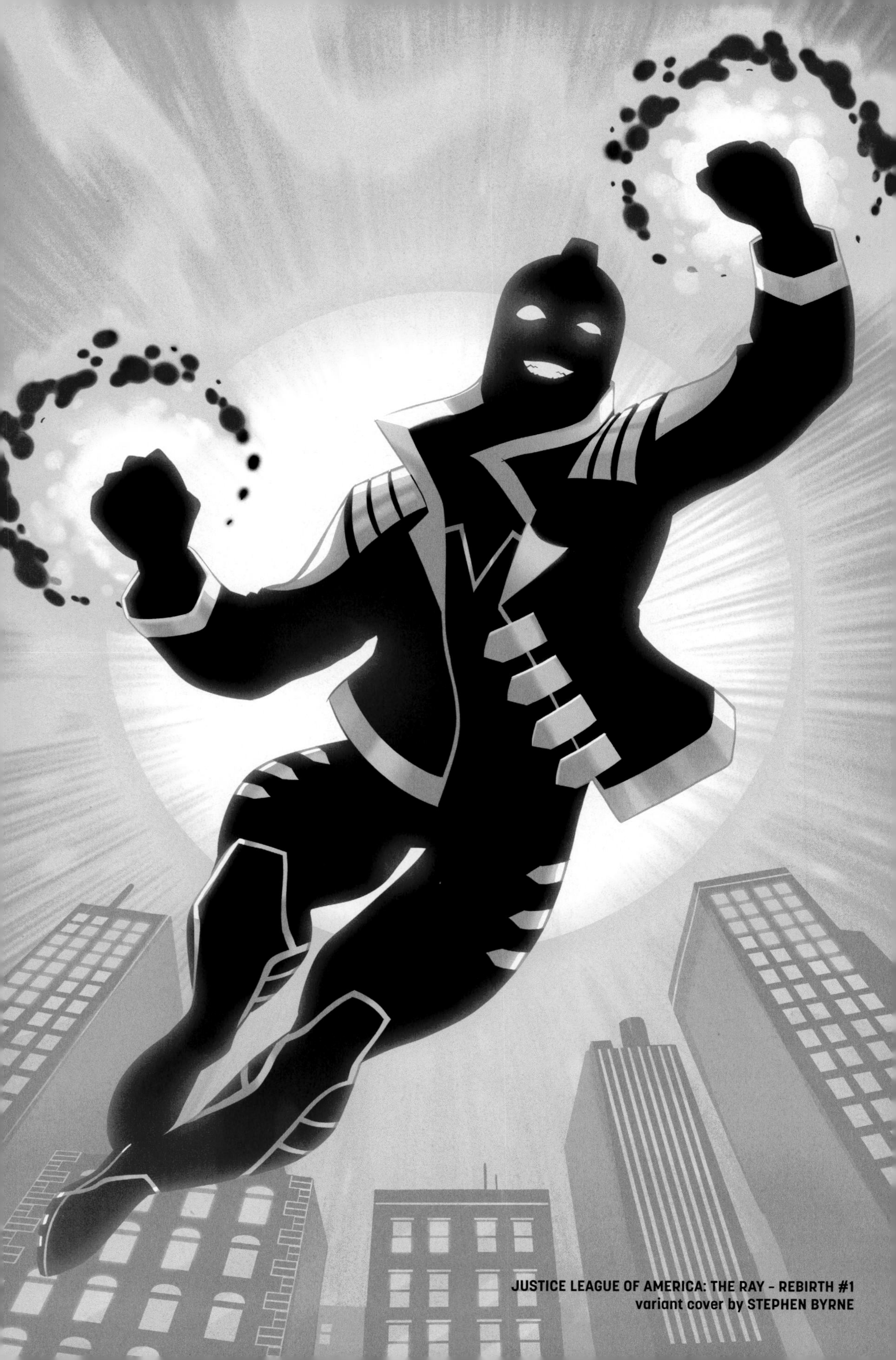

JUSTICE LEAGUE OF AMERICA: THE RAY - REBIRTH #1
variant cover by STEPHEN BYRNE

JUSTICE LEAGUE OF AMERICA: KILLER FROST - REBIRTH #1
variant cover by MIRKA ANDOLFO

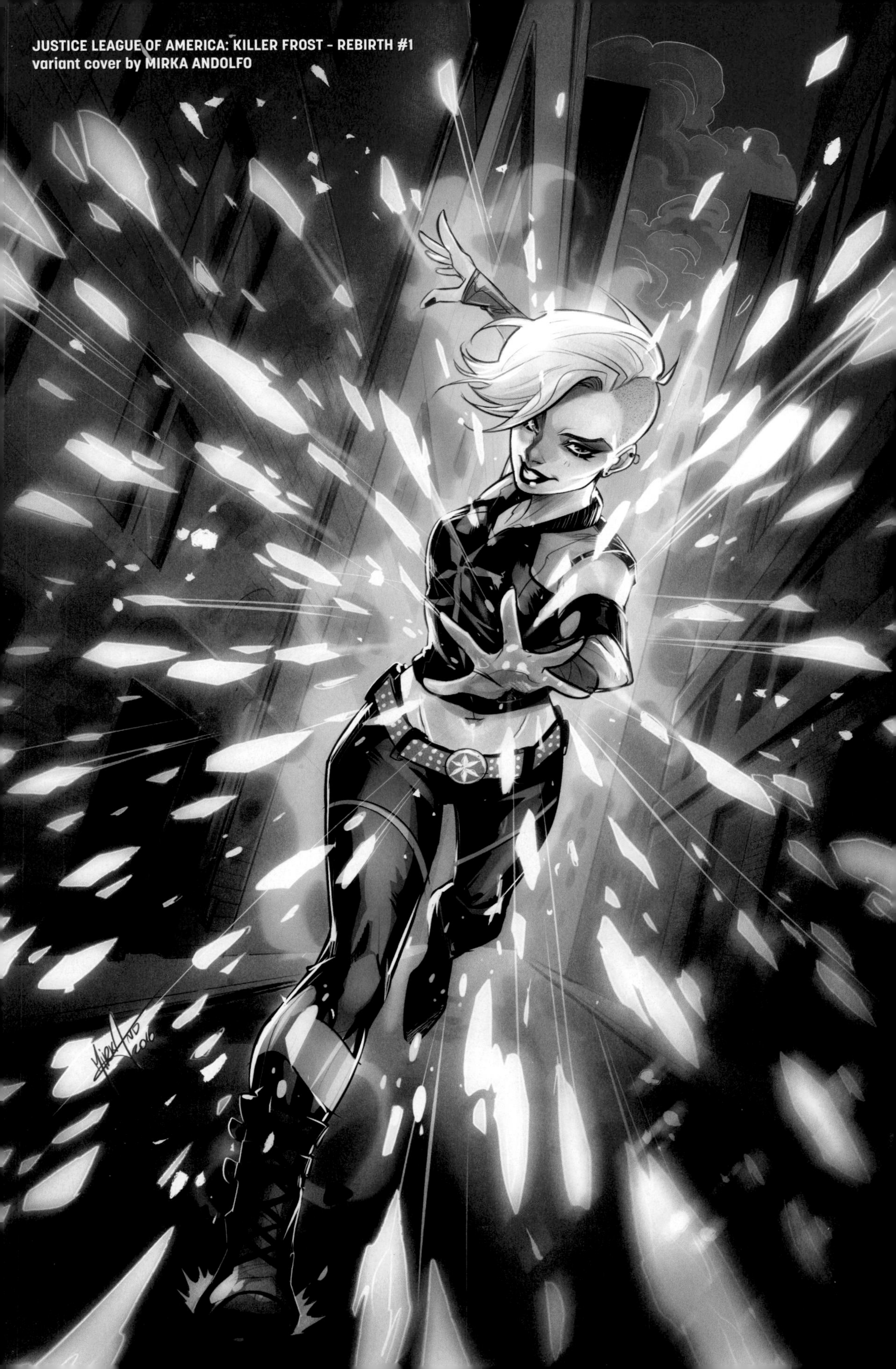

JUSTICE LEAGUE OF AMERICA: REBIRTH #1
variant cover by RYAN OTTLEY and SUNNY GHO

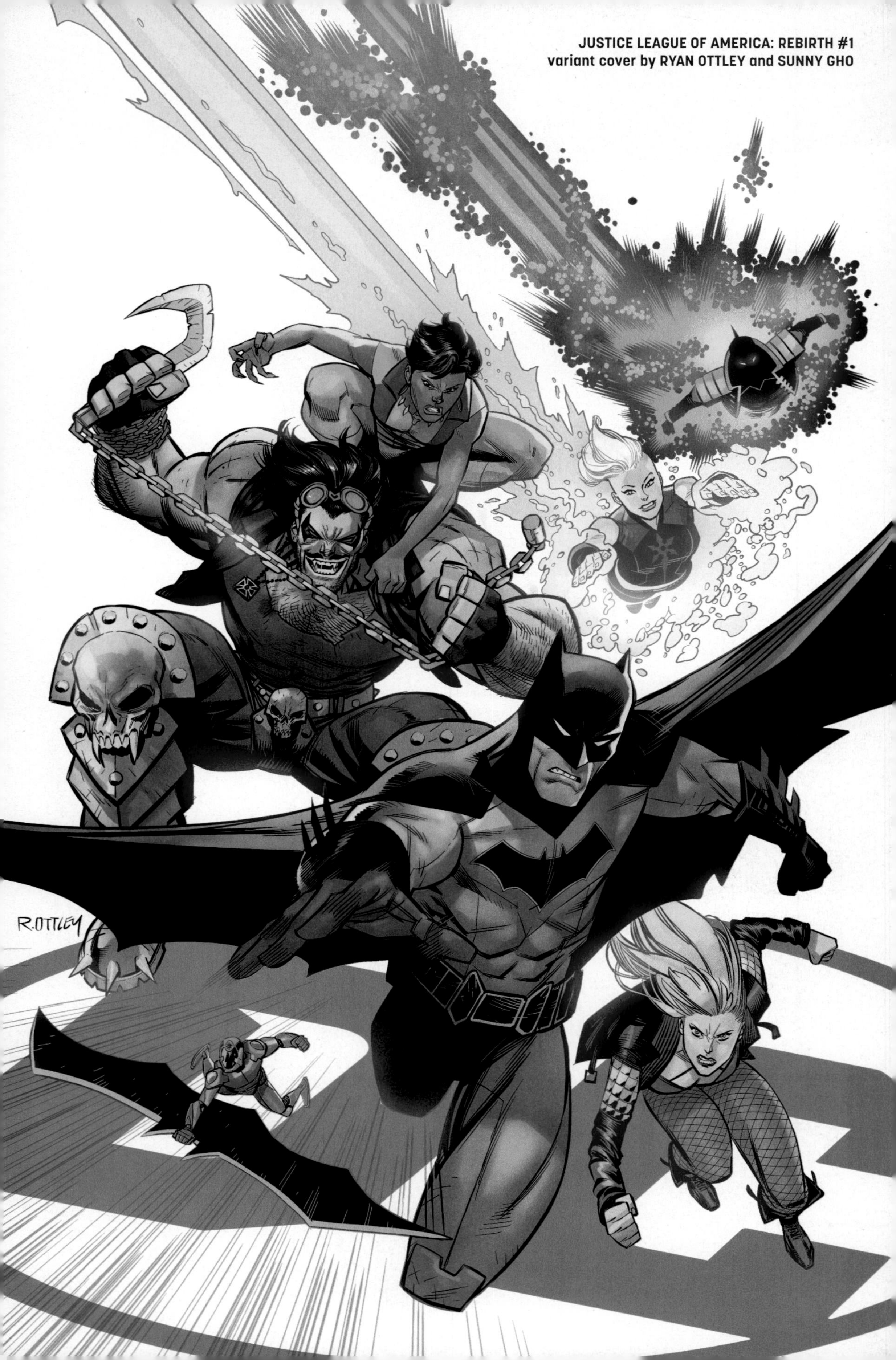
R.OTTLEY

THE ATOM

Character sketch by IVAN REIS

Pencils by ANDY MacDONALD

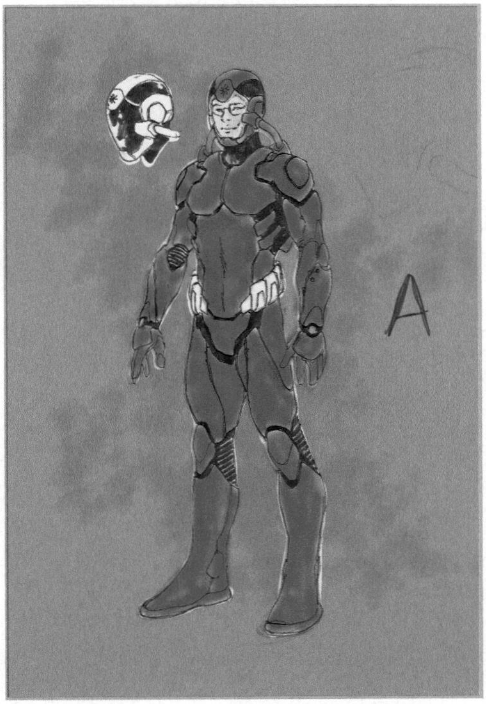
A

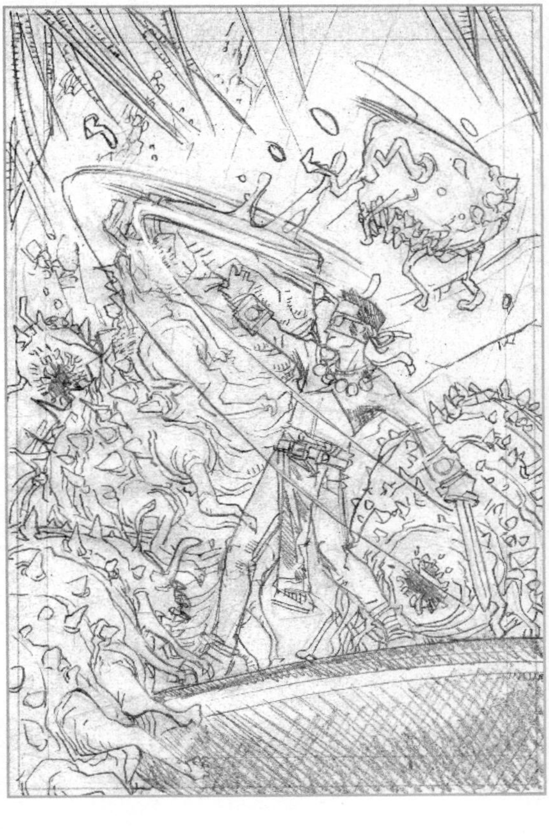

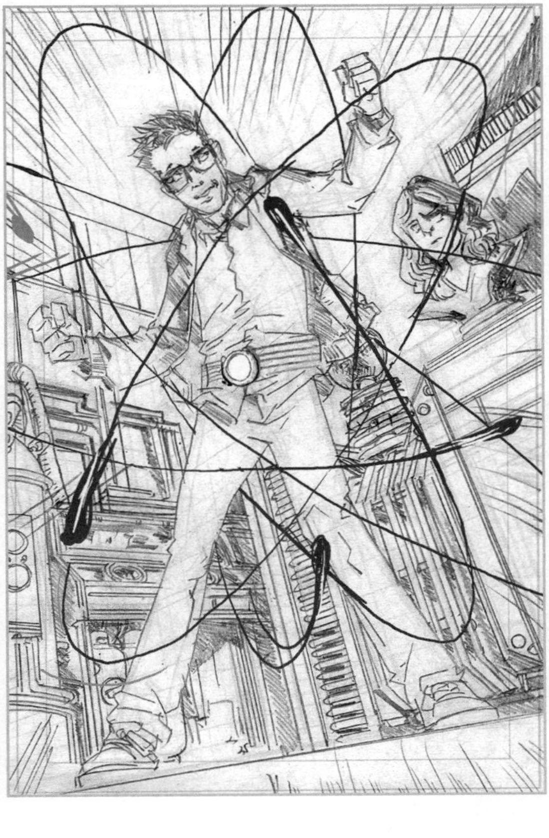

VIXEN

Character sketches by IVAN REIS

Inks by JAMAL CAMPBELL

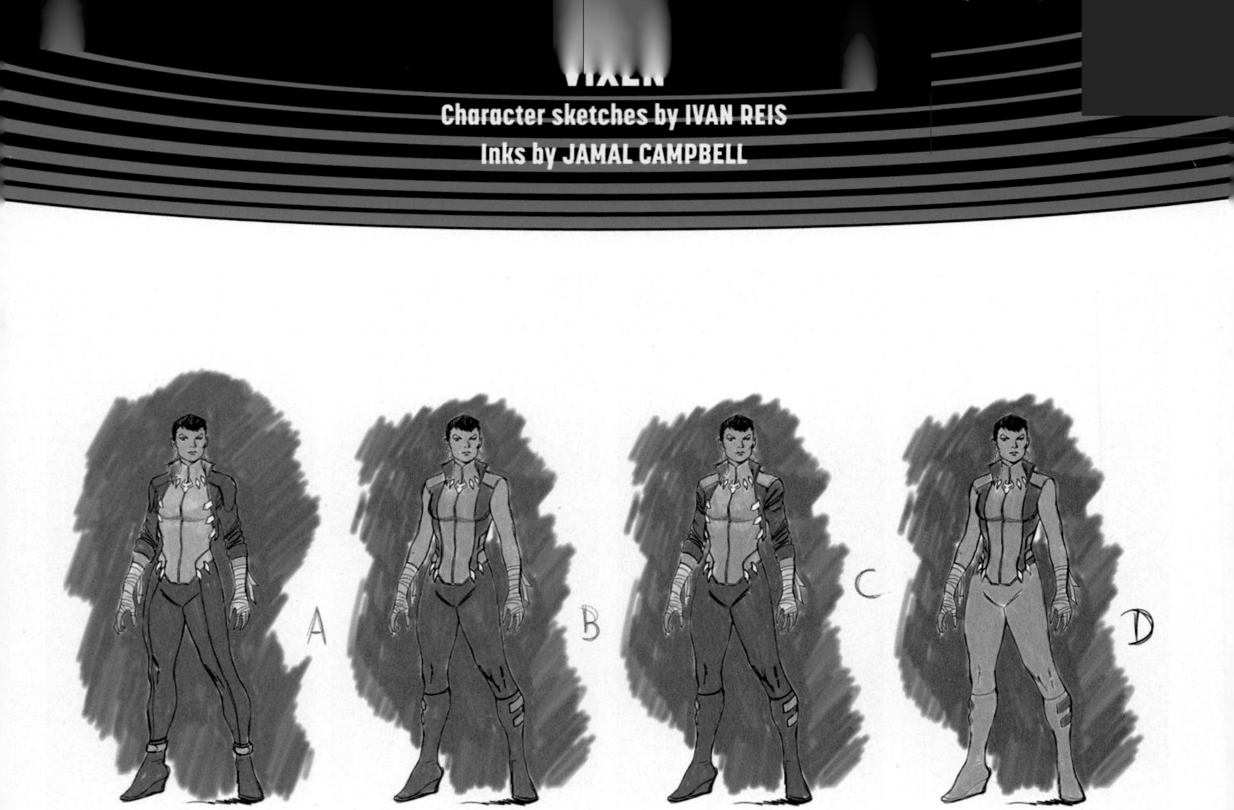
A
B
C
D

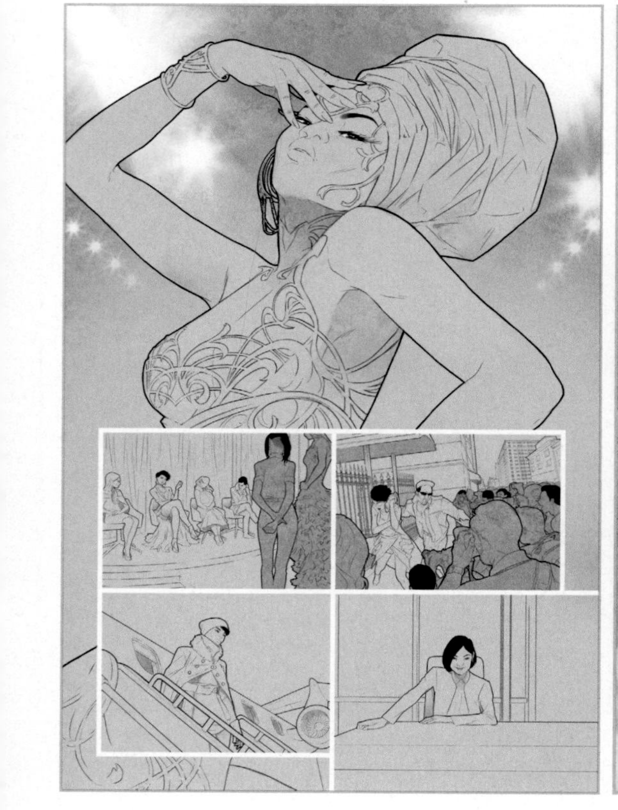

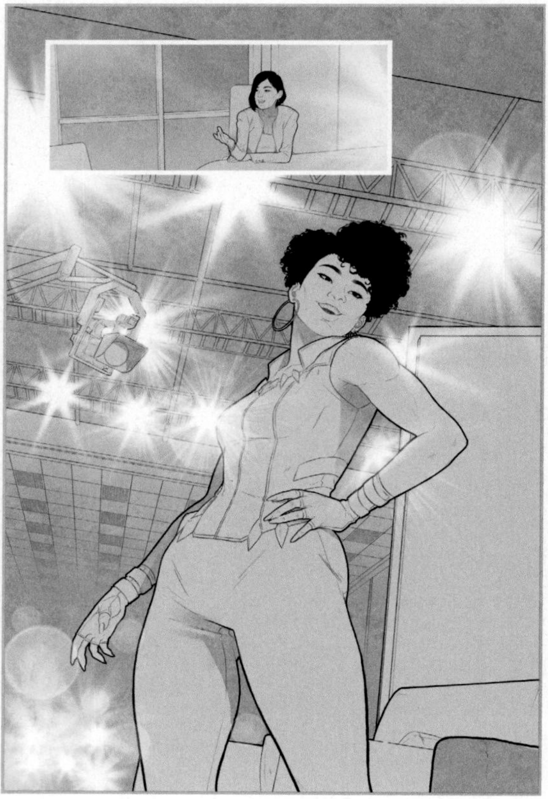

Character sketches by IVAN REIS

Layouts by STEPHEN BYRNE

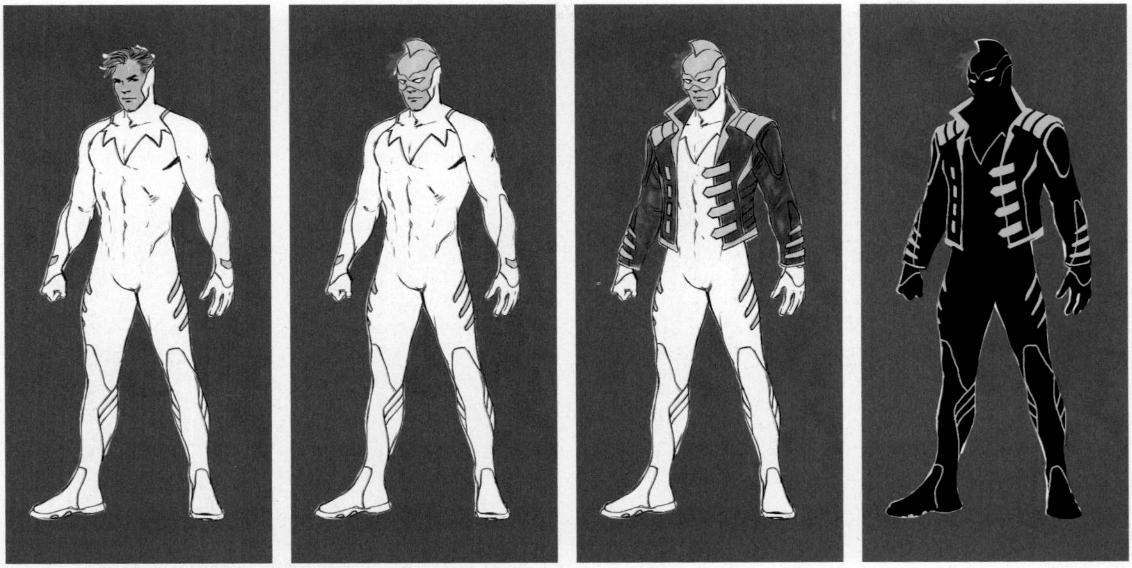

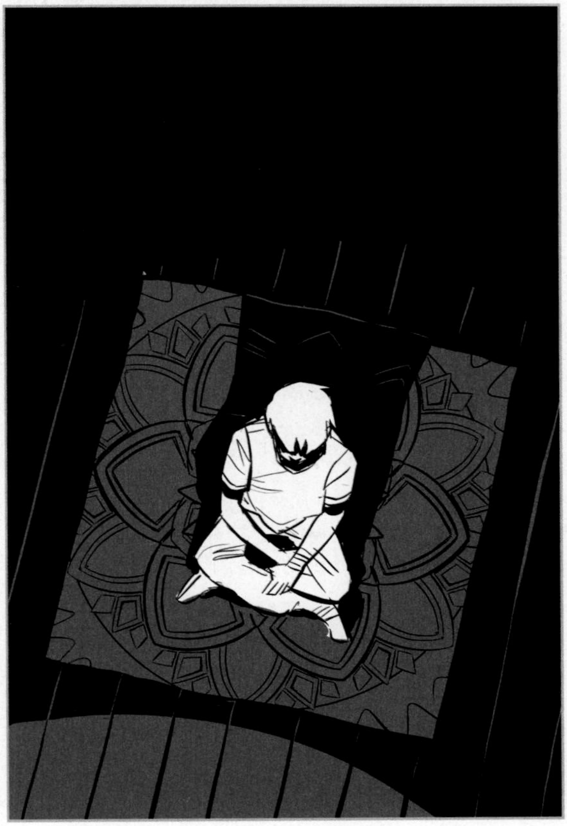

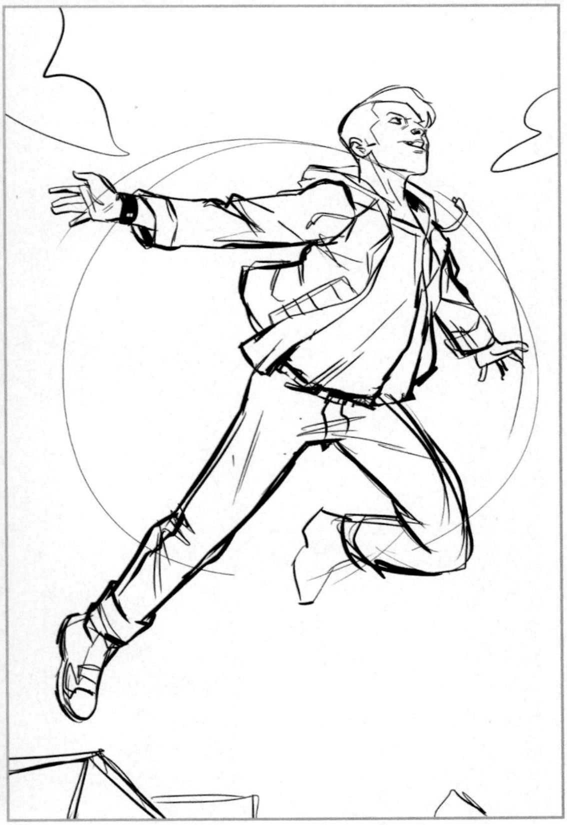

KILLER F

Character design by JASON FABOK and IVAN REIS

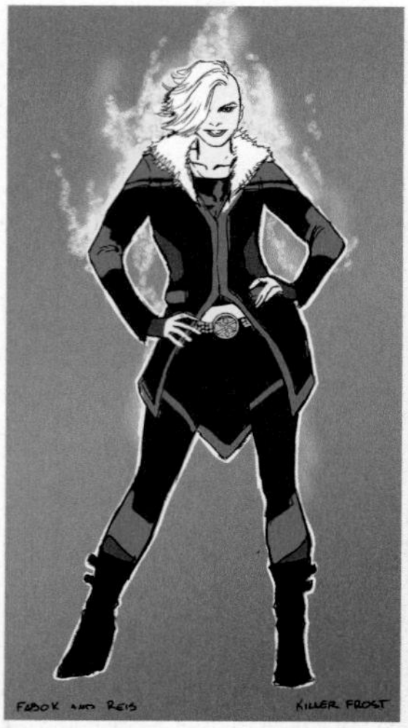
FABOK AND REIS
KILLER FROST

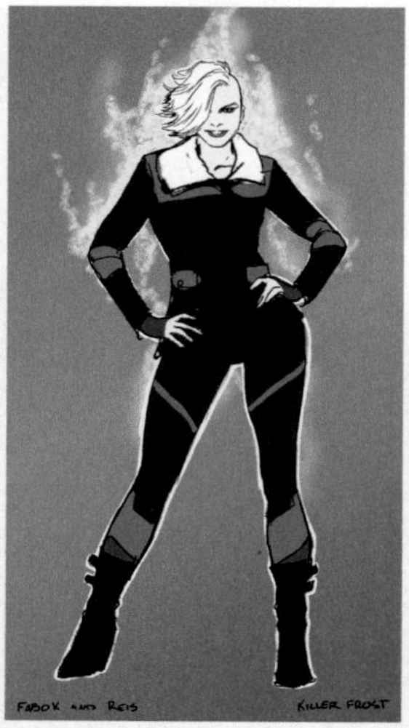
FABOK AND REIS
KILLER FROST

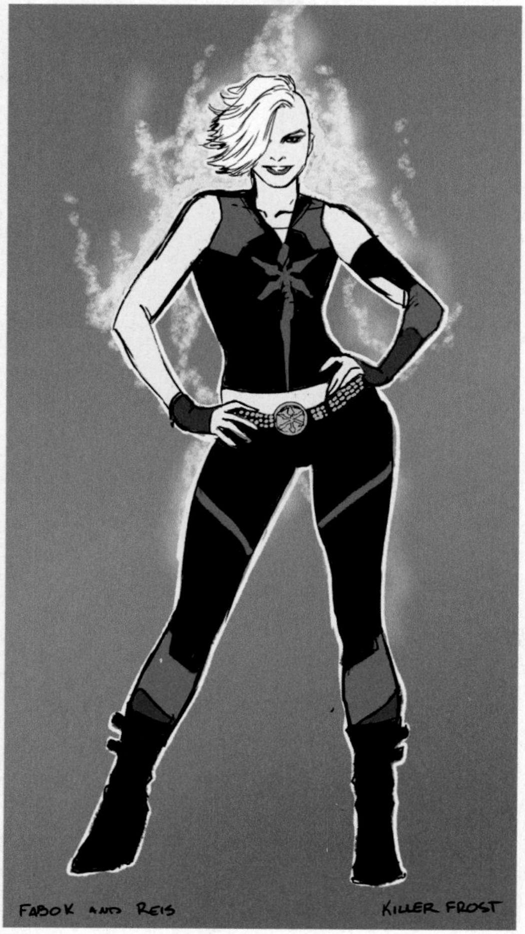
FABOK AND REIS
KILLER FROST

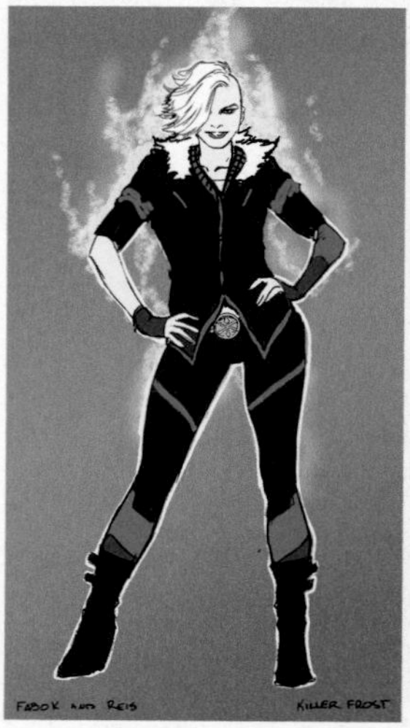
FABOK AND REIS
KILLER FROST

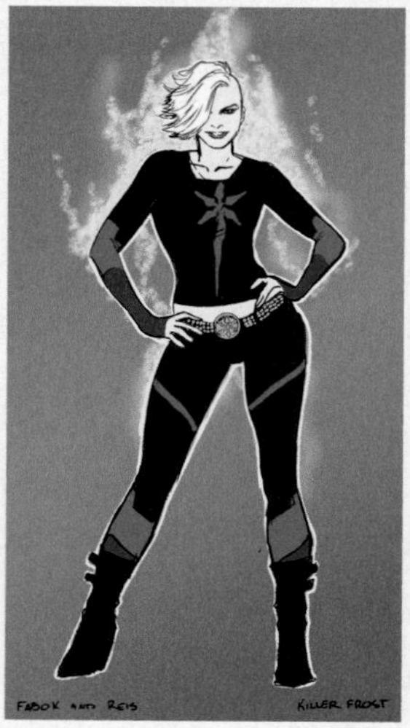
FABOK AND REIS
KILLER FROST

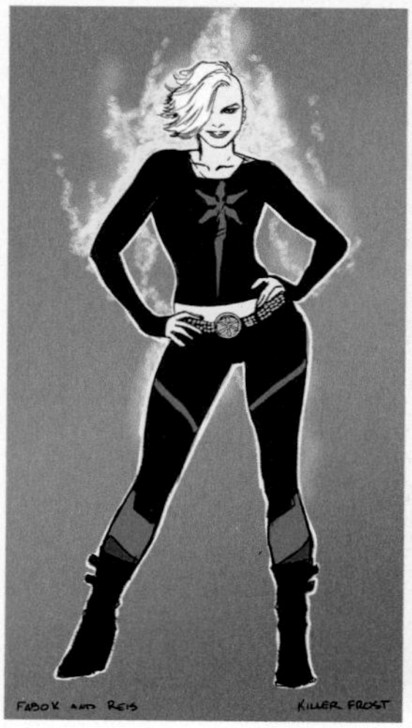
FABOK AND REIS
KILLER FROST

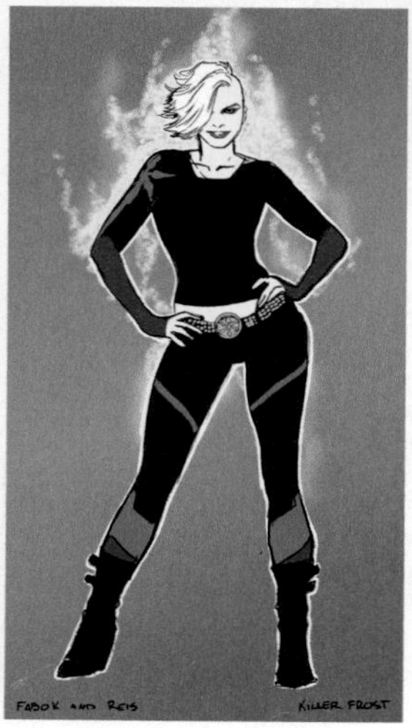
FABOK AND REIS
KILLER FROST

LOBO

Character design by IVAN REIS

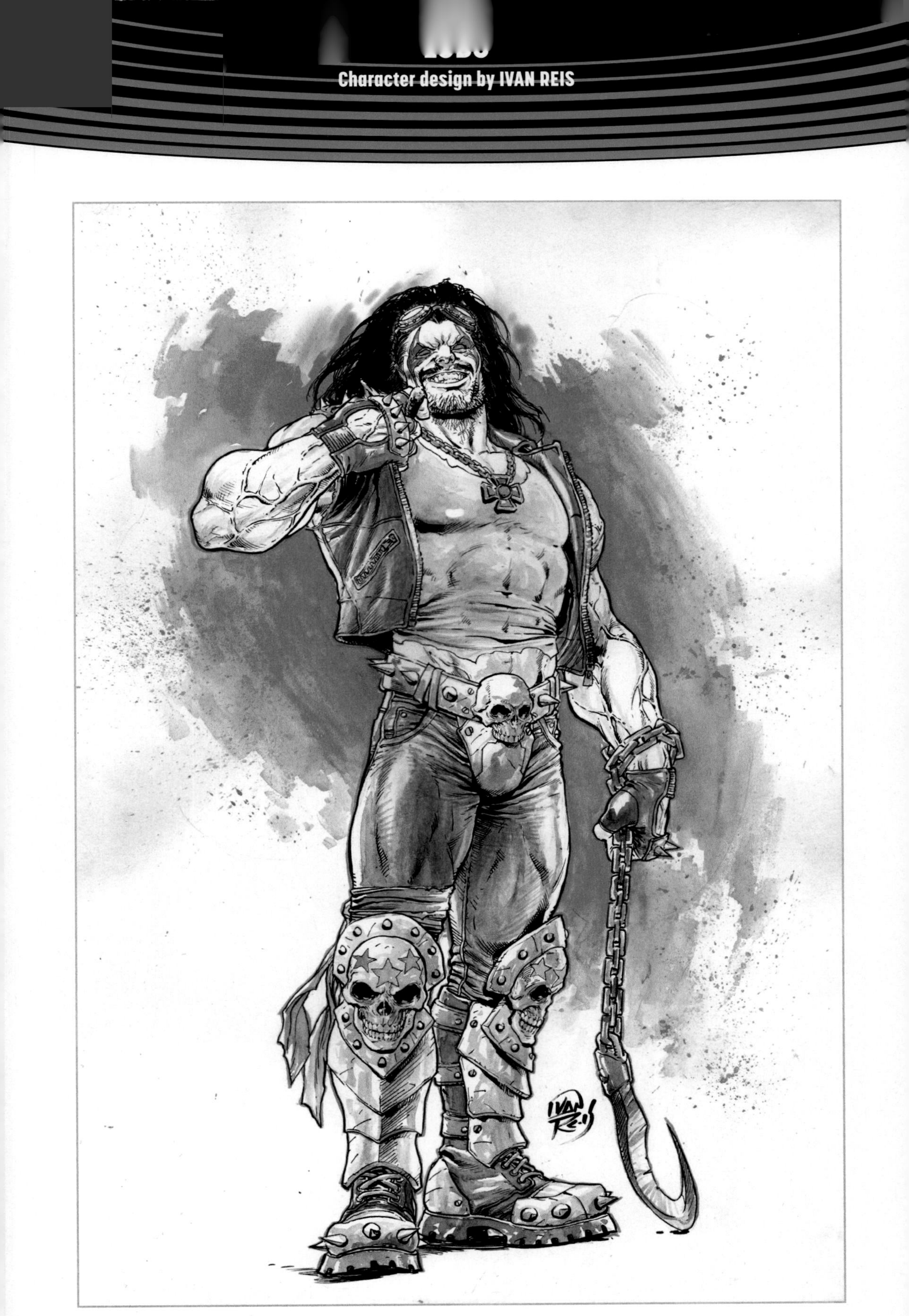

THE ATOM – REBIRTH #1

Variant cover sketches by ANDY MacDONALD

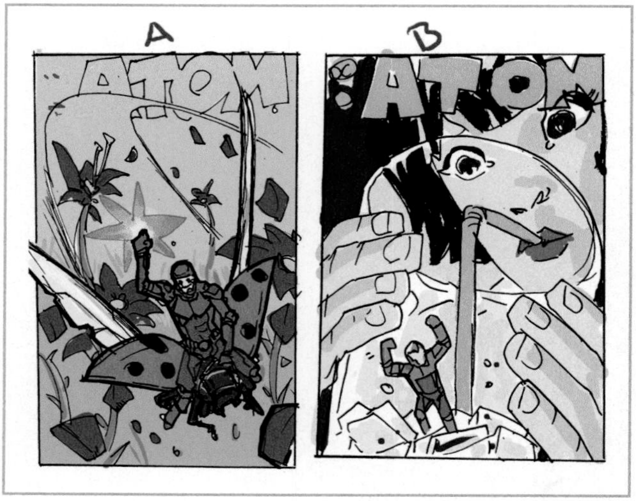
A
ATOM
B
DC
ATOM

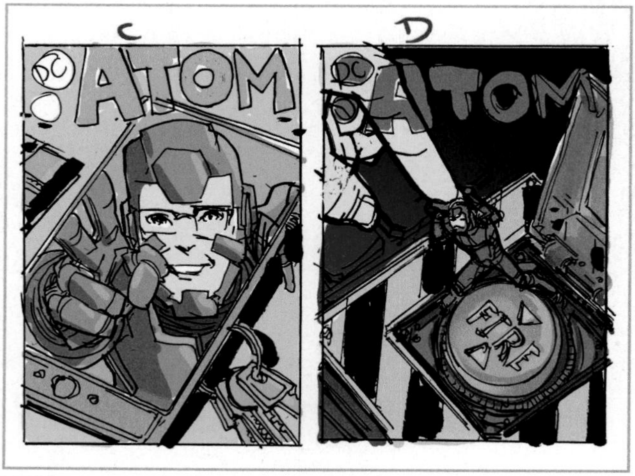
C
DC
ATOM
D
DC
ATOM
FIRE

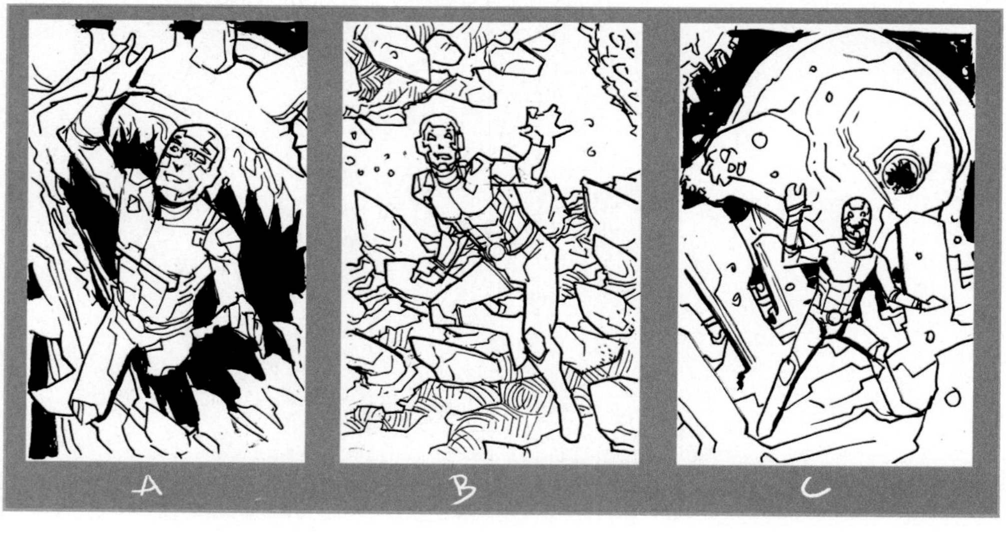
A
B
C

VIXEN – REBIRTH #1 and KILLER FROST – REBIRTH #1

Cover pencils by IVAN REIS

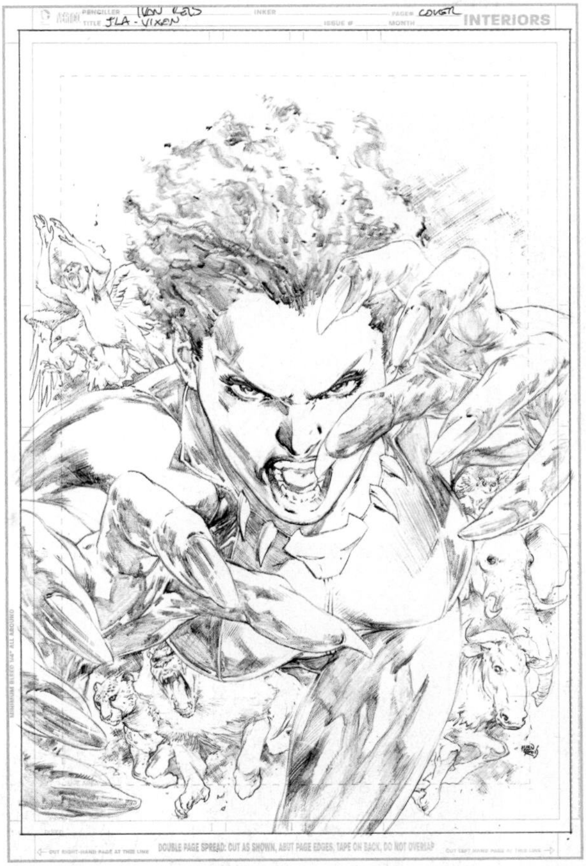
PENCILLER IVAN REIS
TITLE JLA - VIXEN
INKER
ISSUE #
PAGE# COVER
MONTH
INTERIORS
DOUBLE PAGE SPREAD: CUT AS SHOWN, ABUT PAGE EDGES, TAPE ON BACK, DO NOT OVERLAP

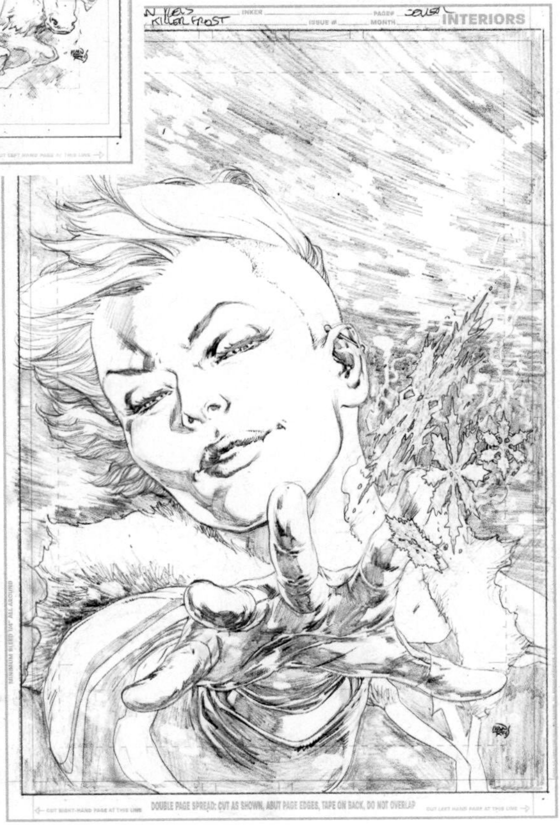
KILLER FROST
INKER
ISSUE #
MONTH
INTERIORS
DOUBLE PAGE SPREAD: CUT AS SHOWN, ABUT PAGE EDGES, TAPE ON BACK, DO NOT OVERLAP

JUSTICE LEAGUE OF AMERICA: REBIRTH #1

Cover sketches by IVAN REIS

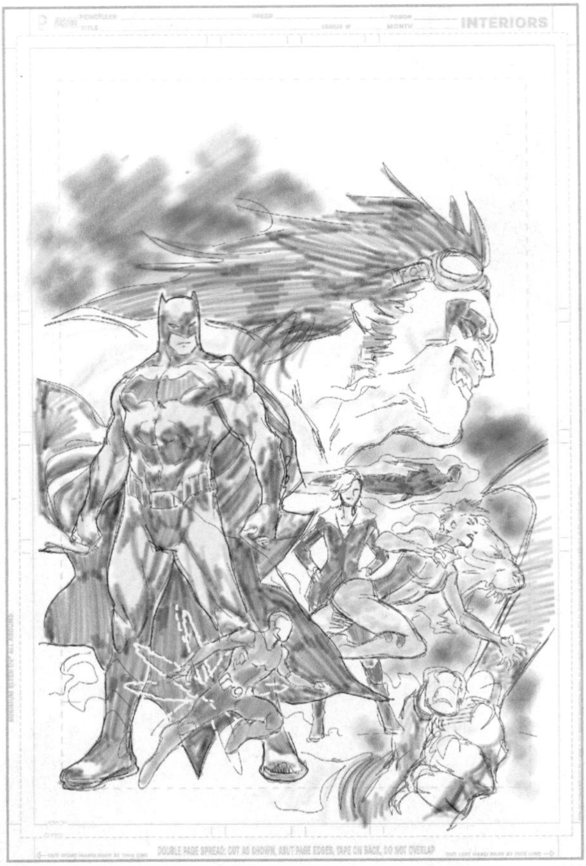
INTERIORS
DOUBLE PAGE SPREAD: CUT AS SHOWN, ABUT PAGE EDGES, TAPE ON BACK, DO NOT OVERLAP

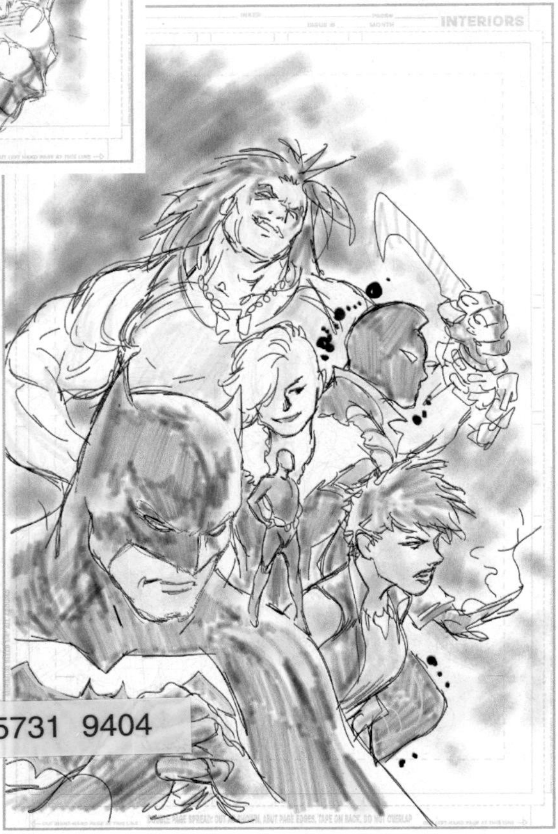
INTERIORS

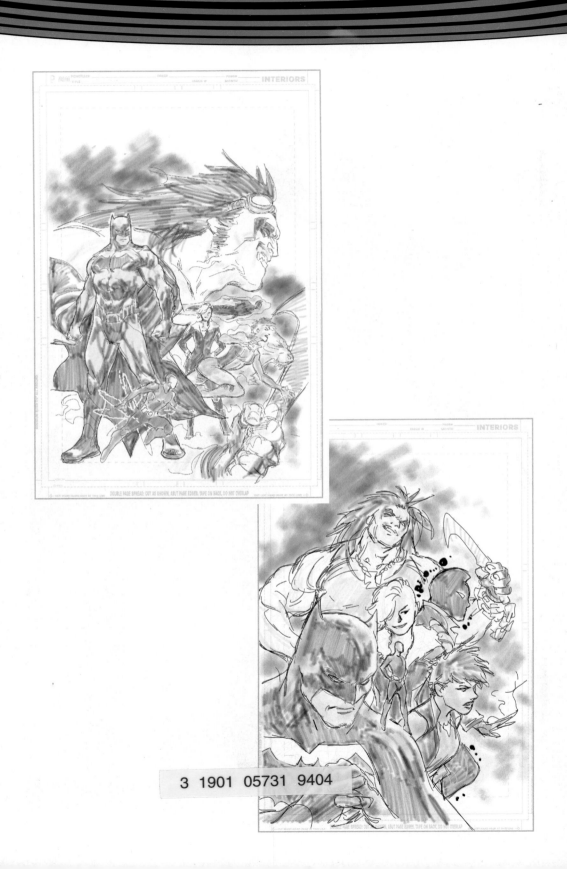

THE RAY - REBIRTH #1
Variant cover sketch by STEPHEN BYRNE

THE RAY - REBIRTH #1
Cover sketch by IVAN REIS

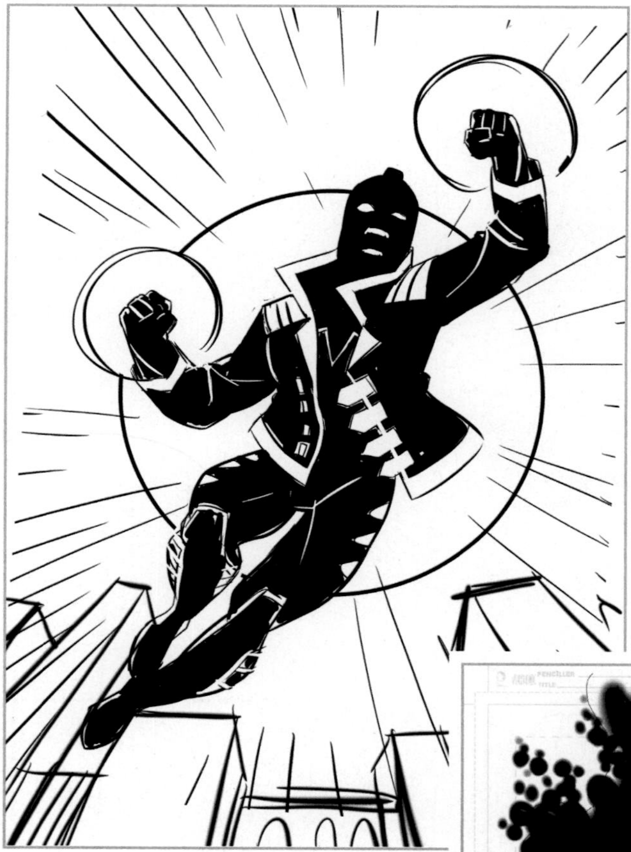

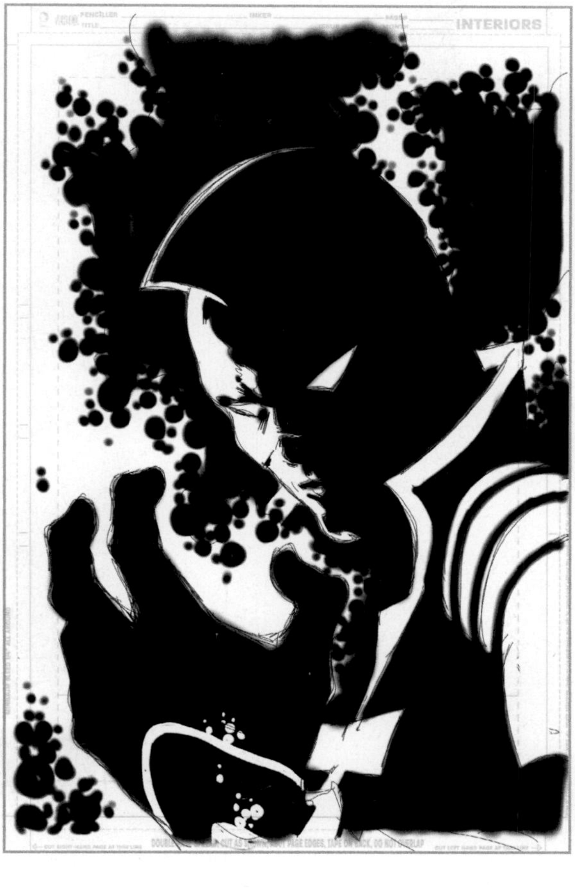
INTERIORS

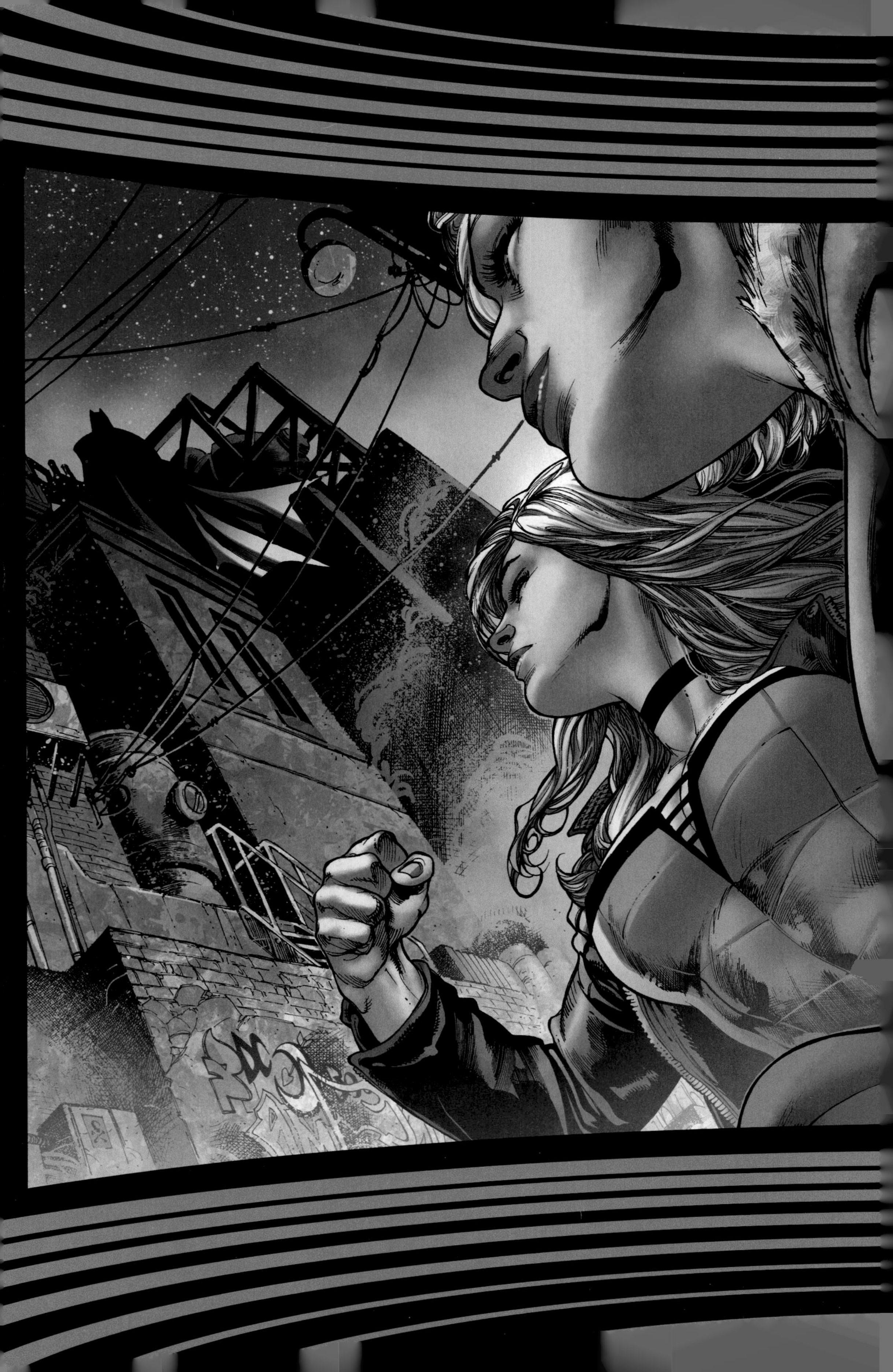

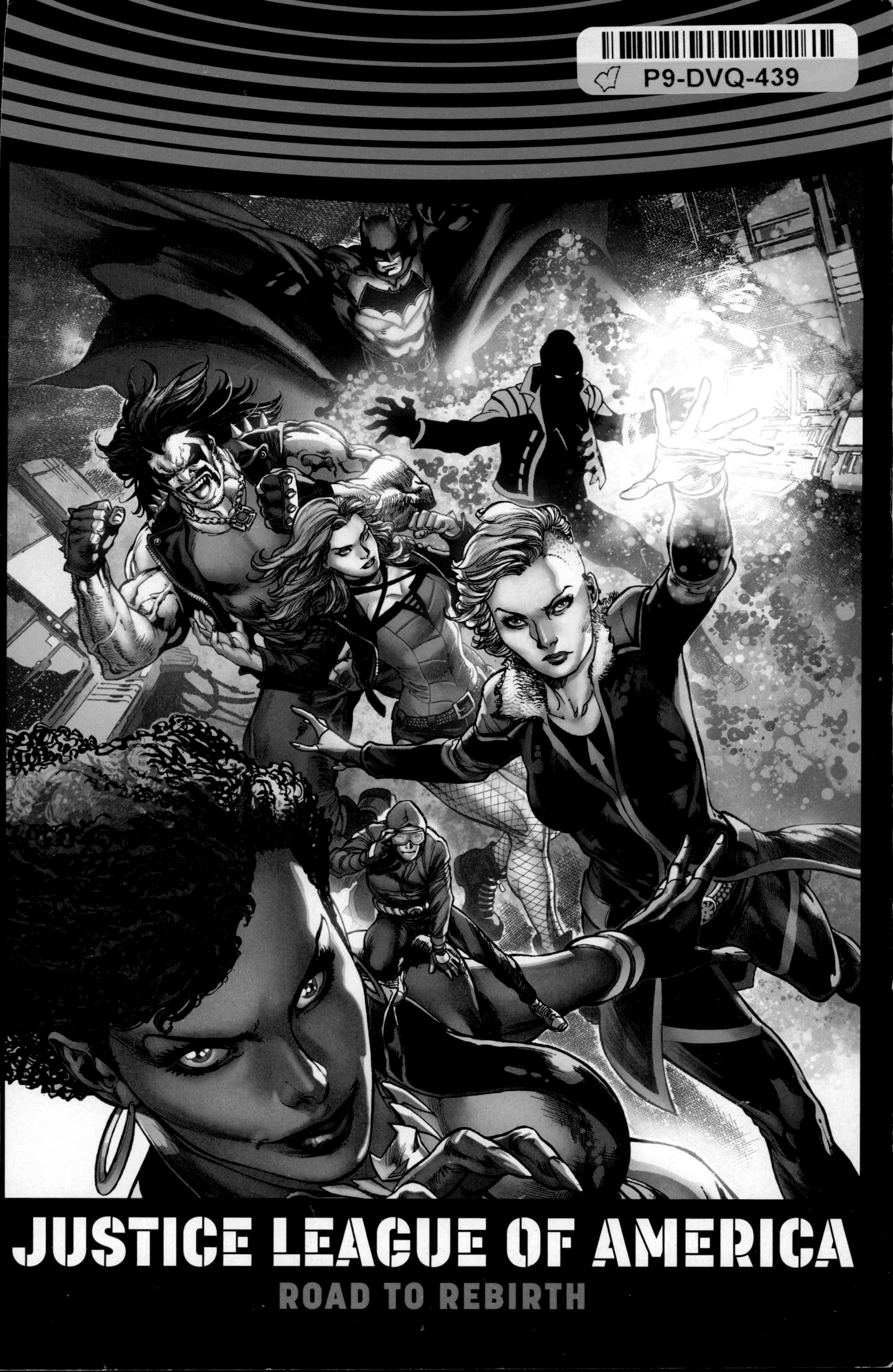

JUSTICE LEAGUE OF AMERICA

ROAD TO REBIRTH